CANADA'S CURLING CHAMPIONS

ICE GOLD

TED WYMAN

Foreword by
GLENN HOWARD

ecw press

Published by ECW Press
2120 Queen Street East, Suite 200
Toronto, Ontario, Canada M4E 1E2
416-694-3348 info@ecwpress.com

Editor for the press: Laura Pastore
Author photo: Jason Halstead

LIBRARY AND ARCHIVES CANADA
CATALOGUING IN PUBLICATION

Wyman, Ted, author
Ice gold : Canada's curling
champions / Ted Wyman.

Issued in print and electronic formats.
ISBN 978-1-77041-247-7 (pbk.)
978-1-77090-644-0 (PDF)
978-1-77090-645-7 (ePUB)

1. Curlers (Athletes)—Canada—
Biography. 2. Olympic
Winter Games (22nd : 2014 :
Sochi, Russia). I. Title.

GV845.6.W94 2014   796.964092'271
C2014-902552-1   C2014-902553-X

Front cover images: (Jones) Al
Charest/Calgary Sun/QMI Agency
OLY2014; (Jacobs) Ben Pelosse/Journal
de Montreal/QMI Agency OLY2014
Back cover images: (top) Al Charest/
Calgary Sun/QMI Agency OLY2014;
(bottom) AP Photo/Wong Maye-E;
ice © Boris Pamikov/Dreamstime
Maple leaf: echoenduring/Vecteezy

The publication of Ice Gold has been generously supported by the Government
of Canada through the Canada Book Fund for our publishing activities, and the
contribution of the Government of Ontario through the Ontario Book Publishing
Tax Credit and the Ontario Media Development Corporation.

Printed and bound in Canada   Printing: Norecob   5   4   3   2   1

This book is dedicated to Chris and Emily.

My heroes.

Foreword by Glenn Howard   IX

Introduction   XIII

ONE From the Coke Machine to the Top of the World   I

TWO Brothers in Arms   29

THREE Breaking Up Is Hard to Do   49

FOUR The Vagabond   62

FIVE A Father's Inspiration   78

SIX The Buff Boys   89

SEVEN Isabella's Influence and Hometown Glory   103

EIGHT The Perfect Storm   117

NINE The Golden Road   131

TEN Gut-Checks and Glory   157

ELEVEN The Greatest of Them All   183

TWELVE Pride of the Soo   203

Acknowledgements   217

FOREWORD
by Glenn Howard

It's every sports-minded kid's dream to participate in the Olympic Games. For most, it remains a dream, and a very small percentage gets close, but for a select few, it comes to fruition and it comes with a gold medal.

When I first started the game at age 10, there was no sign of curling ever being a demonstration sport at the Olympics, let alone a full medal-sport like it is today. My dream was to get to the Brier, our national championship, and to play beside my idol — my brother Russ. We were two "average Joes" who loved to play and loved to win. There was never any talk of nutritionists, sports psychologists, personal trainers, coaches or gym memberships. As long as we had three meals a day, we were good to go. During the off-season we had no thought or consideration for curling whatsoever. We were taught to practise, practise and practise. Have fun and do it to the best of our ability. We maintained full-time jobs and practised as much as we could. We learned at an early age that the only way to get better was to play against the best. Get into lots of bonspiels, and play the "big boys" as much as you can and learn as much as possible. Become sponges.

Times have changed. Curling is one of the most-viewed Olympic sports on television. The days of throwing a few rocks, eating what you want, showing up at the rink and expecting to win are gone! Five years ago, I realized this and made a huge change in my outlook. After turning 47 and wanting to stay competitive and be successful, I had to make some wholesale changes. I hired a personal trainer. He has challenged me, educated me, provided valuable insight and helped with sports psychology. I am still working with him today. I am in the best shape of my life and still on one of the best curling teams in the world. I have worked with nutritionists and sports psychologists and, of course, I now have a gym membership. I learned that with better physical conditioning comes less fatigue and better concentration, which equates to better performance. Welcome to the present-day curler. Today's game comes with greater demands, more time away from home and family, greater commitment to goals and team dynamics and also team preparedness.

The past five years have seen some great successes and some huge disappointments. Our team won the Canadian and world championships in 2012, but we were the Olympic Trials runner-up in 2009 and had a dismal sixth place finish in the 2013 Olympic Trials. Our successes and excellent consistency can definitely be attributed to the "new" work ethic and superb team dynamics created over the past years. But, what was missing? Why did we not achieve all our goals? Why didn't we win the Olympic Trials? These questions are asked by every men's and women's team each year, and every four years for the Olympics, except for two teams. These teams didn't ask themselves, "Why not?" They asked themselves, "Why *did* we win?" This year those two teams are Jennifer Jones and Brad Jacobs. Both were gold medalists at the 2014 Sochi Olympics. Their greatest triumph bar none! Two totally different stories. The cool but wily veteran, 39-year-old Jennifer Jones, and the young, feisty 28-year-old Brad Jacobs. Two differing eras, but two identical results. How did it happen? Why did it happen?

Every curling team assesses their previous year and figures out what to do next.

Do we continue with the same lineup? Do we make changes? These questions burn in every curler's mind at the end of every season. Jennifer and Brad are no exceptions. Both teams made some huge changes that have turned out to be "gold!" Jennifer stayed with a couple of teammates that she had on her team for years, but she did bring on young Kaitlyn Lawes to add some youth and excitement. This combination proved to be lethal to the other teams. Although the change was massive, I believe the biggest reason for Team Jones's success at the 2014 Olympic Games was Jennifer herself. She put on a performance for the ages. She had overcome a few challenges, including a very extensive knee surgery, the birth of her first child, Isabella, and a life-partner change. Jennifer is a very high-profile athlete in Canada, so with all the changes came a lot of scrutiny. This is where she rose to the occasion. Jennifer took all this as another one of life's big challenges. She was going to win, plain and simple . . . and she did! In dramatic fashion, Jennifer, Kaitlyn, Jill and Dawn dominated the field and went undefeated to win the gold medal.

Team Jacobs made some changes as well. Brad and Co. were quite successful over the past few years, but they just didn't have the consistency that the top teams possessed. Brad knew it, as did his cousins E.J. and Ryan. Their big change came with the acquisition of Ryan Fry. Not only was this a big move, it meant Brad's long-time third E.J. Harnden would move down a position to second stone, a position he wasn't that familiar with. They started slowly but it wasn't for long. They quickly did some major damage on the bonspiel circuit, but they took it to the next level winning the 2013 Tim Hortons Brier. They eventually lost the 2013 world final but made a statement they were here and they were for real. The naysayers still questioned Team Jacobs's consistency but they were soon quieted with their 2013 Olympic Trials victory and a berth in the Olympic Games in Sochi, Russia. The exclamation mark came with an undefeated record. With a rough start at 1-2, the Olympic Games didn't go quite as smoothly for the men's team as it did for Team Jones. This was Team Jacobs's turning point; their team dynamic and endless sports psychology sessions came into the forefront at this point. The pressure on Team Canada was huge. They could put their tail between their legs and feel sorry for themselves or they could think positively and do what they do best . . . make shots!

And they did make their shots and started winning more games. To be exact, they didn't lose again. They won the gold medal and capped off a perfect double gold performance for the Canadian curling teams. I'm sure if you ask Team Jacobs what the turning point was, they would say the big win in game 4. Brad, Ryan, E.J. and Ryan were able to perform at their very best when everything was on the line, the ultimate prize in curling . . . the gold medal.

You are about to read about two remarkable curling teams. How the players got their start and how they tick. You will get a better understanding of their quest for Olympic gold and the processes that got them there. They realized the changes they needed to make, the personal commitments and the buy-in from each teammate to achieve their goals. Perhaps you may look at *your* goals that you want to strive for in your personal or professional life and start to make the necessary steps. It can be a short process or it may take many years of hard work, dedication and the involvement of others, but if you don't start with a plan in place, how will you know if you have arrived if you don't know where you are going?

I hope you enjoy this book and are proud of the remarkable accomplishments of these great curling teams. It's taken years of blood, sweat and tears for these teams to realize their dreams and win gold at the Olympic Games. I'm certain all Canadians were extremely proud when our national anthem was played, not once, but twice for our Canadian curling teams.

Glenn Howard
Four-time Canadian and Four-time
World Curling Champion

INTRODUCTION

She settled back into the hack, flipped her hair a few times in customary fashion and triple-checked the bottom of the 42-pound piece of granite in her hands. Decades of experience helped control the roiling excitement in her stomach as the biggest moment of her life stared her directly in the face. History would be made that day and a lifelong dream would come true in spectacular fashion, in the biggest game, on the world's biggest stage. Ever the picture of composure, she lifted her head, contemplated the objective one last time — it was a task she had performed thousands of times before with ease, though with much less on the line — and reared back to throw the stone that would propel her into curling and Olympic lore.

Thousands of miles and several decades away sat a painfully shy little girl, too timid to go outside and make friends but full of dreams she never dared to believe would come true. What would that reticent child think of her older self now? Would she be able to believe that she'd grow up to be a corporate lawyer, a coveted public speaker and a national hero, not to mention one of the greatest female curlers ever to walk the planet? So shy she could barely open her mouth to talk to people her own age, she'd wonder who this intimidating person was: this 39-year-old woman who was the focal point of millions of televisions around the world, this darling of the international media, this icon of a sport who relished performing under the glare of the spotlight.

Little did the girl know that she would soon find a way out of her shell and start chasing her dreams of being the best at something — anything — by taking up sports, trying her hand at many athletic endeavors, simply to have a chance to feel included. She'd quickly find she loved playing sports — the competition, the camaraderie, the feeling of belonging. At age 11, her father would introduce her to curling and the mutual attraction would be instantaneous. She loved the smell of the ice, the sound of the rocks and the brooms and the friendships she started to form with teammates. It was where she felt the safest, and it allowed her to start to believe in her dreams.

Thirty years later that introverted child was still hopelessly in love with the game. She was there with her most loyal friend and curling compatriot, Jill Officer, who she'd known for almost a quarter century, and Dawn McEwen, who had become like a sister to her through years of ups and downs. She had her right hand, Kaitlyn Lawes, who was so much younger, so talented and so strong in the face of cruel adversity. She had a little girl of her own, oblivious to it all on the other side of the world but omnipresent in her heart and mind.

And now the stone was turning in her hand, releasing, carrying a lifetime of hopes and dreams as it slid down the ice, straight and true as usual, about to make contact with history. She watched it, reflected silently, then stood and raised her arms in the air as it met her opponent's last-hope stone with a familiar clack. At that moment, Jennifer Jones became an Olympic gold medallist, the best female curler on the planet, a Canadian hero, a woman who was proud of herself and her teammates and could think of no greater reward than to have won for her country and all the supporters back home.

The shy little girl would be proud, too.

Very few people would call Brad Jacobs and his teammates shy. Perhaps brash, confident or out-of-the-ordinary would be better descriptions. Physically fit specimens who took curling to a whole new level on their rapid ascent to the top of the sport would be most apropos. They're pure winners who put in an effort over and above what everyone else was doing and reaped the rewards. At the beginning of 2013, only hardcore curling fans and those who hail from the mining town of Sault Ste. Marie, Ontario, knew who these guys were. Now, countless fist-pumps, broom slams, whoops and hollers later, their names are indelibly stamped on the curling world's collective memory.

In March 2013, the team, made up of skip Brad Jacobs, third Ryan Fry, second E.J. Harnden and lead Ryan Harnden, barely squeezed into the playoffs of the Canadian men's curling championship in Edmonton. They had all been to Briers before, though never all together, and they looked like newcomers who didn't belong with the big boys in the playoffs. There was three-time Brier and two-time world champion Jeff Stoughton, four-time Brier and world champion Glenn Howard and 2006 Olympic gold medallist Brad Gushue joining them in the mix. It was there, with a who's who of curling's all-time greats standing in their way, that the Jacobs boys began a roll that took them to heights they only dreamed of reaching. It's a roll that's still going strong today.

They were a hungry team: young, fresh, different. Their loud, in-your-face style grated on curling purists like sand on the ice surface, and their ability to throw big weight curling shots frustrated their opponents. Three straight wins made them Brier champions for the first time and a month later they added a silver medal at the world championship in Victoria, British Columbia, but their hunger never dissipated. Out of that taste of success was born a newfound killer instinct, a steely determination and laser-like focus that put them on a path to even greater things.

Hitting the weight room like no others in their sport before them, they became strong, true athletes who belied the common perception of curlers as beer-swilling, cigarette-smoking farm boys. Along with bulging biceps and thick chests, they also developed a mental toughness and resilience that proved to come in handy down the road. At first, no one saw them coming, but when they did, the rest of the men's curling world was caught watching like an animal frozen on the highway, wondering just what this charging vehicle coming at them might be. They soared through the Canadian Olympic Trials with a perfect 7-0 record and then took their intimidating, entertaining style of curling to Sochi, where more greatness and glory awaited them.

Eventually they stood, two brothers, their cousin and a best friend, draped in the Canadian flag, running and jumping around a curling rink in subtropical Russia, celebrating a gold medal few ever thought possible.

Nobody's wondering who these guys are anymore.

In Canada's glorious curling history there have been so many brilliant moments, so many world championships and Olympic medals, but never before has there been a time like February 2014. In that magical month, in the picturesque Black Sea resort of Sochi, Canadian curlers pulled off a feat that had eluded them for 16 years — they won double gold at the Olympic Winter Games. The teams skipped by Jennifer Jones and Brad Jacobs grew up in completely different surroundings and took very different paths to the top of the podium in Sochi, but they'll forever be connected by golden glory.

CHAPTER ONE

FROM THE COKE MACHINE TO THE TOP OF THE WORLD

The shy little tomboy grew up in the quiet Winnipeg neighborhood of Windsor Park, the younger of two girls in a close-knit family that treasured sports and had a deep passion for curling. Born on July 7, 1974, Jennifer Judith Jones kept to herself and her family in the early days, unsure of herself when it came to making friends and happy to dream about shedding the stifling timidness and growing up to do something special. Painfully introverted, a trait that stayed with her for a few more decades, she found refuge in sports, competing in baseball, volleyball, basketball and track and field.

"I was a super shy kid, like *super* shy, so sport was kind of my way to be involved," Jennifer Jones recalled. "I never liked to be the centre of attention."

Her parents, Larry and Carol Jones, had strong family values. They believed in raising children the right way and in keeping them active. Both Larry, who worked in sales, and Carol, a nurse, were curlers and that meant Jennifer spent a lot of time at the rink from a very young age. In fact, there was a daycare at the St. Vital Curling Club and that's where little Jennifer spent her time while her parents were on the pebble. She was not particularly interested in building blocks or Barbie dolls, though; it would not have been at all strange to see the little girl, face pressed against the glass, staring down at the action below. "It was all they could do to keep me off the ice," she said.

"I remember being plastered against the glass and everybody always looking for me," she told the Canadian Press back in 2010. "I would always kind of wander off and watch curling. I loved it from the very beginning."

Long before her parents enrolled her and her 18-month-older sister, Heather, in a curling program, Jones was a student of the game. She watched it, studied it, understood it, was infuriated by it; she wanted to play. By the time Larry decided to teach her the game in 1985 when she was 11, he could scarcely have known how much passion for granite, corn brooms and pebbled ice already burned inside her. He held the broom for her as she took her first shaky slides out of the hack, a 75-pound girl trying to manage a 42-pound rock. It's a tradition that continues to this day. Larry still holds the broom when she practises and some 28 years later, when she was on the precipice of winning an Olympic gold medal, she would think of him. As she prepared to take her last shot, the one that would bring her Olympic glory and realize her dreams, she pictured her dad at the other end of the ice, holding the broom.

It would not be long before curling became the shy tomboy's passion, her refuge from the world, the one place where she could shut everything else out and just be herself. "Back then I just loved playing. I loved the smell of the ice, I loved competing, I loved being in the place in the world where I felt the safest." That holds true to this day. "I feel like I'm almost at a spa when I'm on the ice," she said at the Olympics in Sochi. "It's the one time when I can just focus on one thing. My cell phone's not going off, there's the smell of the ice, the feeling I get when I'm sliding . . . there's no better place for me in the world."

As a kid, she didn't dream of winning an Olympic gold medal. At that time, curling was still mostly a recreational sport in which even the highest-calibre competitors would drink beer and smoke cigarettes while they played. It wasn't until she was in her twenties that curling became an Olympic sport. Regardless, her early dreams didn't involve medals or trophies or glory in any specific sport.

"I never really had a specific dream of doing anything in particular," she said. "I just really wanted to always try my best, to try to be the best at something."

Her parents supported her in that dream and did whatever they could to make it possible. Perhaps knowing what sports did for her psyche, Larry and Carol made sure their daughter had every opportunity to be on the ice. "They are tremendous people," Jennifer told *On Manitoba* magazine in 2006. "They have a generous spirit, both of them, and they were very supportive of me in school and in curling. They never missed one curling event and they often skipped holidays to take me. They are my role models, and saints, too, considering what they sacrificed for us."

Jones went to General Vanier School in south Winnipeg from kindergarten to grade 8 and then moved on to Windsor Park Collegiate, where her sporting career took a major shift. Up until that point she was a multi-sport athlete and was particularly proficient at volleyball. "But curling was what I loved and it was all they could do to keep me from going on the ice all the time," she told CBC. "When I was in high school I really had to make a choice and it was actually my volleyball coach who told me I had to choose either volleyball or curling, and I chose curling. It's worked out pretty well for me."

Her first foray into competitive curling came in 1990, when at age 15 she skipped a team in the Manitoba junior women's championship. That team, which included her sister, Heather, at second, Tracey Lavery at third and Dana Malanchuk at lead and was coached by her dad, won one game in the tournament and lost two before being eliminated. It was to be expected for such a young team, competing against curlers who were five years older, but what wasn't expected was how much attention came the skip's way after the tournament. People recognize talent when they see it, and suddenly Jones was in demand. She was recruited to play third for Jill Staub, who was three years her senior, the following season, and success wasn't far behind. That team, which also included Kristie Moroz at second and 14-year-old future world champion skip Kelly MacKenzie (now known as Kelly Scott) at lead, went on to win the Manitoba junior women's championship and moved on to the Canadian juniors as strong contenders.

The Staub team bulldozed through the round robin with only one loss and made it all the way to the final before losing to New Brunswick's Heather Smith. That loss proved to be important in Jones's development as a curler. She was devastated and didn't handle the situation well in her own opinion. That was something she wanted to learn from.

"It took me a long time to recover but it gave me perspective," she told *Lawyers Weekly*. "You can't let the outcome affect you so much. It took away from the enjoyment of the moment and sport. Ever since then, I've been in the moment. It's helped me have a great perspective in sports and in life. That was the turning point for me. We had lost a heartbreaker. It was there for the taking and it really hurt. I didn't recover from that as well as I should have and I vowed I would never do that again."

Indeed, much later on in life, Jones would often talk about how well her team handled losses, how they could put disappointment aside and move on as well as any team she had ever seen. When she was just 16 and a fledgling competitive curler, Jones recognized her disappointment as a sign of immaturity and immediately started herself on a path to self-improvement.

The following year Jones decided to go back to skipping her own team and set out to piece together the right squad. There was one girl she had seen around the curling scene who she had never met but wanted to play with. She approached the girl, who was a year younger, at the Highlander Curling Club in Winnipeg and pulled her over by the Coke machine. The girl's name was Jill Officer and it would be the beginning of a long, beautiful and highly successful friendship.

Officer was just about to turn 16 at the time and had never even played in a provincial championship at that point. Here was this older girl, who had made it all the way to the Canadian final a year earlier, asking her to join her team.

"I was a bit star-struck," Officer said.

The connection was instantaneous between the two girls, both on and off the ice. They became great friends and curling soulmates. Jones and Officer would curl together for 18 of the next 22 years, making it to the Canadian championship in 12 of those years.

"It really hasn't changed for us over the last 20 years," Jones said. "We got together when we were quite young and had an instant connection on the ice and became really good friends. I think we bring out the best in each other. We have a great work ethic and it's just been an incredible journey for both of us."

Officer also grew up in a sporting family, her father, John, a hockey coach and former player, her mother, Leslie, a sports enthusiast who wanted her children to try many endeavours. In her formative years, Jill took figure skating lessons, gymnastics, baton twirling and played soccer. Her mother signed her up for curling for the first time at age 10 and even put together a team for her. "I was always hanging around a curling club or a hockey rink, so I was bound to take up one of those sports," Jill said in an interview with *Active Life* magazine. From the very beginning, Jill came to understand the value of physical fitness and always kept her body in tip-top shape. "I've learned a lot about myself, not only as an athlete, but as a person. I've learned what is important for me to be at my best — sleep, nutrition, general health and fitness. It all goes together."

They made it to the Manitoba junior women's final in their first year together before losing to Jennifer's former teammate Tracey Lavery, but Jones had a very positive outlook after the game. The 17-year-old bounded off the ice and eagerly told reporters: "I'm young yet, I've still got a few years to go." It wasn't long before the team really clicked. Along with third Trisha Baldwin and lead Dana Malanchuk, Jones and Officer found their first taste of big-time success in 1993, winning the Manitoba championship and competing in the Canadian juniors, where they compiled an 8-4 record and missed the playoffs. A year later, there would be no stopping them. The same team returned to the Manitoba championship and went undefeated. They went on to the Canadian championship in Truro, Nova Scotia, and, this time, they won it all. Jones and her teammates defeated Saskatchewan 8-5 in the final and the skip left the tournament with the battle scars of a long week. After tripping over her feet during the final, she suffered a black eye and bumped her head; she was a bit woozy as she did interviews following the biggest win of her life. "[My eye] is really sore and

I've got the biggest headache of my life," Jones told CBC. "I kinda tripped on my feet and banged my head but we played good so I guess I won't complain. This makes it feel much better." They may not have known that this would be the first of many Canadian titles, but Jones and Officer did know that they loved playing together, and they would endeavour to keep doing so for as long as possible.

"I think we have something special together," Officer said. "We probably bring something out in each other that obviously works because pretty much all of our success has been together. That obviously says something about how it works with us on the ice. We've both grown as people and as athletes, and I feel like she's grown so much as a person and a leader and she's really brought out the best in me and has motivated me to just constantly push to be better."

TSN curling analyst Cathy Gauthier, who played lead for Jones in 2005, said Officer is a huge key to Jones's success, not only because she is a great curler, but also because she is always good for the skip's psyche. She described the relationship between Jones and Officer as "unquestionable loyalty and support."

"It really doesn't matter whether Jen is playing well or not, frustrated or not, they have the longevity and Jen knows that every single game, every single shot, every single time, when she goes to the hack she's going to get that mental support from Jill," Gauthier said. "Jill is a person that is always going to be there for Jen and you don't always have that on a team. Rare teams do. You see people that are with you when things are going well but sometimes they are not so good when things aren't. To have somebody that you know has your back, no matter what happens, is so uplifting. Their friendship is based on complete loyalty."

There may have been times over the years that Jones could have considered going to a different player at the second position. Even if there were a better player out there — which is questionable — there was no way Jones could replace the package of ability and support that came with Officer.

"You've got a best friend that you've also got a chance to play with," Gauthier said. "The friendship was there before and it will be long after curling. The ability, and what's going on, on the ice, is just the second tier."

Jones had made her first big splash on the curling scene with the win at the Canadian juniors. The shy little tomboy had grown into an attractive young woman with long blonde hair, and it was clear early on that the TV cameras loved her. Everything seemed rosy and the future was incredibly bright, but a setback was on the way. Up until 1994, the Canadian junior curling champions were sent to the world championships the following year. Jones and Co., by right, should have been Canada's representatives in the 1995 world junior championship. However, that year the Canadian Curling Association changed the rules and decided it would send the current year's champion to the worlds. The decision meant that Jones's team would now have to win the 1995 Canadian championship just to get a chance to go to the worlds.

First up they would have to get through Manitoba, where an old teammate was standing in the way. Young Kelly MacKenzie, who was the lead on Jones's 1991 team that made it all the way to the Canadian final, was now skipping her own team. When Jones formed her own team in 1992, she chose not to include MacKenzie, instead opting for Malanchuk, and a rivalry that would last for many years was born. In 1995, MacKenzie's team, which included third Joanne Fillion, second Carlene Muth and lead Sasha Bergner, got its first taste of revenge and then came back for seconds. MacKenzie beat Jones in the Manitoba final and earned a berth in the Canadian championship in Regina.

That left Jones and Co. on the outside looking in once again when it came to the world championship, but there was still one last vestige of hope. The Canadian Curling Association decided to give the Jones team another chance to qualify for the worlds and put them directly into the semifinal of the 1995 Canadian junior championship. MacKenzie was once again standing in the way.

It came down to this: Two Manitoba teams, skipped by former teammates, facing each other in the semifinal at the Canadian championship with a chance to go to the worlds on the line. It was both controversial and dramatic and, just like in the Manitoba final, it was MacKenzie who came out on top. She also won the final and earned a trip to the world championship in Perth, Scotland. Her team won that event too and came back to Winnipeg with world championship gold medals.

It was a bitter pill for Jones and her teammates, who certainly were within their rights to believe that trip to the world championship should have been theirs. Since the world junior women's curling championship started in 1988, the 1994 Jennifer Jones team is the only Canadian champion to not participate. Ten years later, when both Jones and MacKenzie were at the Scotties Tournament of Hearts in St. John's, Newfoundland, people were still making a big deal about the rivalry born in 1995.

After a stellar junior career that included three Manitoba junior women's titles and a Canadian championship, it was time for Jones and Officer to move on to the real world. After growing up aspiring to be a doctor, Jones changed gears once she got to the University of Manitoba and decided to pursue a law degree.

Even while earning her degree over the next five years, Jones continued to curl competitively, mostly playing third for Winnipeg's Karen Porritt. Officer curled more, winning a Manitoba mixed title with Chad McMullan in 1996 and playing lead for four years on a team with Porritt and Jones. Officer eventually enrolled in the Creative Communications program at Red River College in Winnipeg, looking to pursue a career in journalism or broadcasting. The results of the Porritt team were somewhat a reflection of how busy the curlers were in their lives away from the rink. They still made it to the Manitoba provincial women's championship three times but didn't find much success at that level.

While she was in university, Jones worked part time at a Winnipeg payroll services company called Comcheq (now known as Ceridian) and there she met Scott Labonte, who would become her significant other for the better part of two decades. Labonte was not a curler but he was a regular in the stands on the curling trail and often brought a group of vocally supportive friends along for the ride. The couple moved in together in September 1999 when Jones was 25.

Jones earned a B.A. in psychology and economics and eventually earned her law degree in 1999. She almost immediately found work, articling with the Winnipeg firm Aikins, MacAulay and Thorvaldson, and started into a highly demanding profession that seemed unlikely to offer much flexibility for a competitive curler. Jones didn't play in any significant championships in 2000, but it wasn't long before she was back on the scene and making noise.

"It's about priorities," she said of juggling curling and her career in an interview with *On Manitoba* magazine. "I learned at a young age that I wanted to be successful and I learned that in order to be successful I had to give up some things. I'm not saying I would do anything differently, but I might, if I could go back, be a little more relaxed in my overall approach."

Officer was in college from 1999 to 2001 and didn't do much competitive curling, but Jones kept it up and even started skipping again in 2001. With Porritt at third, Lynn Fallis-Kurz at second and Malanchuk at lead, Jones made it to the Manitoba final that year before losing to Karen Young, and the following year took it one step further. Jones, with the same lineup as 2001, won the Manitoba championship and qualified for the Scotties Tournament of Hearts for the first time. The Canadian women's championship was to be played just down the road from her hometown in Brandon, where, coincidentally, Officer was now working as a TV reporter.

Jones added Officer as her team's fifth player (or alternate) for the 2002 Scotties in Brandon and promptly announced to the curling world that she was ready to contend with the elite curlers in the women's game. With an 8-3 record they made it to the playoffs, but another one of those challenging moments that helped Jones develop into the cool customer she is today was right around the corner.

Manitoba was playing Ontario in a single-elimination playoff game and Jones had the hammer coming home in the tenth end with the two teams tied at 6-6. Jones had a golden opportunity to win the game with a draw to the four-foot with her final stone. It's the kind of shot every skip wants to make, dreams about making, and needs to make to be the best. This time Jones was just a tad heavy. The stone slid through the four-foot and gave Ontario's Sherry Middaugh a steal of one and a chance to move on in the playoffs. Years later, after she had become a Canadian and world champion, Jones looked back on that moment as a turning point in her career.

"There was a lot of disappointment, but after that, I learned to enjoy the moment," she told the Canadian Press in 2010. "We've been fortunate enough to be on the other side of those games more often than not. You just have to lose the big one to realize it's just a game. Life goes on, the sun comes up the next day."

It was an early sign in Jones's career that she was starting to develop a new perspective on the game. She loved the competition and having the opportunity to be on the ice with the best women curlers in the country. "I told you guys," she said to the media in Brandon, "and I wasn't lying — we had a great time all week and I'd be happy if we played well. Unfortunately I missed my last shot. So, bad timing, but that happened and I have no regrets."

The next two years didn't go well on the curling ice for Jones, though she made it back to the Manitoba final in 2003 (with Kim Keizer replacing Porritt at third) before losing to Barb Spencer. Porritt and Officer rejoined the team in 2004, but they lost in the Manitoba semifinal.

Jones and Labonte were married on May 1, 2004, and they settled down in Winnipeg. "My favourite thing to do on a weekend is to relax at home with my husband," she said in an interview with the University of Manitoba's alumni magazine in 2006. "We'll kick back and rent a movie . . . just relax and enjoy each other's company." Jones would soon find out that being a competitive curler and a driven lawyer presented a significant challenge to maintaining a successful marriage.

It was after that 2004 season that people started to wonder if something was missing. Jones was proving to be one of the finest curlers in the game, but she wasn't dominant all the time and there was a feeling that she should have been. One person who had that belief was Cathy Gauthier, a two-time Canadian champion who looked at Jones and saw unlimited potential.

"I would go out and watch curling and I would see that Jennifer was a brilliant player but because of the circumstances of the team she was with, it wasn't the right fit for her," Gauthier recalled. "Karen's marriage was ending and she had two young children . . . she couldn't travel, they weren't playing as much and I knew Jennifer wanted to play more."

Gauthier also had her eye on a former teammate of hers — Cathy Overton-Clapham — who had already established herself as one of the best thirds in the world. Overton-Clapham, widely known as "Cathy O," won a Canadian championship as third for Connie Laliberte in 1995 (Gauthier was also on that team) but had been struggling to find her way as a skip for a few years.

"Cathy O was skipping and I never felt that was her position, I always felt that third was her position," Gauthier said. "I remember watching Cathy skip a team and she's not doing particularly well, certainly not winning. I'm watching Jennifer skip a team that was on different pages because of their personal lives and that's not going really well either. I went to both of them individually and said 'From my observation, it looks like you two would be good together.'

"I just said to Jennifer, 'In my opinion, if you had someone like Cathy come to your team, somebody fully committed, who has a husband who's super supportive about the kids, who can travel a lot and play a lot, you're going to get to some of the events you want to get to and I think your team is going to be stronger.'"

Gauthier proved to be both an excellent matchmaker and a good judge of curling chemistry. Though Jones and Overton-Clapham didn't really know each other at the time (Overton-Clapham was five years older), they agreed to try it out in a bonspiel. "I didn't know her from Adam," Overton-Clapham said. "We went out to Boston Pizza and sat and chatted — I had never actually had a conversation with her until then. She was keen, we had the same goals, we seemed to be on the same page and went with it." Jones asked her old reliable friend Jill Officer to join them at the test bonspiel and Gauthier played lead just to fill out the position.

"We had a lot of fun and the chemistry was really good," Gauthier said. "About a week later, Jen phoned and said, 'This is the team I want, but I want you to be a part of it.' And I was like, 'But I don't want to play!' I played for the year and I loved it."

In fact, everyone loved it, from Jones and her teammates to curling fans across the country. It took a little while for the new team to click — they struggled in the cash bonspiel season — but once the curlers found their groove, the season evolved into one of the most memorable of their lives. They won the Manitoba championship in January and qualified for the Canadian women's championship the following month at Mile One Centre in St. John's, Newfoundland. It was there that everyone who plays or follows curling came to know the name of Jennifer Jones.

"I see great things happening with this team," Overton-Clapham said as the Manitobans set out for Newfoundland.

Other observers did as well. Four-time Manitoba champion Lois Fowler picked Jones as the favourite to win it all in St. John's, an indication that the curling world was taking notice of this dream team. "I would put my money on Jennifer Jones," Fowler said. "I really have high hopes for them. I think they're a fantastic team."

The field in St. John's was relatively inexperienced but included defending Canadian champion Colleen Jones, who had won the last of her six national titles the previous season, as well as an old friend and foe of Jennifer Jones and Jill Officer. The skip of the British Columbia team was Kelly Scott (formerly Kelly MacKenzie), the very same person who'd played with Jones way back in 1991 and squashed her world junior championship dream in 1995.

Jones got off to a 3-0 start in the tournament before meeting Scott for the first time. Both curlers talked to the media before the game about being old friends and played down the rivalry, but when Scott was asked if that meant she'd have some sympathy for her former teammate, she replied, "Uh-uh, that's out the window."

Jones, always politically correct, was gracious about playing Scott. "Since she moved away we lost touch, but she's a great person and I would consider her a friend. She has come a long way and she went on to win the world juniors so obviously she's a great player and has a great team." Just like 1995's Manitoba final and Canadian semifinal, Scott emerged victorious from the round-robin game in St. John's. Whether she was willing to admit it or not, Jones had herself a nemesis. But the tournament was far from over, and Jones had plenty left to show.

Jones finished the round robin with a 9-2 record and in first place. Scott came in second with an 8-3 mark, while Saskatchewan's Stefanie Lawton was third at 7-4 and up-and-comer Jenn Hanna emerged for a series of tiebreakers to qualify for the playoffs with a 6-5 record. Hanna's team was notable in that she and her teammates were all under the age of 25 and were absolutely fearless. The team also included a young second named Dawn Askin, who fans of the Jennifer Jones team would come to know very well in the ensuing years.

Jones's first date was with Kelly Scott in the Page playoff game between the first and second place teams. The winner would earn a direct berth in the final, while the loser would have to play a semifinal. Jones certainly didn't have her best game, curling only 69 percent, but it was good enough to break the Kelly Scott curse. Manitoba won 8-7 and moved on to the final. Everyone in St. John's was expecting Jones and Scott to clash again in the championship game, but Hanna surprisingly upset Scott in the semifinal and became the only one who could slow down the Jones juggernaut. She very nearly did just that, but Jones was simply not to be denied.

Jones and her teammates played terribly in the Canadian final on that February day on the snowy Rock. They were off their game from the very beginning, and Jones, who battled a nasty cold all week during the tournament, looked worn down. Jones curled just 70 percent in the game, and Overton-Clapham was only slightly better at 76 percent, so it was remarkable that the Manitobans were even in the contest. They were behind for the first nine ends and trailed 5-2 after six ends, giving up steals of one in both the fifth and sixth. They came into the final end with the hammer, trailing 6-4 and hoping against hope that they might be able to get two points and send it to an extra end. What actually happened was something much more rewarding, and it was one of the most dramatic moments in curling history.

The game was virtually over. Reporters on the media bench had their stories written, proclaiming Jenn Hanna as the new, hugely unlikely champion of women's curling and carving Jones and her team for underperforming in the biggest game of their lives. Hanna and her teammates played a bit of a risky end, with lots of rocks in play, but they managed to have one rock on the button behind cover as it came down to Jones's last rock. With three guard rocks in front of the house, it looked nearly impossible for Jones to get to the yellow Ontario stone, and the dream of a Canadian women's championship was seemingly dead. However, Jones found one last sliver of hope. Surrounding the lone Ontario stone on the button were three red Manitoba stones. Sitting off to the side of the house was an Ontario stone that was outside the rings but had not touched the sideboards so was still in play. Jones and Overton-Clapham studied the angle. They looked at it again and again and decided the shot was there. Even if it wasn't, it was their only hope anyway.

There was a buzz in the building as people slowly started to realize what was about to be attempted. Reporters took their fingers off the Send button on their computers, in case some kind of crazy circus-shot changed the outcome of this foregone conclusion. While it looked to many like a low-percentage, last-ditch effort, Jones was as calm, focused and determined as usual. She could picture the path of the shot and the ultimate result in her mind. She knew what was going to happen.

"Well, I remember the ice, the smell of the ice . . . I will never forget it," she said in *On Manitoba*. "I remember looking up into the stands and seeing all the people. I remember seeing my mom and my sister. I remember consciously taking that moment to savour the experience so I would remember it later."

She reared back, let the rock fly and it screeched down the ice, Officer and Gauthier sweeping frantically, Jones and Overton-Clapham both shouting instructions, every one of them sensing the shot's great potential. The red rock made contact with about half of the yellow stone outside the rings and jumped toward the centre of the house, as if on command. It rolled perfectly toward the button and bumped the solitary Ontario stone all the way out of the house. For good measure, the shooter stuck right there and gave Manitoba an astounding four points and the Canadian championship.

"That is the best shot I've ever seen to win a game," CBC curling analyst Mike Harris proclaimed. "Unbelievable."

The entire building was stunned as the Manitoba curlers went wild, realizing what they had just achieved at such a crucial moment. It was a shot for the ages, one that became dubbed both "The Shot" and "the shot heard round the curling world." Few people could remember any shot in women's curling that was better or more dramatic.

"Right now, I can literally close my eyes and take myself there and bring it back," Jones said to *On Manitoba* in 2006. "It's a memory that will last a lifetime. Yes, the shot was amazing, but it was the feeling itself that was overwhelming and stays with me now. At one point, I thought my head would explode from all the adrenalin. I have an image of my mom and my sister: My mom falling on the stairs and sobbing because the feeling she had was so overwhelming for her, too. I still get tears in my eyes just thinking about it."

Jones was ecstatic to have made such an incredible shot, but also to have finally won a Canadian women's championship and, 10 years after the 1995 debacle, to finally qualify for the worlds. The team also earned the right to be called Team Canada at the 2006 Scotties in London, Ontario, and a berth in the Olympic Trials the following December in Halifax. Jones had always dreamed of this moment, of having a chance to make the huge shot with everything on the line and nailing it.

"It was an easier shot in my dreams, but you know what, this is way more exciting," Jones said after giving an uncharacteristic hug to a couple of reporters from her hometown. "I'm glad that I made a big shot under pressure. I'm not going to say it was easy because it wasn't, but it was there and we made it."

"Jen made a fantastic shot," added Officer, who was the first to jump into the skip's arms. "I think we all saw it was going to happen. But it was so exciting that when I was sweeping that rock down there, I almost couldn't see."

Immediately, a debate broke out on media row about the greatness of the winning shot, which many compared to the in-off made by the late, great Sandra Schmirler at the 1997 Olympic Trials in Brandon. That shot essentially won the tournament for Schmirler, though it didn't come in the last end and didn't have quite the same dramatic effect as the Miracle at Mile One.

"The Schmirler shot wasn't for the victory," the late Don Wittman, play-by-play man for CBC, said at the time. "It was a great shot and it assured Schmirler of victory, but there were still a couple of ends after that. This one had everything on the line. This is a shot that will be remembered for a long time as perhaps the greatest ever. To make a shot like that with the final stone in the tenth end is just unbelievable."

Gauthier, still having trouble catching her breath after all the excitement on the ice, went even further in her assessment of the shot's greatness in comparison to Schmirler's.

"The angle here was sharper, it was longer and it was all-or-nothing," Gauthier said. "It was mind blowing. I just want to see that shot over and over again. We might be seeing it for a while somewhere."

"It's a moment that I'll never forget as long as I live," Jones said, at the time having no idea that this was just the beginning of her historic career.

Nine years later, Mike Harris still held up the Jones in-off as the greatest shot in the history of curling. "I've been doing this for a long time now. It's my fourteenth year of doing TV and I don't remember any shot, especially not to win a game of that importance, that was better. I mean, we've seen crazy shots made but nothing to win a game and certainly not to win a national championship. When you combine the importance of the shot and the quality of the shot, there's never been a better shot."

After "The Shot," the world wanted to know more about Jennifer Jones, this pretty blonde with the brains to become a lawyer and a talent for curling that put her in elite company. She was barraged with requests for interviews on TV and radio and in print, but her introverted nature prevented her from really opening up. In many ways, she remained a bit of a mystery. After playing with her for that one glorious year, Gauthier has a decent sense of what makes Jennifer Jones tick.

"She is a very driven person and that affects all parts of her life," Gauthier said in 2014. "She was driven to success at school and to become a lawyer and driven to be a good person for her family and for her very close circle of friends and driven very much to succeed. It wasn't a lot of pressure that her parents put on her to win. She just got out there and felt it.

"She just doesn't accept average and doesn't accept mediocre. I think about all the games that we played and probably in the wins as much as the losses, she would go back to every single shot and analyze where there were mistakes. Sometimes it's hard as a team, when you've come through a game and you've won, to kind of feel like you've not won, but that's the driven part of her that says, 'Just because you win, it's not an acceptable result.' I think that's what has got her to where she is now.

"She is absolutely, very much an introvert. She tries really hard and she's open to talking to people but I realized very early on when she and I played together, it was remarkable to me how tight and how small her circle of really good friends was. She really isn't an open book to the entire world. It doesn't mean that she's false, it just means that she opens up to very few and I would say that is still the same. But what she's learned how to do is realize that there's always going to be critics out there but there are also so many people who want the best for her and want her to win. She's seen that balance now and I think before she only saw the critics."

They were greeted by throngs of enthusiastic fans at the Winnipeg airport when they returned home from St. John's and were feted throughout the city for a few weeks, until it was time to head to Scotland for the 2005 world women's curling championship. Paisley, Scotland, was the birthplace of curling — the game was invented by monks on a sheet of ice just outside the famed Paisley Abbey, which still stands today — but it was ill equipped to host a major championship in 2005. It was in that year that the International Curling Federation decided to split the men's and women's world championships for the first time. The men's event was to be played in Victoria, British Columbia, while the women were in Scotland. As soon as the curlers arrived in Paisley, it was clear this event would not be up to their usual standards. The curling rink was small, held only 1,000 seats and was in the same building as a swimming pool, which caused immense problems for ice-makers who consider humidity to be the work of the devil. The fourth draw of the tournament was actually postponed because the ice melted overnight. There were also no tournament time clocks — a standard at curling events around the world — because of a dispute between the organizers and volunteer timers who wanted to be paid.

Finally at a world championship for the first time after the disappointment of 1995, Jones and Co. embraced the moment and tried to make the most of a difficult situation with ice conditions that simply didn't play into their hands. It didn't go well. The thrill of wearing Team Canada colours soon began to wear off as the team scratched and clawed its way to a flattering 8-3 record and third place in the round robin behind 11-0 Sweden (Anette Norberg) and 10-1 United States (Cassie Johnson). The most humbling moment of the tournament was still to come, however, as the Canadians faced Norway's Dordi Nordby in an elimination playoff game and were crushed 12-5. They finished fourth, out of the medals, a rarity for any Canadian team at a world championship.

"We would have gone 2-9 at the Canadians if we played like we are playing here," Gauthier said, adding that the team felt like they let the country down with their subpar performance.

In this case, the propensity for Jones to call an aggressive game came back to haunt Canada. Because the ice was so soft, it ran much straighter than what the Canadians were used to. Norberg and Johnson played a more conservative style, and it worked to their benefit while Jones tried to put lots of rocks in play and use the finesse game, but she couldn't make it happen in those ice conditions.

"I'd love to start over," Overton-Clapham said at the end of the tournament. "Maybe we would play differently, play more wide open and wait for mistakes from the other team like most of the teams are doing here. We kept lots of rocks in play and it wasn't conducive to the ice conditions."

"I wouldn't have changed anything," Jones said, showing her stubborn side. "We came in with a great attitude and we made a lot of shots. We just didn't make the big ones when we had to. I wouldn't change our approach." Clearly Jones didn't agree with her third, perhaps an early sign that the two were not always on the same page.

"It was an honour to represent Canada and hopefully we will get a chance to do it again. It's very disappointing but it doesn't take away from winning the Canadian championship and having this opportunity. It almost just gives us more desire to have the opportunity to do it again," Jones said.

The poor performance at the worlds notwithstanding, the Jones team had enjoyed a spectacular year, the best of their curling lives, highlighted by a moment in St. John's that will live on in the sport's lore. There was so much more to come.

Around that time, Jones made a move in her career, leaving Aikins, MacAulay and Thorvaldson for a position as in-house counsel for Wellington West Capital, also based in Winnipeg. The company was run by Charlie Spiring, a big curling supporter who wanted to provide both employment and flexibility for Jones. It was yet another dream come true for Jones, who now knew she had the comfort level to make curling a priority in the winter and maintain her career at the same time.

"It's definitely a tough balance but I've worked for some amazing companies that are all about chasing the dream," Jones said in a CBC interview at the 2014 Olympics. "Charlie Spiring was all about chasing the dream and he said, 'Jen, you come and work for us and you go and chase that Olympic dream.' They were super flexible with my schedule. I feel like I've just surrounded myself with these great people that believe in me. I've been very lucky that I've been able to pursue a career at the same time as pursuing the dream of being an Olympian but it's only because these companies have been so flexible. There's no way that you could balance both. They're both full-time jobs and it would just be impossible."

Spiring's friendship and support meant a great deal to Jones, so much so that she told her boss after the Olympic Trials in 2013 that she couldn't have done it without him. That kind of support is not easy to come by and it's a veritable gold mine for competitive curlers.

Despite their success in 2005, changes were afoot for the team the very next season. Gauthier decided to bow out after only one season, knowing how rigorous the schedule would be for Team Canada. It meant Gauthier was passing up the opportunity to play in the Olympic Trials in 2005 and the national Scotties in 2006, but she stuck to her guns. Jones went out of province to find Team Canada's new lead, recruiting Georgina Wheatcroft, who'd won a world championship in 2000 and Olympic bronze medal in 2002 as the second of British Columbia's Kelley Law. Wheatcroft brought a wealth of experience to the team, and the Jones foursome continued to contend in just about every tournament, and while the end results were not as good as the previous year, the new lead had a positive effect.

"I would give Georgina a lot of credit for where the team continued to go from there," Overton-Clapham reflected eight years later. "She certainly brought a lot to the team as far as her experiences go. We learned a lot from her about what we should be doing pre-game, post-game, pre-season, post-season. We continued to bring those things forward every year after. She had been to the Olympics, she was a world champion. We didn't train in the summer, we didn't go to any training weekends as a team prior to Georgina joining our team. The following year we started to do that."

First off were the Olympic Trials in Halifax in December 2005. It was the first time Jones had qualified for the Trials, and after winning the Scotties the previous year, her team came in as the obvious favourite. Things didn't go well at the arena and were even worse away from it; the Olympic dream was quickly dashed. That the Jones team managed a 5-4 record in the Trials, which were eventually won by Alberta's Shannon Kleibrink, was impressive in itself considering the extenuating circumstances that were revealed late in the event. Jones's team was plagued by problems. There was an uncharacteristic hogline violation by the skip and a burned rock by Wheatcroft, both of which cost the Jones team games. But the most severe and concerning problem was a case of kidney stones — Jones woke up ill in the middle of the first night of the Trials and had to be taken to hospital.

"It was the worst pain I've ever had," Jones said after the Olympic Trials. "I wouldn't want to wish that on anybody."

If nothing else, Jones proved herself to be tough and determined by not missing a single draw at the Trials. "Yeah, I toughed it out," she said. She was given morphine at the hospital but chose not to have immediate surgery because she would have had to miss games. Still, her resilience didn't get the team where it wanted to be. The Olympics would have to wait at least four more years.

"Things just went wrong the whole week and obviously it wasn't meant to be for us," Officer said through tears at the end of the Trials. "There are lessons to be learned from everything in your life and what doesn't kill you makes you stronger. Now we can set our sights on the rest of the season and Olympic-wise, we're going to have to look forward to Vancouver in 2010."

On the bright side, the Jones team still had the 2006 Scotties Tournament of Hearts — where they would be Team Canada — to look forward to. Unfortunately, what resulted at the Canadian women's curling championship in London, Ontario, was more disappointment. Jones and Co. were in contention all week and made it all the way back to the final. Another trip to the worlds was just one win away, but once again old nemesis Kelly Scott was also in the house and posed a familiar roadblock. Scott and her teammates from Kelowna, British Columbia, pulled out another huge win and ended the Jones team's reign as Team Canada after just the one year. Jones was philosophical in defeat, perhaps becoming even more level-headed after tasting both success and disappointment in big events over the past year.

"We had a great year," she said. "It was a great experience to be out there, win or lose. I mean, we were in the final and every team wants to be there. We had a great time out there, we fought for it and it just wasn't our day and there's not really much you can do about it. Obviously, we're disappointed. Being Team Canada was just a thrill of a lifetime and I never wanted it to end. But we'll be back." She had that right, though it would take more than a year and more personnel changes to make it happen.

Jill Officer has always been an adventurous woman and she takes her fitness more seriously than many other curlers. At the end of the 2005–06 season, she was looking for a new challenge and a way to take her mind off the disappointments of the Olympic Trials and Scotties Tournament of Hearts final. She found it in the form of a trip to Nepal with her older brother, Rob. The siblings hired a Sherpa guide and went on a 28-day hike to the Mt. Everest Base Camp.

"It's more challenging than anything — a mental and physical challenge," Officer explained before hitting the trail. Still living in Brandon at the time and working as a communications manager for the city, she trained for the trek by hiking up and down a steep bridge with a heavy backpack. There was no plan to do any mountain climbing with picks and ropes, just a rigorous climb up 19,000 feet to the base camp. Getting to the camp was expected to take 21 days, while coming down would take just seven.

They set off in the spring and completed this extraordinary feat. "It definitely was not easy," Officer said. "It was physically very demanding and you really need to push yourself. At first I thought 'What did I get myself into?' But after a couple of days I got used to it. And the scenery was second to none."

More than anything, Officer said the trip gave her perspective about her own world while mingling with Sherpas who had never heard of a sport called curling. It was a chance to clear her mind, cleanse her system (the trip was so physically demanding that she lost 10 pounds) and realize how lucky she was to have everything in her life, even if her curling team did not qualify for the Olympics or the world championship that year.

"We're really fortunate to live where we do," Officer said after returning home, refreshed and ready for another run at curling greatness. "This was really hard, the challenge of a lifetime, both mentally and physically. I have no regrets." That would become a mantra for the Jones team as they continually tried to climb mountains in their curling careers over the next eight years.

At the end of the 2006 season, Wheatcroft left the team and returned to Vancouver, where her family was residing. Once again, Jones needed to find a new lead, and in April she announced it would be her old friend and teammate Dana Allerton (formerly Malanchuk). Allerton had stepped away from competitive curling for a few years to raise a family, but she was ready to give it a go again and the timing was just right to join her old friend's team. It was a nice story, but it wound up being highly controversial, and by the end of it, Jones was viewed as a ruthless individual by many fans and curlers.

On the eve of the 2007 provincial women's curling championship, Allerton was unceremoniously cut from the team. The lead was stunned, disillusioned and felt betrayed. "I worked really hard and felt like I was part of the team but they felt they needed to go in a different direction," Allerton said at the time. "I had sacrificed a lot and was shocked that they would ask me to leave. I was pumped to go to the provincials and now I won't get the chance."

Though Jones was leading the cash tour at the time, she decided Allerton wasn't working out and replaced her with the team's fifth player/coach Janet Arnott, who was a three-time Canadian champion with her sister Connie Laliberte and had won a world championship in 1984. Though there was an outcry from some curlers and curling fans over her treatment of Allerton, who she called a best friend, Jones maintained there was nothing personal about the decision. "It's just business and we are trying to put the best team possible together," Jones said. "[Allerton] is one of my best friends and I'm hopeful we will remain friends." Still there were lots of boos for the Jones team at the provincial championship. The wild popularity Jones had earned by making "The Shot" in 2005 was waning.

Though 49 at the time, Arnott proved a capable replacement for Allerton and she helped get the Jones foursome another provincial title in 2007. They went on to finish third at the Canadian Scotties Tournament of Hearts in Lethbridge, Alberta. Amazingly, it was once again Kelly Scott who eliminated the Jones team in the semifinal before going on to win her second straight Canadian women's championship.

That off-season brought another significant change for the Jones team. Arnott had no interest in continuing to play but was happy to stay on as coach, so Jones went searching for yet another lead. A young player with considerable ability, motivation and commitment to the cause practically fell into her lap. Dawn Askin, who was second on the Hanna team that Jones beat back in 2005, was moving to Manitoba with her curler boyfriend and was looking for a team. The only women curlers she really knew in Manitoba were on the Jones team so she called them up. It couldn't have worked out more perfectly. Askin slid into the lead position at the end of the 2007 season and has been entrenched there ever since.

"I thought it was fabulous because in 2005, honestly, that team outplayed us badly in the final," Gauthier said. "It worked out so well for Dawn to be able to come to Manitoba because of [now-husband Mike McEwen] and become part of such a great team."

Askin was born in Ottawa in 1980 and started curling at age seven at the RCMP Curling Club. Introduced to the game by her parents, Jane and Wayne Askin, Dawn flourished at an early age and was a competitive junior curler whose aspirations took off when Sandra Schmirler won the inaugural women's curling Olympic gold medal for Canada in 1998. Though she was working on a communications degree at the University of Ottawa, she continued to hone her skills on the pebble and eventually hooked up with Hanna to form part of an exciting young team. When she was just 19, her family billeted a young curler from Manitoba named Mike McEwen during a junior bonspiel at the Granite Curling Club in Ottawa. The pair became a couple eventually, and the relationship drew Askin to Winnipeg.

"To come out here, I couldn't ask for a better situation to be in," said Askin, who was 27 at the time. Little did she know that her addition would be the spark that sent this team on one of the greatest runs in the history of curling. Back then she was just the quiet redhead who really knew how to curl. Before 2007 was over, the reconfigured Jones team had already won two major titles — the World Curling Tour's Players Championship and the Canada Cup. Early in 2008 they won yet another Manitoba championship, meaning Askin would play in her second Canadian Scotties Tournament of Hearts with the very team that beat her in her first.

"How ironic is that?" she said. "I'm so pleased right now. I'm ecstatic."

The 2008 Scotties in Regina didn't start out well for the Jones team as they lost four of their first seven games and looked to be on the brink of elimination early in the tournament. This team had been in tough positions before, and they started their comeback, winning four straight games to finish at 7-4 and earn a spot in a tiebreaker against Newfoundland and Labrador's Heather Strong. They won that game, beat Quebec's Marie-France Larouche in the first Page Playoff game, stole a point in an extra end to beat Ontario's Sherry Middaugh 9-8 in the semifinal and earned berth in the final against 2006 Olympic bronze medallist Shannon Kleibrink from Alberta. It would take an eighth straight win against a team that was 11-1 up to that point, but there was something about the roll the Jones team was on that suggested it could happen.

The final came down to the last rock, as always, and Jones did not have the hammer. What she did have was one lonesome rock in the four-foot, buried behind her own guard after a stellar draw, with a daunting five Alberta stones surrounding it in the house. Kleibrink had an opportunity to score a big end for the win and the Manitobans could only watch helplessly as she tried a runback double with her last rock. That anguish turned to joy moments later when Kleibrink's shot jammed, removing one Manitoba stone from four-foot but leaving another sitting right there to give Jones a steal and a 6-4 win. For the second time, Jones, Overton-Clapham and Officer were Canadian champions. It was a first for Askin, who was immediately asked about how it felt after losing in 2005.

"This is a completely opposite feeling," she gushed moments after the rocks came to rest. "I was quite upset after that '05 final and this is the best feeling in the world. This is unbelievable!"

While the curling world will always talk about the last shot Jones made in St. John's in 2005, her final stone in 2008 was just as important. Jones made a perfect draw through a port to hide her last rock at the top of the four-foot. She could not have drawn it up better on a telestrator.

"This one we absolutely had to make and we had to put it exactly where we put it to make [Kleibrink] think about it," Jones explained. "In '05, it was probably the harder shot, but still, the game's on the line and you've got to make it. [This time] it wasn't a shot to win, it was a shot not to lose; whereas in '05 it was a shot to win the game. I compare '05 to the bottom of the ninth with two out and hitting a grand slam. This one was like the bases are loaded and you strike somebody out.

"It felt absolutely amazing to win, like, a total adrenalin rush. It doesn't get old. It felt as good as it did when we made the great shot to win in 2005. It's an amazing feeling."

Officer had a slightly different feeling after that win. The second was still shaking with excitement when she got tapped on the shoulder to go to the back of the arena for a drug test. The Jones team had earned a berth in the 2009 Olympic Trials in Edmonton that day and that meant Olympic standards for drug testing applied. It didn't go well for Officer, though not because of a positive drug test. "I peed all over my hand," she blurted out to reporters with a hearty laugh. "I mean, I was still shaking from winning the game and there's someone there watching you pee. But don't worry, I washed my hands really, really well!"

So it was off to the world championship again for the Jones team, this time on home soil in Vernon, British Columbia. Canada had not won a world title at home since Marilyn Bodogh did it in Hamilton in 1996, but for the Jones team there was something comforting about the thought of playing at home, and they certainly knew it had to be better than the less-than-ideal situation in Paisley in 2005. "There were no people there, there were no time clocks, the officiating was terrible — it was all a nightmare," Overton-Clapham said. "So many things have changed. We weren't prepared for anything in '05."

One of the things that had changed for the team was the fact that they now had access to the top coaches, athletic therapists and sports psychologists in the land. They worked regularly with noted sports psychologist Dr. Cal Botterill and planned to add him to their entourage for the 2008 worlds. They also now had a technical coach and a national team coach who would help organize their daily schedules. All in all, the team had more going for it than it had the last time. "We're better than we were in '05," Jones said. The proof of that came out in their play in Vernon.

Canada had a few ups and downs at the that world championship round robin, the ups including wins over perennial contenders Switzerland and Sweden, the downs losses to up-and-comers China and Denmark. The most challenging time came when they lost 9-7 to Bingyu Wang of China, a game after which the Chinese players threw their brooms in the air and celebrated as though they had won the

Olympics. The Canadians were slow to recover and found themselves down 6-1 after four ends in the next game against the American team, skipped by former world champion Debbie McCormick. That's when coach Janet Arnott really made her presence felt.

"I heard Janet say something once and it really stuck in my head," TSN analyst Cathy Gauthier said. "It was at the world championship and they were really, really struggling and they were all down and looking pretty blue and Janet walked out at the fifth-end break and she just said to them 'Remember this is a choice that you make. You don't have to curl. You're choosing to do it because you love it. Don't forget that you love to play.' There was dead silence and they were a different team in the second half."

They scored three in the very next end, came back to win that game 10-9, and almost everything went their way after that. They lost just one more game, 6-3 to Denmark's Angelina Jensen, but made very few mistakes the rest of the way, finishing the round robin with a 9-2 record. Next up was the team from China (also 9-2) that had over-celebrated after beating Canada in the round robin. The Canadians frowned upon the Chinese exuberance but they had a bigger problem on their hands: this opponent was good and wasn't going to go away easily. Bingyu Wang's team showed its mettle once again, beating the vaunted Jones team 7-5 to earn a berth directly into the final. Just like in the Canadian championship, Jones wasn't making it easy on herself and now had to play a semifinal game against Japan, skipped by Moe Meguro. The Japanese, who had never won so much as a medal in world curling, actually led 8-5 after eight ends and things looked bleak for Canada . . . but curling fans know never to count out a team skipped by Jennifer Jones.

The Canadians scored two in the ninth with the hammer, stole the tying point in the tenth and then stole the winning point in the eleventh for a 9-8 victory. It was a stunning comeback by a team that had been doing just that all season long. If ever there was a team that had to work for its rewards, this was it. From 3-4 at the Canadian championship and coming through the tiebreaker to win on a steal, to stealing the tying and winning points in the world semifinal, the Jones team was all about resilience. "We had to work hard for it this week but that's just one of the great things about our team," Officer said. "It says a lot about our team and how tough we are and how proud we should be because we never give up. Never."

There was one more huge test still to come though — another matchup with China, the very team that had beaten them twice already in Vernon. This time, the Comeback Kids needed no miracle. Canada scored a big three after Wang made a mistake in the second end and added a key deuce in the seventh when Jones made a tremendous double-raise takeout to make the score 6-3. The nervous Chinese team, in the world final for the first time, could not mount a comeback, and Canada simply had to run them out of rocks in the tenth end for a 7-4 victory. That world championship, the one that had been eluding Jones, Overton-Clapham and Officer since way back in 1995, was finally theirs. Overton-Clapham had been part of Connie Laliberte's Canadian team in 1995 when they lost the final to Sweden on a poor last draw by the skip. Jones and Officer had, of course, been cheated out of their chance to represent their country in 1995, and all three had finished fourth at the Parody in Paisley. Now they were on top of the world and had reached yet another new height in their sparkling curling careers.

"It feels pretty darn good," the then 33-year-old Jones said. "You always dream of it and never know how many chances you are going to get. We went out and controlled that game, and I thought we deserved it."

All four of the Canadian curlers, their fifth player Jennifer Clark-Rouire and Arnott stood arm in arm on the podium to receive their gold medals and belted out "O Canada" as tears streamed down their faces. "Loud and proud, baby," Officer exclaimed. "I just totally had chills all the way down my body."

This was the culmination of a lifetime of effort, time away from families, travelling, practicing daily, being consumed by the game of curling. This was for parents, husbands, children, bosses and fans who'd supported the curlers for so many years. Overton-Clapham, at age 38, could barely put it into words. "It's been a long time waiting. There was a lot of time put into the game and a lot of time away from home and practicing hard and trying to get better. It finally paid off and it feels great, very exciting."

Jones was particularly happy for her third, the woman she'd joined forces with in 2004 to make this dream come true. "Cathy's like a sister to me and this was her [third] world championship, and I know she really wanted to win. We all wanted to win and we were all in shock when it actually happened."

That sister-like relationship between skip and third would be put to the test in the coming years, but nothing could take away from this moment. The curlers returned home to Winnipeg to a crowd of 200 fans at the airport and celebrated once again with their home city. "This makes up for all the bumps along the way in Paisley," Jones reflected. "No matter what happens in curling now, we've achieved everything that we wanted."

Of course, that last statement wasn't true. Jones and her teammates still had one more thing they wanted more than anything else — an appearance in the Olympics and, better yet, an Olympic medal. There were many times they thought it would never come. It would take years and many wild twists and turns in their lives before it finally did.

CHAPTER TWO

BROTHERS
IN ARMS

If you happened to stop by the Soo Curlers Association Club on any random winter day in 1990, you might have seen the most unusual sight of two young boys tearing around the ice surface with their hockey helmets on. The youngest was just four years old, the oldest seven, and they loved to hang around the curling rink with their dad. His name was Eric Harnden, and he was a competitive curler who needed to practise and wanted to introduce his boys to the game at the same time. Eric Harnden and his brother, Al, were due to compete in the Brier that winter in their home town of Sault Ste. Marie, and he wanted his young sons to understand what he was doing and enjoy the experience.

"I'd go out and practise and I'd bring them out," Eric Harnden said. "We'd put hockey helmets on them. They'd have a blast."

The boys were Eric Jr. (E.J.) and Ryan Harnden, and their father couldn't possibly have known what the experience would eventually mean to them. The Harnden brothers, just like their dad and uncle, took to curling immediately and some of their earliest memories came from the Soo Curlers Association Club. There was a home video, shot on Beta of all things, of four-year-old Ryan running through a house full of rocks, stepping on one of the stones, slipping and falling. "Thankfully, he had that hockey helmet on," E.J. laughed decades later. "We sent it in to *America's Funniest Home Videos* at that time when it was really popular, but we never heard back from them, so I guess it wasn't funny enough."

Ryan remembers the fall in the house, though it's hard to know if it's a memory of the incident or the video. E.J. remembers pushing a rock down the ice surface with both hands while his father practised. They carried cut-down brooms with them everywhere they went and couldn't wait to get on the ice for a chance to slide curling rocks up and down the sheets. They both recall falling in love with the game at an early age. Perhaps it was because they got to spend time with their father while they did it, or because they got to watch their dad and uncle compete in club play-downs, provincial championships and even the Brier.

"I don't think there's anything cooler than being a little kid, growing up and watching your dad play in a national championship and watching 5,000-plus people chant your last name," E.J. told the *Sault Star*. "I don't think it gets any better than that."

"I remember being up there and admiring him," Ryan added. "He is still my hero and still the best curler in the world in my mind."

In other years you might have seen another young kid, a self-described rink rat named Brad Jacobs, hanging around at the Soo Curlers Association Club. Brad was a first cousin to the Harndens — he was the son of Eric and Al's sister Cindy — and he shared their passion for curling from an early age. He worked as an ice boy at the curling club under ice technician Ian Fisher and loved to watch his uncles play the game. He was more like a brother to the Harndens — all three of the boys crawled around the floor together as babies and grew up wrestling and roughhousing, organizing ball hockey games and getting into the usual active-boy trouble.

"We were all considered 'rink rats,' eager to learn from the family members who introduced us to the sport and never wanting to go home until we were forced to leave," said Jacobs.

Brad Jacobs was born on June 11, 1985, in Sault Ste. Marie, the first child of Robert and Cindy Jacobs. He was raised in the city of about 75,000 along with his younger sister, Lyndsey, and was involved in sports as far back as he can remember. "Healthy, active living is something my parents really believe in and practise, and I'm glad for that," Jacobs told ActiveForLife.com. "I pretty much did every sport as a kid, in school and outside of school. I tried it all." The Sault was always a sports town and was the birthplace of Hockey Hall of Famers Phil Esposito, Tony Esposito and Ron Francis. The Soo Greyhounds of the Ontario Hockey League are a big part of the sports fabric, having once been home to hockey icons like Wayne Gretzky, Paul Coffey, Joe Thornton and Jeff Carter. And the people there love their curling.

Though they are three years apart in age, the Harnden brothers were best friends from a very young age. They had separate groups of friends, but they always gravitated back to each other when it came to sports. They played street hockey in front of their family home, baseball in the nearby park, strapped on the skates at the local rink and hit the links together for some golf in the summer. "We were always there for each other," E.J. said.

Both boys played hockey growing up and were good enough to make travelling teams. Brad played hockey, baseball and golf and practiced gymnastics. But all three always seemed to gravitate back to curling. E.J. played his first game at age eight, Brad at 10. Ryan remembers daydreaming about the game even as a young child: "I remember practicing and playing a draw and I'd be pretending that the shot was to win the Brier." This thing called curling was clearly pumping through their bodies like the very blood they inherited from their parents.

Brad Jacobs started working with a coach named Tom Coulterman in 1995, when he was just 10 years old. Coulterman had 20 years of curling and coaching experience, and he saw something special in some of the young curlers in Sault Ste. Marie. Coulterman was the junior curling coordinator at the Soo Curlers Association and would later go on to work for 13 years as the team leader for the Canadian Junior Men's National Team. Coulterman's influence on junior curlers across the country, and particularly in the Sault, cannot be overstated. He knew a good curler when he saw one and he loved what he saw in Brad Jacobs and Ryan Harnden, who were around the same age and were good candidates to form a team together. Ryan, though he was the youngest of the boys, was chosen as the skip and Jacobs was tapped to play third. They were joined on the team by Matt Premo and Scott Seabrook. At the time, Ryan was just 12 and Brad 13, and Coulterman couldn't believe how good they already were.

"At their age, they're the best rink I've seen," Coulterman told the *Sault Star* in 1998. "First of all, their technical ability impresses me. They're all excellent shooters and they have a good knowledge of the game. They're just so far ahead of any one team I've seen, girls or boys, at the same ages."

Interestingly, Coulterman could only think of one other boys' team he'd seen that was even in the same class as the one skipped by Ryan Harnden — the one skipped by E.J. Harnden, then 15 and preparing for the Northern Ontario Curling Association junior championships. "When you see them very young, those [two] stand out," he said. "You can tell they've got the potential to be something special."

Eric Harnden saw it too. His sons shared his passion for curling and were willing to do what it took to get better. Ryan, for instance, was a curling junkie, who watched as much of the game on television as he possibly could. He was a student of the strategy, the line calls, the way players slid out of the hack and performed their in-turns and out-turns. "I want to see how the players call the game," he said at the age of 12. "Our goal is to get really good and one day make it to the Brier."

"Ryan knows the game well," Eric said. "When he's watching on television, he's always asking me questions about the calls being made. And he has a very, very good memory. He'll remember certain shots played in certain situations and he takes that out onto the ice and utilizes it."

It was still so early in the development of these young curlers, but there were so many reasons to be excited. Coulterman was certain the boys were destined for big things. "How far they go is up to them," he said. "It depends on how hard they want to work at it. The sky is limit."

E.J. Harnden played hockey until he was in his early teens — even dreamed a bit about playing in the NHL one day — but knew he was at a point where he would need to make a choice. In 1998, curling was introduced as an Olympic sport in Nagano, Japan. When E.J. saw that, he immediately knew what course he wanted his athletic career to take. "We played on travelling hockey teams, but then it got to a point where we were curling competitively and we needed to make a choice," he said. "We needed to put all of our time or nothing into one or the other.

"So I chose curling, thinking that I had a little bit of a better shot having my dad alongside to help me. I grew up with my hero being my dad. Really I wanted to get into curling just because I wanted to be like him and make him as proud of me as I have always been of him. I think that was the deciding factor for me."

It didn't take long for Ryan and cousin Brad to follow E.J.'s lead. As they entered their high school years, all three were competitive curlers taking it very seriously. With Coulterman and Eric and Al Harnden showing them the way, they found it easy to think big when it came to curling. "We were all very fortunate to have someone in our lives who participated in national-level competitions and individuals who not only helped us develop our own game, but more importantly acted as inspirations for us to model ourselves around and strive to achieve similar success," Jacobs said.

By the year 2000, when Jacobs was 15 years old, he was curling regularly with his cousins, even though they were both skipping their own teams, and working at the Soo Curlers Association with Ian Fisher. "Certainly it helped him because he was able to access ice any time he wanted to at that point," Fisher said in 2014, looking back on those early days. "He'd be coming to work and if there wasn't a lot to do or at the end of his shift, he'd be out there throwing rocks. He was able to do it whenever he wanted to so he used that to enhance his game. You could tell that he really loved the game and liked to spend a lot of time out on the ice practicing. He threw rocks all the time, even by himself." Jacobs wanted to know everything there was about the game, including how to judge rocks, how to gauge ice, even how the temperature in the building could affect shots. "I've known Brad for a long, long time," Fisher told CBC Radio. "He has learned all the little aspects around the club about the rocks and the ice, and he was very, very keen at a very young age. You could see that he was going to blossom into something special."

In the early months of 2000, Brad played second for Ryan in tournaments for curlers aged 16 and under and played second for E.J. on the Sir James Dunn high school team. In the fall, they all hooked up together to form a team for a junior cash bonspiel in London, Ontario. E.J was the skip, Ryan the second and Jacobs threw lead stones as they finished third in the tournament. Because he was oldest, E.J. handled the skipping duties in those early days, and by the fall of 2001 they were starting to feel comfortable as a team — so comfortable in fact that they entered the Regal Capital Curling Classic men's bonspiel at their home club. They weren't supposed to play in the event but signed up when there was a last-minute cancellation. E.J. would handle the skipping duties, with Caleb Flaxey at third, Ryan at second and Jacobs at lead. The bonspiel included most of the best teams from the region, including one skipped by their uncle Al and featuring Eric Harnden, and also had a special guest: 1998 men's Olympic curling champion Patrick Hurlimann of Switzerland. Hurlimann had beaten Toronto's Mike Harris in the gold medal game in Nagano, and his mere presence in the Soo bonspiel created a major buzz.

As luck would have it, on the very first draw of the event, E.J.'s team went up against the Olympic champion. Of course, no one gave the four high school students, with an average age of just under 17 years, a snowball's chance in hell. Wouldn't you know it though, there they were, hanging in with Hurlimann, tied at 2-2 through six ends. What a great story it was to have these local kids merely competing with an Olympic champion. What happened next was almost unthinkable. Harnden stole one in the seventh end and another in the eighth and wound up winning the game 5-3. It was almost as if all the other games on the ice that day were irrelevant. "I don't think it's sunk in yet," said a stunned E.J., now 18. "On the ice, I didn't think about them having Olympic gold medals. But right now, I'm thinking about it and I'm saying, 'Wow.' It's definitely one of the biggest thrills since we've been curling."

It was almost surreal — a junior team beating the defending Olympic champion. Who had ever even heard of such a thing? "Once we got the lead, they were kind of shocked," Flaxey told the *Sault Star*. "They were losing to a junior team and they got out of their rhythm."

It was a bit like taking a curling broom to the forehead for Hurlimann, but he was gracious in defeat. In fact, he saw something in his opponent that others, like Eric Harnden and Tom Coulterman, had eyeballed years before. "The kids played well," he said. "I didn't realize they were that young. I'm sure they have a bright future."

High school curling is a big deal in Northern Ontario, and E.J. Harnden viewed it as his own personal quest. In his time at Sir James Dunn Collegiate, he had always been a contender for the provincial high school title but had never been able to win the big one. His team was doubly frustrated because it also failed to qualify for the provincial junior curling championships and that made the high school playdowns all the more important. In 2002, E.J. and Caleb Flaxey were in grade 12 and had one last chance to win the high school crown. They went out to Thunder Bay in March 2002 and got the job done, beating John Epping of Toronto 7-2 in the final. "It feels great to win, especially because this is our last year," E.J. said, and Flaxey added: "This means so much to me and E.J. It was big for Ryan and Brad too, but this was our last chance so we really wanted it."

The following year, Flaxey accepted a golf scholarship to a university in Missouri, so he was replaced on the junior team by Jamie Morphet. E.J. had graduated from high school, so Ryan moved up to skip the Sir James Dunn team and Jacobs moved up to third. Neither team found much success, and soon enough, even bigger changes were in the offing. In 2004, Jacobs broke away from the Harndens and played third for Matt Seabrook at the provincial junior championship, making it all the way to the final before losing to a team skipped by Morphet. Then in 2005, Jacobs took over as skip and took a team with Brady Barnett, Scott Seabrook and Steve Molodowich all the way to the provincial title. At the time, it was the highlight of his life — at age 19 he was on his way to his first Canadian championship.

"I'm just ecstatic . . . overwhelmed," Jacobs told the *Sault Star*. "This is unbelievably hard to explain. It's surreal right now. The guys are so happy."

The first foray into a national championship didn't go as well as Jacobs would have hoped. His team got off to a 1-3 start in Fredericton, New Brunswick, before they were able to bounce back and finish with a respectable 8-4 record, but it was not enough for them to make the playoffs. However, Jacobs and his teammates had little difficulty holding their heads high after going 7-1 in their last eight games of the tournament; it seemed this was just the beginning of big things for the skip with the impeccable curling bloodlines. Not that there weren't setbacks. A year later, Jacobs recruited his cousin Ryan Harnden to play third and went back to the provincial junior championship one last time. However, they lost the final. It was a disappointing end to his junior career, but Jacobs was already finding a way to get over it — by playing on a men's team with his uncle Al, even throwing skip stones while playing third, and trying to get to his first Brier. They lost in the semifinal at the Northern Ontario playdowns, but the 20-year-old Jacobs showed well and let everybody know the future had arrived. "He was the talk of the week," Al Harnden said.

Ryan Harnden had one more year of junior eligibility and made good use of it by skipping a team to the provincial championship and finishing with a 7-5 record — out of the playoffs — at the national championship. Ryan had stuck with other sports longer than his brother and was still competitive in golf and hockey. However, he knew it was time to turn his focus to one sport, and it was an easy decision. "I lost passion for golf and hockey, and the passion always stayed there with curling," he said. "I didn't love the other sports. I hated going to practice, I hated going to the range. With curling I just love being at the rink, and I want to get better and get to a higher level."

Ryan was ready to join his relatives on the men's curling scene and there was little question that he and his brother and cousin would be making headlines in the sport for years to come. The only question now was: Where would everybody play and would they find a way to all play together? Curling was a family affair in the Jacobs and Harnden households. It was all-consuming, a passion that could not be sated. In 2007, there were four curlers named Harnden (Eric, Al, E.J. and Ryan) — plus their nephew/cousin Brad Jacobs — wanting to pursue provincial supremacy. There was no way they could all play on the same team.

E.J. and Ryan fulfilled a lifelong dream by joining forces with their father, playing third and second respectively (with Caleb Flaxey, now back from university in Missouri, at lead). Brad stayed with his uncle Al and continued to throw skip stones. Despite having curlers who were barely out of junior, both teams were successful — the Al Harnden team, however, found the more immediate success.

Al Harnden was 52 and had not been to the national men's championship for 17 years, but one season with Jacobs throwing skip stones seemed to make all the difference. The team beat Tim Phillips in the Northern Ontario men's championship in 2007, which meant at the tender age of 21, Jacobs was heading to his first Brier. While his composure and shooting ability belied his age on the ice, his emotions after the game reflected it. After the handshakes, Jacobs was overcome and buried his face into his uncle's shoulder. Growing up in a family like his, where everyone dreamed of winning the Brier like it was the Stanley Cup, this meant so very much to him. "You curl your whole life trying to get to a national championship," Jacobs told the *Sudbury Star*. "You play the game for the right reasons, and you love the game, and when you win something like this, it's so special, you can't hold tears back."

Al Harnden knew this was likely his last run at the Brier. There were young, stunningly talented curlers on their way up and there was little room for a skip in his 50s. He relished the opportunity to guide his nephew through his first Brier experience, however. He truly believed Brad Jacobs had a brilliant future and this was just the very beginning. "Like I told him after the final, this is one of many for Brad," Al said. "To be able to share this with someone just starting out in the men's game is incredible. He's one of the finest players in the country, I believe. He has a lot to look forward to in this game."

Jacobs got his first chance to show all of the curling fans in Canada just what he had in his somewhat unheralded but potent arsenal at the 2007 Brier in Hamilton. Throwing skip stones for his uncle Al's team, Jacobs showed flashes of brilliance but also struggled at times, making for a roller coaster round robin. The Harnden team was certainly in the mix for a playoff spot until it lost both games on the final day of the round robin to finish with a 5-6 record. While Jacobs wasn't quite ready for the rigours of the Brier playoffs, his performance was not without effect. Al had entered the Brier thinking he would retire at the end of the event, but he had so much fun playing with his talented young nephew that he decided to play one more year. The feeling was mutual for Jacobs. He was learning so much from his savvy uncle and believed it would be hugely beneficial down the road. "He taught me how to be a skip, how to be a good teammate, believing in myself, to never give up, how to curl with men and that curling is just a game at the end of the day."

The next year, however, it was Eric Harnden's turn. Playing with his two sons and their lifelong friend Caleb Flaxey, Eric went on a big-time run and won the Northern Ontario championship. At age 52, he qualified for his fourth Brier — the 2008 event was in Winnipeg — but this one was much more special than any of the previous three. This time he was going to the national championship with his boys, 24-year-old E.J. and 21-year-old Ryan.

"I'm just lost for words . . . this is amazing," Eric told the *Sault Star*. "It's tough to put into words just how much this means to me, how special it is going to be to go to the Brier with the kids. I'm really looking forward to it. It's going to be great to curl with my two boys and, in fairness, Caleb's like a third boy to me. I've known him since he was knee-high to a grasshopper. I've coached him in hockey, in curling, even in T-Ball."

The younger Harndens were over the moon as well. For as long as they could remember, their father had been their hero and the man they trusted more than any other on the planet. Now he was their skip and would be leading them onto the ice at the Brier, the competition they had dreamed about participating in since they were running around the rink in hockey helmets as tots. "This was the ultimate goal," E.J. beamed as the team prepared to head to Winnipeg. "That was a dream for all us, to have the chance to play together. Obviously it's extra special for me. It's something I've run through in my thoughts many times, that it would be the perfect situation. And this is just as good as it has been in my thoughts." As if this Brier wasn't enough of a family affair for Eric and his boys, they added another familiar face to the team to serve as fifth player — Brad Jacobs.

It did not go well. While Kevin Martin was rolling unbeaten through the round robin and the playoffs to win his third Brier title, the Harndens faltered badly. They were only able to muster a 3-8 record and finished well back in the standings. About the only bright spot came on the very last day when Flaxey stepped aside and allowed Jacobs to join his uncle and cousins on the ice for a game against Saskatchewan. They won 7-6 against a Pat Simmons–skipped team that was destined for the playoffs. Then, when Eric's knee locked up, Flaxey stepped back in along with Jacobs and the Harnden brothers for the final game. It was more than fitting, almost symbolic of what was about to come.

"You can print that I'm retiring," Eric told the *Sault Star* moments after the final game. "That's it. I knew before I came here. It's time for me to walk away. I had a good run but it's time to let the kids take over. They're ready to go on their own now, ready to carry on."

In a 2008 Brier field that included former world champions Martin, Glenn Howard and Kerry Burtnyk and 2006 Olympic gold medallist Brad Gushue, the Northern Ontario team managed to draw a fair bit of attention. It didn't go unnoticed with the veteran curlers that the Soo Crew included four players (the Harnden brothers, Jacobs and Flaxey) who were under 25, were in the best physical shape of any curler in the field and could make all the shots. If anything was missing, however, it was maturity, and with Al Harnden joining his brother Eric in calling it quits after that season, the younger curlers were going to have to develop on their own. They all were known for having bad tempers, for sometimes being petulant, for broom slamming and cursing. More than anything they were known for their bickering.

"Because we're so close, because we were crawling around on the floor as babies together, we can get away with a little bit more honesty and being a little bit more open with one another than some other teams," Jacobs explained years later about the on-ice jawing between him and his relatives.

Jacobs took over as skip of the team full time in the fall of 2008 and the foursome had a collective chip on its shoulder. At the Brier in Winnipeg, a long-simmering subject came up that was very sensitive to Northern Ontario curlers. There were some in the Brier field who believed Northern Ontario was a non-province and therefore should not have a representative in the Canadian men's championship. Martin was one of the most vocal supporters of a plan to kick Northern Ontario out — making them compete against all of Ontario for a Brier spot — and replace it with the returning champion from the previous Brier, wearing Team Canada colours. All Northern Ontario curlers were affronted by the suggestion, which was championed by some media members from across the country.

There was a legitimate argument to be made against Northern Ontario's continued inclusion in the Brier. It was the only non-province in the event other than the combined Northwest Territories–Yukon team, and there were many curlers who thought teams coming out of Northern Ontario had it too easy in qualifying for the Brier each year. Northern Ontario had not had a team make the playoffs since Al and Eric Harnden had done so in 1990. But Jacobs and his teammates were fiercely proud of representing the region and they felt they had something to prove. The integrity of their region was at stake and there was even more to it; as provincial playdowns and Briers were now essentially part of the qualifying trail for the Olympics, it would be a massive blow to a Sault Ste. Marie team if they were forced to compete against teams from the entire province of Ontario each year. The members of the Jacobs foursome believed it was partly up to them to prove Kevin Martin and the other naysayers wrong.

"I've been thinking about that since the moment we left the Brier," E.J. Harnden said as the team prepared to embark on the 2009 season. "It does kind of anger us when people talk about that," Jacobs added. "It's a respect thing, like they're saying there aren't any teams in Northern Ontario that are good enough to compete at that level, and it angers us." Jacobs and his teammates recognized they were a big part of the future of curling in Northern Ontario and would need to work even harder to gain respect. As a result, they planned to take their curling up a notch in 2008–09 by competing more regularly on the World Curling Tour. That meant significant travel and a serious commitment from all four members of the team. That fall, they hit WCT events in Switzerland, Norway, Scotland and Western Canada with the goal of qualifying for the Grand Slam events and improving enough to be consistent contenders for the Brier title. They also had their eyes on the Canadian Curling Trials pre-trials competition in 2009. Like all other teams in competitive curling, the Olympics were becoming the primary focus.

"If we can't play in these events, then we have no chance," E.J. said. So now, on top of regular jobs and keeping fit in the gym four or five times a week, the Jacobs team members needed to embark on a fundraising campaign to help pay for their travel expenses and entry fees. The companies around the Sault Ste. Marie area likely didn't realize how significant their investment would be, not just for a young team with very real Olympic aspirations, but for an entire region of curlers.

The returns were not immediately felt. In fact, the team suffered a major blow in that first season of re-imagined dedication to the game — they lost the Northern Ontario final to Mike Jakubo of Copper Cliff and failed to reach the Brier at all. "We're really bummed right now," Jacobs said to the *Sault Star*. "It's going to take a while to get over this. I'm thinking the season is pretty much over at this point. We're out of money." It was mid-February and they had already played 80 games but had come nowhere close to reaching their ultimate goal. Still, Jacobs liked what he saw with the team and planned to keep it together for the next season.

The most significant change that off-season was bringing an old friend and mentor back into the fold. Jacobs brought in Tom Coulterman, the highly decorated Soo coach who had picked Jacobs for a team way back in 1995. When asked by an interviewer for a Canadian Curling Association blog who the most influential person on his curling career had been, Jacobs said Tom Coulterman: "He taught me the basics in curling at a young age." Though they resumed the ambitious schedule set out the season before and saw much more tangible results, they didn't get into the pre-trials event for the 2009 Olympic Trials in Edmonton and had to watch as all the other top teams in Canada chased that carrot. They were such a young team and so freshly minted that it was no surprise, but for a team that so desperately wanted to run with the big dogs, missing out on the pre-trials was a major disappointment.

Undeterred, however, they qualified for their first Grand Slam — the National — to be played in January 2010 in Guelph, Ontario. That cash bonspiel, which included a top-quality field, including Olympic Trials champion Kevin Martin, turned out to be both a humbling experience and a major turning point for the team. They laid a gigantic goose egg in the tournament, losing all five of their games, but they were able to look at a much bigger picture when they returned home. Like sponges, they soaked up everything they could from the world-class competitors in the field and came away a much better team. "It's hard to make people understand how you can go 0-5 and still have a really good experience," E.J. Harnden said.

Less than a month later they were already seeing the payoff for their perseverance. Their attitude coming out of The National was just right and the team started to click right away. They plowed through the Northern Ontario championship in Sudbury with a 10-1 record and beat Matt Dumontelle of the host city 5-2 in the final. They were going back to the Brier to represent Northern Ontario, for the first time under this team configuration and for the first time without one of the elder Harndens calling the shots. "This is so special," Jacobs said. "We're all related. We have two brothers and a cousin here. There's a lot of family love. Our uncles were here for us. Coming into men's curling, they helped us get ready to play on our own. That was the goal, for them to teach us and for us to take over."

The fact that they had all been to the Brier before allowed them to go into the event in Halifax with a bit more confidence than a team of curlers in their mid-20s would normally have. They were serious about going there to win, not just to show up and put a scare into some of the heavyweights of the curling world. They celebrated their provincial championship win for one night and then hit the gym and the practice rink for daily training. They might have still resembled wide-eyed rookies, but they were more experienced than most of their competitors realized, more committed to fitness than most curlers and had the calming influence of Tom Coulterman in their corner.

Sun Media's Terry Jones picked the Jacobs outfit to finish ninth in Halifax, behind the likes of Ian Fitzner-LeBlanc of Nova Scotia, Darrell McKee of Saskatchewan, James Grattan of New Brunswick and Jamie Koe of the Territories. On paper, it looked like this Brier would be all about the four top teams, including Ontario's Glenn Howard, Manitoba's Jeff Stoughton, Alberta's Kevin Koe and Newfoundland's Brad Gushue, who had been revitalized by the addition of a young Manitoban named Ryan Fry as his second. After a few draws, nothing had happened to change people's minds. Jacobs was 1-2 through the first three games and had already lost to Howard and Koe. However, the one win did come against Stoughton and was a boost to the confidence of the young foursome. "I know I was way nervous the first couple of days," Jacobs said. "We feel way more comfortable now and a lot of nerves are out of the way."

What happened next was something nobody saw coming, not even the four Northern Ontario curlers. Jacobs and Co. went on an absolute tear, reeling off eight straight wins and pummelling many of their opponents in the process. When the dust settled, Northern Ontario had a 9-2 record and was all alone in second place, behind only the great Glenn Howard at 11-0. Behind them were Alberta's Koe (8-3) and Newfoundland's Gushue (8-3), and out of the playoffs was Stoughton at 7-4. Almost as impressive as their run on the ice was the team's confidence. They weren't even close to qualifying for the Olympics, had only played in one career Grand Slam and started the Brier 1-2, and yet they felt right at home just a couple of wins away from a Brier championship. "I'm not surprised by our record," Jacobs said. "We believe in ourselves and our abilities. We came here to do as well as possible and to make a statement. This is a phenomenal feeling but we have two more wins to go and we're definitely looking to win this thing."

The statement they made was not only for themselves but also for the entire region of Northern Ontario. It had been 17 years since a team from the region qualified for the Brier playoffs and all the curlers wanted to prove they belonged. It would be awfully tough to take the regional Brier berth away from a "province" that had just won the Canadian championship. If Northern Ontario — its fans famous for making moose calls by pulling a rope through a hole in a tomato can at the Brier — was an endangered species, Jacobs had a chance to provide some protection. "I'm hoping we're proving a point that Northern Ontario deserves to be in the Brier. Everyone back home from Thunder Bay to the Soo to Sudbury is absolutely thrilled . . . we're thrilled," Jacobs said. "We were hoping to do this by coming here and playing the way we've played. Northern Ontario has been here forever and I don't think it deserves to go out."

Jacobs was still just 24 years old, a greenhorn in a curling world dominated by men in their 40s. He was an up-and-comer in the game but was surely not expected to do this well this early and with such a young team. Jeff Stoughton, for one, was very surprised, as were the reporters and analysts who cover the game regularly.

Sure, Jacobs and his teammates were a bit of a novelty — physical specimens in curling uniforms who had bad tempers and massive potential — but they had no real chance of winning, the thinking went. Depending on whom you talked to, of course. "I would rate their performance as a mild surprise, not a shocker," Al Harnden, uncle to three of the team members, told the *Sault Star*. "They worked hard at getting to where they are."

Glenn Howard was 23 years older than Brad Jacobs and had already won three Briers and three world championships. It was not expected to be close, but nobody told that to Jacobs and his teammates. They led the first versus second Page Playoff game 4-2 after four ends and 5-3 after six. They had the game in their hands but nerves and inexperience eventually came to the forefront. Jacobs started making mistakes in the seventh end and eventually lost the lead. The game went to the tenth tied 6-6, but Howard had the hammer and the savvy of a champion and wound up winning 8-6. It really came unravelled after that. Northern Ontario got another chance, in the semifinal against Alberta's Kevin Koe, another up-and-comer with a few more years of experience. It wasn't even close and Alberta moved on to the final and an eventual Brier championship with a 10-3 win.

It was a difficult-to-swallow loss that was made much easier by the optimism of youth. In the long run, Jacobs and his teammates were pretty happy with the bronze medals they had hanging around their necks as they left the Brier. "We're pretty proud of how well we did, and we're going to keep our heads high," Jacobs said. "It's a huge positive. We've never been in this situation before and if we're lucky, one day we'll get back here, and hopefully we'll handle it better. We're young, and we'll keep plugging away."

They were truly the pride of Northern Ontario after that Brier in Halifax, coming home with a bronze medal after quieting the critics who wanted their region kicked out of the house. They were celebrated in the Soo and took great pride in their achievement, but they couldn't truly feel satisfied. One thing they weren't about to do was sit back and wait for more success to come to them. Recognizing some of their faults, they enlisted the help of sports psychologist Arthur Perlini to help them control their emotions in the big games and the big ends. "He's helped them a lot," said Ian Fisher, one of Jacobs's mentors. "They're growing with it. They're still awfully young." There was a sense in the curling world that the Jacobs team would be better if they could control their tempers, keep cool in key situations and not get down on themselves, and they hoped Perlini would help them work through those issues. "Personally for myself, it was the temper that needed to get better," Ryan Harnden said a couple of years later. "It's a lot better than it was in previous years. We've been working with a sports psychologist and Arthur has helped me a lot, like he has the whole team."

While curling was their all-consuming passion, members of the Jacobs crew did have lives outside of the game. Brad had studied geography at Algoma University and wanted to become a police officer, Ryan was also studying geography, and E.J. had a business administration degree, specializing in marketing. Jacobs was working at Future Shop, selling televisions in order to make ends meet. Flaxey, meanwhile, moved to Calgary for work and was replaced on the Jacobs foursome by Scott Seabrook. They picked up right where they'd left off, still drinking their Blue Lagoons before games (a combination of Red Bull and Gatorade), still carrying their intensity on the ice, still feeling a deep desire to win in the wells of their curling-hungry bellies. They watched football on Sundays, played golf, went camping and boating and hung out with their girlfriends, but no diversion could keep them from their ultimate goal — somehow, some way, they had to win a Brier.

The highlight of their 2010–11 season was a remarkable comeback against Joe Scharf in the final of the Northern Ontario provincials in Thunder Bay. Jacobs trailed 6-2 heading into the ninth end, an almost insurmountable obstacle in competitive men's curling, but somehow came all the way back to win. They scored two points in the ninth end and then stole three in the tenth to win 7-6. It was the kind of resilient performance that so many people — Al and Eric Harnden, Coulterman, Perlini included — believed would lead the Jacobs team to great things. "We went absolutely crazy," Jacobs said after becoming the first skip in more than 20 years to win back-to-back Northern Ontario titles. "Saying we took the long way home is an understatement. We took the impossible way home."

It was perhaps the highlight of his career, a comeback win that would be remembered for ages in Northern Ontario, but Jacobs was not happy a few days later. A curling writer from Thunder Bay, named John Cameron, had written a scathing article in *The Chronicle Journal*, depicting Jacobs and his teammates as arrogant prima donnas. The headline of the article said, "Northern champs could have been more gracious" and took the Jacobs team to task for their wild celebration at the end of the comeback victory. The win was the result of an opponent missing his last shot and giving up a steal, and it's customary in curling to not over-celebrate in such situations. "We went nuts," Jacobs admitted. "I threw my broom and we all jumped on each other and hugged and screamed. I mean, that's to go to the Brier!"

There was more to it than just the poor etiquette of the celebration, however. Jacobs and his teammates had earned a reputation for being hotheads, and they gained no friends with the fans in Thunder Bay when they were involved in a broom-smashing incident earlier in the week. Both Jacobs and Ryan Harnden broke their brooms after a loss that would have guaranteed them a spot in the Page Playoff first versus second game. "The on- and off-ice demeanor of the Sault Ste. Marie squad left a lot to be desired," Cameron wrote. Jacobs was defiant about that incident too, saying it was simply a sign of frustration from an athlete who takes his sport seriously. "Ryan and I take full responsibility for the broom-smashing incident. I barely missed a shot that would have guaranteed us the 1-2 game, so there was a lot of built-up frustration. I smashed my broom off the ice and it broke. Ryan hit his broom against a rock and the head flew off. Other curlers hit their brooms like we did and were warned in Thunder Bay, too. When you're playing for a spot in the Brier, and when you dedicate your life to the sport, sometimes tempers flare and you can't help but get upset. Look at golf, tennis or hockey. You ever see those guys break their sticks, racquets or clubs? Of course you do. And they do it with millions of people watching. But Brad Jacobs, Ryan Harnden, they break a broom and it's the worst thing that's happened in the world."

Though angry, they had no choice but to put the stinging criticism of their behaviour in Thunder Bay behind them. Jacobs and his teammates were working on their tempers with Perlini and didn't want to change too drastically what was working for them. Intensity was a big part of their game even if it sometimes belied their true nature. Jacobs once described E.J. Harnden as one of the nicest guys on the planet: "People think differently because of how intense [he is]." They weren't about to let people guilt them into changing their style just to preserve their reputation. Winning was the only thing that was important.

Jacobs went 7-4 at the 2011 Brier in London, Ontario, and narrowly missed the playoffs. Brad Gushue, with Ryan Fry at third, Jeff Stoughton, Glenn Howard and Kevin Martin took the four playoff spots and Stoughton wound up winning his third Brier. Jacobs and his teammates decided to stick together for at least another year. E.J. Harnden was now working as a brand manager for the Ontario Lottery and Gaming Corporation and Ryan was working as a real estate appraiser. E.J. was married to his wife, Rachelle, that June. Everyone was putting down roots in the Soo and though Jacobs knew he might have to leave Sault Ste. Marie to pursue his goal of becoming a cop, he didn't want to give up the curling dream with this team just yet.

The goal was to get back to the Brier — Jacobs said he wanted to play in at least 10 before his career was over — in 2012 and they did just that, beating Mike Jakubo in the final of the Northern Ontario provincials. More incredible than their third consecutive provincial title — a rare feat in Northern Ontario — was their semifinal win over Sault Ste. Marie's Rick Elliott. Playing the game at their home club, the Soo Curlers Association, the Jacobs foursome scored an incredibly rare eight-ender during a 14-3 victory. *An eight-ender in a provincial championship? In the semifinal?* You could almost hear the cries from the Northern Ontario naysayers who suggested Jacobs and Co. didn't have to deal with much competition to get out of their province. Eight-enders are rare in Wednesday night beer leagues where some of the players are rookies and others are drunk. At a provincial championship, they're unheard of. "I've heard stories about guys making them, but that's probably the first time I've seen a guy make a shot in order to get it," Soo Curlers Association ice technician Ian Fisher said. "It's one of those things you never expect to see and you'll probably never see it again. That's just the way the game goes sometimes, eh."

"It felt awesome," Jacobs said with a sly smile, but not too much exuberance.

The Jacobs team was piling up the achievements: Three straight provincial championships, a Brier bronze medal and now an eight-ender in a meaningful game. It wasn't even close to enough for them. What they desperately wanted was to win a Brier, to bring glory back to Northern Ontario for the first time since the mid-'80s. They all believed they'd get there someday, but that day was not in 2012. They went 5-6 at the Brier in Saskatoon and finished out of the playoffs for the second straight year. "It's like the worst feeling we've probably ever felt in our curling careers," Jacobs said. "Right from the beginning of the week, we weren't as sharp as we normally are, and it was frustrating for everybody on the team."

As good as the Jacobs team had become, there was still something missing. They knew they had all the talent to be Brier champions and they were working on their temperament. They were in better shape than anybody, but they just couldn't find a way to get over the hump. They had taken steps in the right direction by having a coach and a sports psychologist, but until they found a way to make the playoffs at the Brier and win a game or two, they couldn't count themselves among the elite teams in Canada. That's where they wanted to be — not just among the best curlers in the world, but right at the top of the heap. Team dynamic was something they had always been trying to build, so they could get to the point where the chemistry was just right. That, they believed, was the secret to success.

That off-season, they went looking for the missing piece of the puzzle.

CHAPTER THREE

BREAKING UP IS HARD TO DO

Winning the 2008 world championship started the Jones team on a roll that took them from perennial contenders who couldn't quite win the big one to a lofty status among the all-time greats of the sport. Over the next few years, Jennifer Jones, Cathy Overton-Clapham, Jill Officer and Dawn Askin wore Team Canada colours practically everywhere they went. They returned to the Scotties Tournament of Hearts in 2009 in Victoria as the defending champions and went through another character-building experience, finishing at 7-4 and having to play through a tie-breaker and two elimination games before reaching the final and eventually winning their second straight national title. Their reputation as Comeback Queens held true and they flirted with danger throughout the tournament before finally flipping the switch at the end and showing the rest of the field who carried the hammer in women's curling.

In the tiebreaker, the Jones team had to face Rebecca Jean MacPhee of Prince Edward Island and, though heavily favoured, found themselves down 3-0 early and 5-3 with only two ends to play. By this point however, the curling world had learned never to count Jones out. After taking just a single point in the ninth end, Jones entered the tenth down one and without the hammer. Apparently, she had the Islanders right where she wanted them. Jones made a come-around draw with her last rock in the tenth, which led to a steal of one and a 5-5 tie. Then, in the extra end, Jones did the exact same thing, stole one again and wound up with an unlikely 6-5 victory. Those kinds of comebacks, without the last rock, just don't often happen in curling. With the Jones team, they seemed to be becoming a regular occurrence.

"This team just seems to come together and pick it up a notch whenever we get into these situations," a relieved Jones said. "It's so much fun to be a part of. We just make the big shots whenever we have to."

The rest of the road to the final was not nearly as difficult; Canada upended Saskatchewan's Stefanie Lawton 8-6 and then topped Quebec's Marie-France Larouche 12-8 in the semifinal before dispatching British Columbia's Marla Mallett 8-5 in the final to win a second consecutive Scotties title. It was an early indicator that the Jones team was one that could not be stopped when it got on a roll. In fact, the *Winnipeg Sun*'s longtime curling writer, Jim Bender, compared the Jones team to Jason from the Friday the 13th movies.

"These Manitoba monsters are masked with comely smiles that belie a gritty determination seldom seen on the curling sheets," Bender wrote. "After watching Jennifer Jones repeatedly rise from the dead to kill again, their opponents must be wondering what kind of wooden stake they need to keep her team in the curling coffin."

The resume was starting to get full for Jennifer Jones: Canadian junior champion, world champion and now three-time Canadian women's champion. Cathy O could even boast a fourth Canadian title, having won one as third for Connie Laliberte in 1995.

"We've done it before and it never gets old," Jones said. "You think the last time will be your last and then we do it again. When you've got that Maple Leaf on your back . . . it's completely the most glorifying experience you've ever had."

There would be more greatness in store for this team, but not before they had to endure bitter disappointments. The curling world had become increasingly focused on the Olympics, and Vancouver 2010, the most important Winter Olympics in Canadian history, was looming large. The Canadian championship was nice for Jones and Co., but they had much more grandiose goals in their minds.

Before the Canadian Curling Trials, which were slated for December 2009 in Edmonton, the Jones team had another world championship to compete in and headed to Gangneung, South Korea, to defend its title. Canada compiled a 9-2 record but that was only good enough for third place in the round robin. China's Bingyu Wang, who was hungrier than ever after losing the world final to Jones in 2008, put up a stunning 10-1 record in the round robin and the surprising Angelina Jensen of Denmark went 9-2, including a win over Canada in the round robin that earned her team second place. Canada had to play an elimination game against the great Anette Norberg of Sweden and lost 5-4 on a last-rock draw to the four-foot. Though the Canadians believed they were the best team in the tournament and had curled their best, they were now out of gold medal contention and would have to play for bronze against Denmark. They lost that game 7-6 and finished out of the medals for the second time in three appearances at the world championship.

"We played unbelievable all week," a frustrated Jones said. "There were just a handful of ends that cost us in the end. Hopefully we get it figured out. It was uncharacteristic of our team. Obviously we're disappointed. I don't know between third and fourth if there's much of a difference, but we wanted to get a medal."

It was a difficult loss to swallow but not nearly as devastating as it might have been had the Jones team not already won a world championship. There was history made that year as well, as Wang's team became the first from outside North America or Europe to win a world championship, beating Sweden in the final. Jones the competitor never liked to lose, but Jones the curling enthusiast could certainly see the value in what China's win did for the growth of the game. It seemed, also, that the Canadian skip knew there was still a bigger prize to be won that year, and her loss at the world championship could only serve to motivate her more for the upcoming Olympic Trials.

"I don't think it takes anything to get us more fired up," Jones said. "We're going to play our hearts out next year."

They already knew they'd be returning to the Scotties Tournament of Hearts in 2010 as Team Canada, which allowed them to enter the Olympic Trials with one less thing to worry about. It was their tournament to win, the favourites on every reporter's ballot. The bitter sting of the 2005 Trials, where Jones was afflicted with kidney stones and had to be hospitalized, was still in their system, and all they had done since was win. Nobody could have predicted what would happen in Edmonton in mid-December 2009. The Olympic dream was over before the rapid eye movement even started.

Jones compiled a stunningly poor 2-5 record and finished tied for sixth place in a field of only eight teams. Though she later revealed she was sick all that week, there was nothing at the time that could explain the dramatic fall at the Trials. Two draws into the event, Jones was already 0-2, having been crushed 9-3 by Ontario's Krista McCarville and 8-5 by Saskatchewan's Amber Holland. They simply could not recover from that start and had to watch as 43-year-old Cheryl Bernard of Calgary, who had never won so much as a Canadian championship, captured the Olympic Trials and earned the right to wear the Maple Leaf in Vancouver.

"We worked really, really hard and wanted to excel at this event, but it just didn't work out . . . it just wasn't meant to be," a stoic Jones told reporters. "Yeah, I want to go to the Olympics, and so does every Canadian, but you can't sometimes make things happen. We just didn't make enough shots and couldn't get things going. It's very disappointing."

For all its greatness, it was obvious that this team could be better. They had only one medal in three tries at the world championship and had dismal finishes in a pair of appearances at the Olympic Trials. This time there was a sense that something wasn't quite right with the team. Jones, perhaps feeling the effects of the flu, was not as sharp as usual and Overton-Clapham, who is usually among the leaders at her position at every event, finished fifth among thirds at 78 percent. Cathy O was able to shrug off the situation at the time, seeing her team's dreadful performance as somewhat comical.

"Obviously, we're extremely disappointed, but what do we do?" she said, and then laughed. "What am I going to do, cry? We worked very hard for this but didn't play as well as we could have."

Overton-Clapham's performance at the Trials would loom large in the coming months, but there was at least the consolation prize of another trip to the upcoming Scotties. The Jones team had a couple of months to try to get over what went wrong in Edmonton and refocus on winning another Canadian championship in Sault Ste. Marie, Ontario, in early February 2010.

"It's going to take a while to figure out," Jill Officer said right after the Trials. "We're going to have to go back and debrief, I guess. I'm not sure what it was. At the provincials, the Scotties and the worlds, we've always been able to perform but not at the Trials."

Jones promised the team would recover quickly. She always maintained her foursome knew how to lose better than any team and that's why it could always bounce back. History would eventually prove her to be correct.

"Going to the Olympics is not what it's all about for us," Jones said, in a statement she might have found humorous a few years later. "Obviously we're disappointed. But to dwell on it? We'd drive ourselves crazy."

Around that time, Jones was going through some significant personal issues. She and her husband of six years, Scott Labonte, were struggling to hold their marriage together. Between her job as a corporate lawyer and her schedule as one of the top curling skips in the world, Jones and her husband were apart a great deal of the time.

"He was not a curler and he tried to support her by coming, but she was on the road a lot and they just really became two people with very separate lives," Jones's friend and former teammate Cathy Gauthier said. "He would take winter vacations without her because her winter vacation was curling. When you start to do that as a regular habit, pretty soon the life that you have together isn't much."

For many years, Labonte was a regular figure at the women's big curling events. He was there at the 2009 Olympic Trials and it didn't sound like there was anything wrong at the time.

"Jennifer is obviously very competitive and very intense on the ice and very driven, so when we spend our time at home, we spend our time away from the rink, relaxing." Labonte told the *Edmonton Sun* and then joked: "She doesn't scream at me when I don't do the dishes like she does when we need to make a big shot.

"I would not dare offer her any advice with anything to do with curling. All I can do is be supportive and enjoy the time we spend together."

Jones had talked for years about one day taking a step back from curling to start and raise a family, and at those Olympic Trials in 2009, it certainly sounded like that was part of the plan with Labonte. The nature of Jones's competition schedule had simply gotten in the way up until that point, with such an intense focus on trying to qualify for the Olympics in Vancouver.

"The preparation for this has been a few years now," Labonte said. "You can't always time these things but we'd like to start a family and when the time is right that will happen."

It never did happen, at least not with Labonte. The marriage disintegrated not long after that and the personal troubles weighed heavily on Jones as she seriously re-evaluated her future following the Olympic Trials.

"For Jen, because she's so conscientious and always wanting to do the right thing, I think what drove her as much crazy as the marriage breaking up was that feeling of failure," Gauthier said. "With someone like Jen who is very driven and has done very well — has her law degree, has done very well in curling — having something in your personal life be a failure would have been a dark cloud hanging over her head for a long time. Not even the issues with her and Scott, but just that it was something she wasn't able to complete properly."

Despite the inner turmoil, Jones showed none of it on the outside as her team prepared to compete in yet another Scotties Tournament of Hearts. It was not known publicly at the time, but there was unrest on the Jones team as well, which was exacerbated by the poor performance at the Trials. For the first time, cracks were showing in the team's solidarity and those in the know realized there were issues off the ice. This team had been together a long time and it was starting to get stale.

Still, the foursome had something left in the tank and it showed when they went to the Scotties in The Soo and did something they had never done before — they dominated at a Canadian championship. This time there were no tiebreakers, no steals needed to win extra-end games. Jones and Co. went 8-3 as Team Canada in the round robin and played the Page Playoff game against Kathy O'Rourke of Prince Edward Island, with a trip to the final on the line. They won that game 8-5, which set up another matchup with P.E.I. in the final.

Of course, it just would not have been the same for this Jones team if there were no adversity at all and, as such, Team Canada fell behind 6-3 through six ends, thanks to the sharp shooting of Prince Edward Island's 21-year-old fourth Erin Carmody and a few slip-ups from Officer (69 percent) and Overton-Clapham (73 percent). Once again, many observers would have been tempted to write Jones off, especially when she scored just one in the seventh end and gave the all-important hammer back to P.E.I for the eighth. In typical fashion though, Jones stole one in the eighth to make it 6-5 and then stole two more when Carmody came up light on a draw in the ninth to make it 7-6 for Team Canada. The Islanders tied the game with a single point in the tenth but Jones once again had the chance to make the glory shot with her last one in the extra end, picking a yellow P.E.I. stone out of the four-foot to score one and claim a third straight Canadian championship. With this team, it just wouldn't have been the same without the drama.

With four Canadian championships to her name, Jones was now second only to the great Colleen Jones of Nova Scotia (six) in all-time titles. Only Colleen Jones had ever won more consecutive titles at four and Jones was now tied with the great Vera Pezer of Saskatchewan with three straight Scotties crowns.

"Unbelievable . . . just winning one is what everybody dreams about," Jones said. "It's pretty incredible and the way we won, the way we came back, is pretty awesome. It blows my mind. I never, ever in a million years, dreamed that this would happen and here I am standing in a dream come true."

"This is the one I felt the most shock about right away," Officer added. "I just can't believe that we did this. Like, three times back-to-back, I just can't explain it. I'm totally beside myself that we were able to come through in the end. We were obviously disappointed in the Trials, but after Christmas, we were just like, 'Okay, we're better than that. It was one event.' Unfortunately, it was a big one but we knew we'd be able to come back and play our game. So I think that three in a row is kind of big."

The win cemented Overton-Clapham's status as perhaps the greatest third in the history of the game. It was her fifth Canadian championship, and while she clearly struggled at the Olympic Trials, she was one of the best players at the Scotties in Sault Ste. Marie. In fact, she was named to the first all-star team at the third position. Still, as the Jones team prepared to compete in yet another world championship, there were whispers that Cathy O was going to be replaced. She was 41 years old and had to receive occasional cortisone shots in her knees just to keep playing. Clearly though, if Overton-Clapham was on her way out, it certainly wasn't by her own volition.

"As long as I can keep playing at the level I can curl, I'll keep playing," she said, denying she had anything to prove at the upcoming worlds in Swift Current, Saskatchewan. "I love to curl. It's what I do."

As soon as the Scotties ended, Jones was off to Vancouver, having been given an opportunity to work for Yahoo! Canada as a reporter at the 2010 Olympic Winter Games. She didn't know it at the time, but the experience turned out to be invaluable. Jones rubbed shoulders with Olympians and celebrities and got a much better idea of what it was like to be on the other side of the microphone while working as a reporter. Among Jones's highlights of the Vancouver fortnight was getting a chance to visit with Canadian crooner Michael Buble, who sang at the Closing Ceremony, and teaching him a thing or two about curling.

"It was his first time on the ice and he said he liked it," Jones recounted. "He was pretty good actually.

"The whole experience was actually great because I got a good perspective of things from a reporter's point of view. Obviously, being an athlete at the Olympics is a lot more fun and what I really wanted to be doing, but it was still an experience of a lifetime."

The trip to the Olympics proved to be a turning point for Jones, who later revealed the bitter disappointment of the 2009 and 2005 trials, plus her marital troubles, were causing her to re-evaluate her future. Even after her team won the 2010 Scotties, Jones was seriously thinking about quitting at the end of the season. Perhaps going out on a winning note would be perfect.

"I was serious," Jones said. "I was burnt out, I was just done. I was just not enjoying curling. I just thought it was maybe time to do other things. But then I went to the Olympics and then it was too hard to not want to curl. The Olympics helped me gain perspective. It made me realize that if I left the sport before I thought I was ready, I knew I would regret it later on."

Much to the delight of her teammates, Jones returned refreshed and motivated from Vancouver and was ready to take another run at the world championship in Swift Current. Officer was now married to Devlin Hinchey and was eager to start a family. Perhaps that put her on board with her longtime skip, considering a break from competitive curling. However, the rest of the team wanted to keep going and there was an immediate task at hand to worry about. This was very likely the best women's curling team in the world but it was not nearly as decorated as it might have been. Winning another world title would go a long way toward changing that.

The Jones team went to the worlds as the favourite once again and showed exactly why, steamrolling through the round robin with a 10-1 record. Each member of the Canadian team led her position in curling percentage through the round robin, with Overton-Clapham coming in at an impressive 88 percent, tops amongst all seconds, thirds and skips. This looked like a coronation for the Canadians, who were finally making things easy on themselves at a major tournament. It all came crashing down with a resounding thud once the playoff round began.

It all looked fine for Jones and her teammates until the ninth end of the first playoff game against Germany's Andrea Schopp, who was appearing in her seventeenth world championship and had won it all back in 1988 when Jones, Officer and Askin were barely old enough to throw a curling rock. In that fateful ninth end, Jones led 3-2 but made a crucial mistake with her last rock and left Schopp a hit for four points. Many observers were stunned to see Jones — she of the famed in-off, the icy cold draw, the late-end stolen points — miss a big shot and have the tables turned on her, but her teammates had her back.

"I've never seen anyone who can make the big shot under pressure like she can," Dawn Askin said. "She just thrives in those situations." Overton-Clapham went one further, suggesting this was the perfect situation for Jones, with her back against the wall once again. "She's pretty determined. She's very goal oriented and if there's something there that she wants, she's going to do everything she can to get it."

Germany won that game 6-3 and advanced to the final and, once again, Jones and her teammates were in a position where they would have to do things the hard way. They would have to play a semifinal against Scotland, skipped by 19-year-old Eve Muirhead, and it would be an immense test of their mettle. It would also be a massive test of Jones's resolve to stick with curling after contemplating retirement earlier in the year. Did she still have what it took to win these big games? She didn't have it at the Olympic Trials and she didn't have it in the playoff game against Germany. She most definitely didn't have it in the semifinal against Scotland.

Scotland hammered Canada 10-4 and the dream of a second world title was over for another year. Jones shot a woeful 59 percent in the game and completely lost her draw weight, one of the staples of her elite game. While Schopp went on to win the world championship at age 45, 22 years after winning her first title, Jones and Co. had to settle for a spot in the bronze medal game against Sweden. The disappointment in the skip's voice suggested her curling career was once again at a crossroads.

"We got outplayed and it's very disappointing," Jones said. "We actually had a great week and got into the semifinal and we just didn't come out and play."

To their credit, the Canadians rebounded the next day to beat Sweden's Cecilia Ostlund 9-6 and claim a bronze medal, giving the Jones team its second trip to a world championship podium. It was small consolation for a team that had experienced so many ups and downs that season, but some of the perspective Jones had absorbed during her Olympic experience came through at that moment. "I don't think fans expect gold," Jones said. "I think the media does and I think that's unfair. When I was at the Olympics, Canadians were proud of any colour. I think it's the media that scrutinizes it and I don't think that's right."

It would not be the last time Jones would speak about her belief that medals of any colour were significant and deserved to be celebrated. She would carry that attitude with her for the next four years, even up to the eve of the biggest game of her life.

The months after the world championship in Swift Current were troubled times for Jones and her teammates. There were lingering doubts after the discussions about retirement came up a few months earlier, the skip's marriage was falling apart and there were deep concerns about the team's ability to ever qualify for an Olympics. More than anything there was unrest with some members of the team, a certain feeling about the foursome's chemistry that was creating an unspoken strain within the team. It would be fair to say things were getting stagnant.

The Jones foursome ended their 2009–10 curling season with an appearance in the World Curling Tour's Players Championship in Dawson Creek, British Columbia. They lost in the quarter-final, missing out on a chance for a $50,000 payday. That game was played on April 16 and just six days later, the Jones team shocked the curling world by making a major change to its lineup, one that angered fans and other curlers, but ultimately put the team on course with destiny.

On April 22, Jones, Officer and Askin informed longtime third Cathy Overton-Clapham — the woman Jones once said was like a sister to her — that she was no longer part of the team. The veteran third, now 41 years old but still feeling like she had plenty left to offer, was stunned. Not only was she off the team, but she was going to be deprived of a chance to represent Canada for another year. She would have returned with the team to the Scotties in 2011 as well as other major bonspiels like the Canada Cup and Continental Cup. It was devastating for her to hear that the team she helped to win three consecutive Canadian championships and one world title, thought it was better off without her.

"I was totally blindsided and obviously very disappointed," Overton-Clapham recalled. "They just said things were getting stale and they needed more excitement and vision."

The reaction was swift. Many curling fans hated the move, thought it was unfair and vilified the Jones team for being ruthless, just as they did when Dana Allerton was cut years earlier on the eve of the provincial championship. Jones, perhaps relying on her skills as a lawyer who has to deal with difficult situations all the time, held firm. Jones and her remaining teammates wanted to build a team that would contend for the next Olympics, in Russia in 2014, and they didn't believe

Overton-Clapham was the correct fit. "It was the right move at the right time," Askin said. "It's been a wonderful partnership, but to build for the future, any team needs to keep injecting new energy and maintaining the right balance."

While Jones tried to play the diplomat, talking about how Overton-Clapham was one of the best thirds in the history of curling, was a big part of the team's success and was a great friend who taught them all how to win, she knew the only way to fix this stale piece of bread was to cut out the mold. No one on the team was getting along with Overton-Clapham as well as they once did.

"It was the entire team, it really was," former Jones team member Cathy Gauthier said. "It really was a situation where they had been together for a long time and there started to be issues off the ice. They had been together a long time and I think it was getting really stale."

The practice of changing up teams at the beginning of Olympic quadrennials is common in curling, more so on the men's side, but in this case fans had very little interest in forgiving Jones. She was attacked through social media and on comment boards on news and sports websites. People were particularly angry with the timing, as it left Overton-Clapham without a team at the end of April instead of preparing for another season as a member of Team Canada.

"If it had not been a Team Canada situation, I don't know that anybody would have cared," Cathy Gauthier said. "It was because they had a chance to play on. Even if it was perfect, sooner or later teams have to change. It was just the timing of it that was bad because they won and they were going back."

Overton-Clapham was bitter and couldn't see it that way. "There may never be a right time to do this but there *is* a better time," she lamented. "You know, I get that things have to be done to get better and I get that this is a business team, but if we are all business partners, don't you think you should talk to your business partner too?

"I guess what's so hurtful is that they knew when we were curling in Dawson Creek and I was oblivious to the whole thing. And to actually face me like they did every day is hurtful. I put in as much as the three of them did. They're taking that away from me and that's hard to take."

The decision had been made and the Jones team was moving forward, but the strong feelings about the nasty split with a longtime teammate would not subside any time soon.

"We hope that at some point — and it's going to be up to Cathy — we hope we can move forward somewhere down the line and have some sort of friendship with her in the future," Officer said.

Friendship would not be the right word — to this day they still do not communicate — but they certainly did meet up again down the line.

Overton-Clapham's replacement had not yet been named, and the Jones team was about to make a splash that would take them in a whole new direction. The team had two things in mind when they considered recruits to replace Overton-Clapham in the lineup: Find the best third available and perhaps nip a potential future challenger in the bud by bringing her into the fold. There was talk they would try to recruit up-and-coming skip Rachel Homan of Ottawa, who had just gone 13-0 at the Canadian junior championship and won a silver medal at the worlds. It would have been an excellent choice, given that Homan would soon become the top contender in the women's game. In the end, the Jones team decided to go in a different direction, staying much closer to home and picking a young curler with an equally solid resume. Her name was Kaitlyn Lawes.

CHAPTER FOUR

THE VAGABOND

It would not be a stretch to say Ryan Fry was born to be a curler. He was introduced to the game while he was still in diapers and grew up around curling rinks. His father, Barry, was not only a curler but a great one, who won the Brier in 1979 when Ryan was just seven months old. Barry Fry was known as The Snake because of his quick delivery from the hack and his ability to slither out of trouble. He only won the one Brier — in fact only appeared in the one — and took home a bronze medal from the world championship that year in Switzerland, but The Snake was a legend in Manitoba and the Fry name was synonymous with curling success.

Ryan Fry was born on July 25, 1978, in Winnipeg, and he always knew what he wanted to be when he grew up — a curler. At an early age, he learned the famous "Manitoba tuck" delivery from his dad and was soon using it in competitive curling events. Anyone who saw him play knew the potential for greatness was there. He mastered the tuck, and the long, effortless slide down the ice — he simply looked like a curler.

"I grew up watching my dad," Ryan Fry said. "I was in the curling clubs when I was six, seven years old. As I got a little older I made sure I was at every game. He was a member at the Granite Curling Club and I pretty much lived there for 10 years, all through school. My dad and I have a special relationship, just based on the fact that we both love the sport so much. He instilled passion for the game in me and I've run with it."

Ryan spent many of his early days around curling with his family and with his "second and third families," which included curling legends Don Duguid and Ray Turnbull, his dad's good buddies. He started curling competitively at the age of eight and by the mid-'90s he was already one of the top up-and-comers in Manitoba. He played skip for the most part, like his old man, and found success early, winning both the 1996 and 1997 Manitoba junior men's championships. "From early on, once he got started, he just loved the game," Barry Fry said. "When you grow up in a curling family, and the old man has accomplished a few things, well . . . I remember Ryan once telling me as a kid that he was going to do bigger and better things than I did."

While he was already proving to be a highly skilled and knowledgeable curler by his teen years, he was also fiery, perhaps somewhat petulant and prone to emotional outbursts. Nicknamed "Small Fry," he developed a reputation very quickly for being immature and overly demonstrative with his intense behaviour on the ice. It was a trait that made him somewhat difficult to play with and he was not the kind of teammate every curler could handle.

"He was really edgy and he had a bad temper when he came through juniors," TSN analyst and family friend Cathy Gauthier said. "He was just known as this kid who was hard to play for and was mad all the time."

One person who had no problem handling him was his father, and as soon as Ryan was old enough to graduate from the junior curling ranks, the two started playing together. Barry was 60 years old in 2000 — and had suffered a mild heart attack the previous year — when he and 21-year-old Ryan first played together and qualified for the Manitoba men's curling championship. "Father-son combinations can be like oil and water," Barry said at the time. "But, by and large, we get along good on the ice, and he's a real good thrower."

The team didn't click at that provincial championship in 2000 but the Small Fry gained some valuable experience while playing with one of the best curlers the province had ever produced. Not long after, Ryan tried his hand at playing third for the first time with another home province legend, three-time Manitoba champion Vic Peters. That configuration didn't last long however, just the 2002–03 season, but Fry made it to another provincial championship with skip Kyle Werenich in 2004. Again success was tough to come by, and a season later, Fry was back skipping with a team that included Werenich at third, Jason Smith at second and Cory Naharnie at lead. They travelled and played on the World Curling Tour cash circuit to gain experience, and they qualified for the 2005 Manitoba championship in Selkirk. There, with Barry Fry coaching, they served notice to the province's top curlers that they were a team with all the tools to win a Manitoba title.

Now 26, Ryan was the star of the 2005 championship. To that point he had always been considered a player with tremendous potential who was just too intense for his own good. That year he seemed to calm down quite a bit, thanks in large part to his father's presence. "He's a steadying influence for all the guys on the team." Ryan said. "He's a great friend of mine and has been a great friend of all the guys on my team for a long time. He pretty much lets us go according to plan and he'll throw his two cents in when it's asked for and even sometimes when it's not asked for."

In the playoff round, Ryan Fry beat Manitoba's legendary five-time provincial champion, two-time Brier champion and 1995 world champion Kerry Burtnyk, not once, but twice. The young team was right on the cusp of winning the Manitoba championship but fell 8-5 to Randy Dutiaume in the final. It was a very tough loss to swallow after they came such a long way, but Ryan came away with a positive outlook. "It's very disappointing, but we're all pretty young guys and we're all very committed to trying to compete for this province for many years to come, so hopefully we'll just keep on going and maybe find ourselves back here in a year or two, and it will be different then."

They were back the very next season, seeded third in a field of 32 teams, for the provincial championship. After having a spectacular cash tour season, in which they beat the likes of the great Randy Ferbey of Edmonton, the Fry team stumbled badly at the provincial championship, losing out quickly and heading home terribly disappointed after showing such promise a year earlier. Again, they still felt confident they would one day contend for that elusive Manitoba title and trip to the Brier and were sure they would be back. Ryan would certainly find his way back, but not with the same teammates.

His performance at the 2005 provincial and on the World Curling Tour in 2006 made Ryan a hot commodity. So hot, in fact, that it was the greatest curler Manitoba has ever produced who came knocking at his door. Fry was added to 10-time provincial champion Jeff Stoughton's team as the third for the 2005–06 season, replacing the rock-steady Jon Mead. It was sure to be an interesting dynamic — the fiery, ultra-intense Fry paired up with the unflappable and mild-mannered Stoughton. The veteran Stoughton took the game very seriously and left the after-game partying to the other teams. With the addition of the fun-loving Fry and new second Rob Fowler of Brandon, Stoughton's "boring" demeanour was about to be put to the test.

"When he curled with me for a couple of years, he was a great guy, but he loved to have a lot of fun," Stoughton said, looking back in 2014. "He liked to go out and enjoy the evenings. It was fun at the time because I wasn't used to anything like that on the team, so it was a little bit of an eye-opener for me to see a guy who's just loving life and living it to the fullest.

"I don't think it affected our team. The first year we sort of sat down and set out guidelines of what we could or couldn't do. It was kind of a funny situation where both Ryan and Rob Fowler were realizing early on that they actually couldn't drink during events because the next morning they weren't very good at all. They actually knew they couldn't go out and party. There were actually quite a few good little evenings after events where we were knocked out that Rob and Ryan would let loose a little bit and enjoy the festivities. Ryan played hard, he partied hard during my time, and I have no complaints.

"It wasn't something I would have stood for, for years and years."

While Stoughton said all the right things, there were others on the curling circuit who thought Fry was just a little too wild to be a good teammate. "He went hard," Gauthier said. "He was a young kid and bonspiels were not just about what was going on on the ice. He was going hard off the ice and there were a lot of players, including Jeff Stoughton, who looked at the game a bit differently. They expect you to go hard on the ice but want you to maintain that balance off of it, so that they know the shape you are going to show up in the next day. There was a feeling amongst Manitoba skips that he was a bit of a risk to take on because he liked to go really hard."

At the time though, at least, Stoughton was thrilled to have recruited two young, energetic players who really knew the game, especially with another Olympic quadrennial just underway. "The youth of them is kind of nice, because they're excited," Stoughton said of Fry and Fowler. "I was getting a lot of phone calls during the summer when I wasn't too in it, so they got me all pumped up, which is good. That's exactly what I needed."

The team didn't click immediately on the ice, even though Stoughton found much of his same old success in terms of winning money on the cash circuit. The skip admitted it was a difficult adjustment, going from Mead, who had been his vice-skip and confidant for many years, to Fry, with his relative inexperience and hotheadedness. "It's hard," Stoughton said before the team's first provincial championship appearance. "I mean, Jon was like your right-hand man for so many years. He was always there and you always knew exactly what you were going to get out of him and that's sort of been the learning curve with Ryan. He's a great player and he's doing all the good things that he can do. We're just getting very comfortable with each other. You can't replace a guy like Jon Mead but Ryan is stepping in and trying to fill those shoes."

Fry did a fine job of filling those shoes at the 2007 provincial championship in Dauphin. He was one of the best thirds in the tournament and the Stoughton foursome won it all, meaning Fry, at age 28, was heading to the Brier for the first time, looking to duplicate the feat his father pulled off way back in 1979.

"It sort of validates the way I set up my life, actually," Fry said. "My dad got me into the game. I've learned from him and it's taken quite a while to be able to win a championship and get myself there. But it feels great to be going and I'm sure he's very proud, and I'm very proud to be able to carry on the tradition he started."

Things didn't start off very well for Fry at his first Brier. He struggled mightily early on, curling only 66 percent in a loss to Ontario's Glenn Howard, but started to heat up as the tournament went along. With his father watching in the stands, he curled 96% in a win over the Yukon–Northwest Territories and helped his team into first place with a 4-1 record. "I like having my dad around because it's fun to talk about curling. And it's another pair of eyes to notice if anything's going wrong." As for Barry Fry, he was perfectly happy to be sitting in the stands and not having to deal with the pressure down on the ice. "It's exciting to watch him here after having been there myself," he said.

In the end, the 2007 Brier proved to be more learning experience than success story for Fry. He didn't play as well as he would have liked, but he helped the team make the playoffs and win its first playoff game against legendary skip Kevin Martin of Edmonton. Unfortunately, they lost to eventual world champion Glenn Howard of Ontario 8-4 in the semifinal and had to settle for a bronze medal. Fry was named to the second all-star team in his first Brier appearance and went home with a medal around his neck, both factors that helped him hold his head high upon returning to Winnipeg.

"Any time you lose, you're going to be a little bit frustrated when you had a shot to go to the final but didn't make it," he said. "But we're all hoping we're going to have a lot of opportunities to come back to the Brier next year. If someone told me I was going to come here and place third at the beginning of the week, I would have been pretty happy with it. Once we got here, obviously it's a little disappointing."

The following year would bring more disappointment, but Fry wouldn't be so patient this time. The 2008 Brier was slated for Winnipeg's MTS Centre and all the Manitoba teams wanted desperately to have the home-ice advantage. Stoughton's team never really had much of a chance though, as they could get no further than the playoff round at the provincial men's championship in Brandon. When they were eliminated and had to watch rival Kerry Burtnyk go on to earn the right to play in the hometown Brier, Fry was already thinking that perhaps he needed a change. He did a lot of soul searching over the rest of that season and realized that if he wanted to reach the pinnacle in curling he was going to have to work harder at it than everybody else. What he decided to do rocked the curling world and was a bold step that ultimately paid off in ways few people would have ever envisioned.

In April 2008, Fry announced that at age 29 he was leaving two-time Brier champion and former world champ Jeff Stoughton and heading as far east as one can go without leaving North America. Fry had decided to hit the road in search of the perfect curling mix and his choice was to join 2006 Olympic gold medallist Brad Gushue's team, based out of St. John's, Newfoundland. His plan was to move to the Rock over the summer and find a job so he could play second with Gushue the following season. People in Manitoba were stunned, and Stoughton was left looking for a capable replacement at a very late date, but Fry was undeterred. He was certain this was what it would take to achieve his dreams. It started him down a road that earned him a reputation as both a curling vagabond and a picture of determination.

"I wanted to play with three guys who were closer to my own age and a team that can win a Brier," Fry said. "Jeff's still one of the best players in the game today but you look at his longevity and you don't know how much longer it is. Hopefully, we'll win lots of provincials, then the Brier. Then there's the Olympics. Jeff is a solid guy and there were no hard feelings. He did a lot in helping to develop my game and we had a good couple of years together."

His assertion that 44-year-old Stoughton was over the hill was way off the mark — Stoughton won his third Brier and second world championship in 2011 — but Fry had a vision, and he was compelled to follow it.

"I would say it was gutsy for sure," Gushue said, looking back in 2014. "It shows his level of commitment to the game and the passion for it. The fact that he's willing to put his career ahead of everything else, even starting a family, it shows that curling was the main priority for him."

Even Stoughton respected Fry's decision, "He was in an enviable position of not having any ties so why not? He loves the game, I know that. He loves it with a passion. He wanted to try to improve himself and improve any team that he went to. He was trying to find that right mix of guys and make it all connect.

"He was moving on to a younger team, which was more than understandable. He always mentioned he appreciated the couple of years with my team. We went to a Brier together and came away with a bronze medal in his first Brier, which was pretty exciting for him. He just wanted to move on and play with another team that he felt was going to get to the Brier and another team where the guys were definitely younger and more his generation. I had no problem with it at all."

Fry moved to Newfoundland in the summer of 2008 and lined up a job working as a bartender on the famed George Street in St. John's. More than a few curlers were familiar with the strip of bars that was full of revellers just about every night of the year, where newcomers to the Rock could be "Screeched in" through a ceremony of drinking high-alcohol rum and kissing a cod fish. The hard partying Fry fit right in, both on his new team and in the George Street lifestyle.

"He's been having a lot of fun down there," Gushue told the *Winnipeg Sun* in January 2009. "I don't go to George Street at all, but he's had some good times and I get some good stories when we get on the road."

Fry admitted the job was tiring but said he was having "a blast." He managed to work into the wee hours and still function as a competitive curler by going through a lot of Red Bull energy drink. If any of it was affecting his play on the ice, his teammates certainly weren't saying so. "He's a pretty easygoing personality," Gushue said. "He's a good team player. He's a positive guy and he's intense, so you know he's into the game each and every time you play."

"The chemistry is great," Fry chimed in. "We're all relatively the same age and we all have the same goals. The three of them have become three of my closest buddies. The teams that seem to win seem to be that way."

Eventually Fry would leave the George Street lifestyle and take a job as an events manager for a golf course in St. John's. It was a source of pride for his family that he was willing to travel across the country to make a serious go of curling. "He wasn't like some of the guys we've seen, who pretend they've moved to another province to fulfill the residency rules," Barry Fry said a few years later. "When he moved from Winnipeg to St. John's, Newfoundland, it was lock, stock and barrel."

In the early days of his tenure with Gushue, both second and skip were feeling positive about the match and saw this team, which included third Mark Nichols and lead Jamie Korab, as a potential Olympic contender. Gushue, Nichols and Korab had won an Olympic gold medal with veteran Russ Howard — who won world championships as a skip in 1987 and 1993 — playing second in 2006 in Turin and talked about taking a run at 2010 or 2014 with a new lineup. Gushue had never won a Brier but had finished second the previous year in Hamilton, losing the final to Glenn Howard, and few people doubted he was capable of winning plenty of events with the right mix of curlers. They qualified for the Brier in 2009 in Calgary and set their sights on winning it all. As soon as his team qualified for the Brier, Fry took a quick look at the schedule. His old skip, Stoughton, had won Manitoba again, and he wanted to know when they'd meet in the round robin.

"It's going to make for an interesting little battle with them, for sure," Fry said. "Me and Jeff got along well. There were no real hard feelings. He knew what I wanted. I'm excited to play against them. Both of our records are going to dictate how important that game is."

They quickly showed they were a contending force, finishing the round robin with an 8-3 record. However, one of those losses was an 8-3 drubbing at the hands of Stoughton, and that was not the last they would see of Fry's former skipper. The Gushue foursome finished in third place, while Stoughton was 7-4 and had to play a tiebreaker against Quebec's Jean-Michel Menard just to get into the playoffs. Stoughton won, and that set up another big game against Gushue, one with all kinds of storylines. For one, there was the Fry connection, but more importantly, it was Gushue who beat Stoughton in the final of the 2005 Olympic Trials and it had been a bitter pill for the Manitoba skip to swallow. This time, Stoughton was the dream-killer. He scored two in the tenth end with the hammer for an 8-7 win and a berth in the semifinal. Gushue and Fry were heading home empty-handed. Playing second for the first time, Fry didn't have a great tournament — his poor shooting percentage put him out of the top five seconds.

Fry was certainly making a name for himself in the sport though. He was as good a shooter as anyone out there on any given day and was known for his dedication to physical fitness, a key attribute for a front-end player who needed to do a great deal of sweeping. He viewed himself as an athlete first and a curler second and hoped that attitude would catch on with curlers around the world. "The sport has a bad rap in terms of guys not being in shape," he said. "The thing that has contributed to the sport getting better is guys taking better care of themselves.

"Fitness is huge on two sides. It obviously keeps your body able to compete at this high a level but it's also very good for you mentally. You are able to find some peace in the gym and when you're there and you're pushing weights and you're with the guys, it forms a brotherhood and it really makes you able to cope with certain things mentally. You know you've put that type of work in that perhaps some other teams might not have. When you're stepping on the ice and you know that you might have given a little bit more than what they have, it's an edge."

Gushue laughs when he looks back at how hard Fry worked in the gym to get ready for curling. Skips generally don't need to be in as good shape as front-end players, so Gushue admittedly didn't spend as much time hitting the weights as his teammate.

"Ryan's got big arms," Gushue laughed. "I can run circles around him but he can lift me up pretty easy. We used to joke with Ryan when he'd go to the gym that he just did arm curls . . . but in reality he really brings a different aspect to the game."

What he really brought to the game was a ton of skill. Gushue knew it and the rest of the elite curlers in Canada knew it. Fry could curl with the best of them and had the unique ability of being a great hitter who could make the finesse draws, sweep and play any position. "His technique is a big part of it," Gushue reflected. "If you can get into the position that he does in that tuck delivery, it makes it a little bit easier. Hitting becomes much easier in that position and the fact that he grew up in the game and learned from a lot of great curlers, not only his father but guys like Ray Turnbull and Jeff Stoughton, means a lot. He's a pretty good student of the game and works hard at it."

The rest of 2009 did not go well for the Gushue foursome. Though Gushue was the defending gold medallist and had been in the playoffs at the Brier the previous two seasons, he still didn't have a berth in the 2009 Olympic Trials in Edmonton and needed to go through a pre-trials qualifier in Prince George, British Columbia. The team won only one game in the triple-knockout pre-trials event and then lost three straight to be eliminated. Gushue's dream of repeating his Olympic gold medal was dead and Fry's primary reason for joining the younger team — taking a run at the Olympic Trials — was never really even born.

They bounced back fairly quickly however, as all the great teams do, and earned a berth in the 2010 Brier in Halifax. Once again they were solid contenders, making the playoffs one more time (Gushue's fourth time, Fry's third) with an 8-3 record and edging out the 7-4 Stoughton for fourth place. For the third time in his career, Gushue was eliminated in the first playoff game, this time by Alberta's eventual champion Kevin Koe, and once again the team was heading home without any hardware.

Gushue was disappointed, but he still liked his team and particularly his association with Fry. At that moment, he believed his team would still be together for a run at the 2014 Olympics in Sochi. "I personally want to continue," he said. "I don't want to play at a half-ass level. If all four of us want to come back and attempt to curl at this level again, if we have the sponsorship and the family support, then we'll do it."

At that Brier in 2010, a new name emerged among the contenders. Brad Jacobs of Northern Ontario, a 24-year-old upstart, surprised a lot of people by going 9-2 and making it to the Page Playoff game against Glenn Howard of Ontario. Jacobs, who was playing with his cousins E.J. and Ryan Harnden, lost that game and later the semifinal to Koe, but still took home the bronze medal and showed the curling world that his team had a bright future. No doubt, Fry took notice — the Jacobs boys were a lot like him in terms of intensity, demeanor and physical fitness — but there was something brewing in Newfoundland that he still wanted to be a part of.

Just a month after the Brier, the Gushue team made a gigantic splash by announcing that it was adding six-time Canadian and four-time world champion Randy Ferbey to the mix. Ferbey was breaking up his Edmonton team, the most successful in the history of men's curling, to join Gushue. He planned to skip and throw third stones, just as he did for years with fourth Dave Nedohin and his Alberta team. He had no plan to play for Newfoundland in the Brier, just to tour with the Gushue team during the cash bonspiel season and hopefully stay together long enough for an Olympic run. The move meant Jamie Korab was off the team and everyone else would move down a position. Fry was now the lead on this dream team and had played every position in high-level curling.

The experiment was an unmitigated disaster; just five months after they started curling together, Gushue and his original teammates split from Ferbey in spectacular fashion. There was a public war of words, much of it vitriolic, and a great deal of embarrassment for both sides. Fry was right in the middle of things, telling Sun Media's Terry Jones that it was time for the 52-year-old Ferbey to retire. It was a stunning comment about a curling legend from a young player who had never won a Brier, but Fry stuck to his guns. He was angry that Ferbey suggested in the media that the rest of the team quit on him and it was an "experiment gone wrong."

"They are comments by a very immature man in Randy Ferbey. I believe it is time he decided to retire. It takes a very special person to take the frustrations of a poor season out on former teammates, no matter what the case. His recent vent is one that shows the need to stay current in the media in a game that has passed him by. The sport has changed and the class of players have evolved. We have become athletes. There is very little room in the sport now for competitors like Randy Ferbey. I wish Randy the best and hope maturity comes with retirement."

Fry's comments stunned the curling world and brought an immediate reaction from Ferbey: "A little young puke like that is going to push me into retirement? Yeah, whatever."

Given Fry's reputation for being immature himself, for throwing and banging brooms and showing his temper on the ice, it would have been easy for curling fans to dismiss his sentiments. But Gushue, an Olympic gold medallist, backed him all the way. "According to [Gushue] I'm the worst piece of shit in the history of the world," Ferbey said. Still there were some curlers who thought Fry owed an apology to the legend of curling.

"For Ryan to say that Ferbey should retire and the game has passed him by is completely offside," four-time world champion Glenn Howard said. "It's unjustified and unfair. I have the utmost respect for Randy Ferbey. He is the most decorated curler in the world as far as I'm concerned. I heard what was said and I was shocked. I was very disappointed to hear this and very, very disappointed in the two of them [Gushue and Fry]. It makes me sad."

The entire incident was somewhat surreal, but Gushue and Fry did not let it derail their team. They simply added Jamie Danbrook to the lineup and resumed their old positions, Gushue at skip, Nichols at third and Fry at second. They made it back to the Brier in 2011 and this time finished on top of the standings with a 9-2 record, tied with none other than old friend Jeff Stoughton. It said something that the Gushue team had been to the Brier three times with Fry in the lineup and had made it to the playoffs each time. This was their best chance yet to win it all, but it simply wasn't meant to be. Stoughton was on his way to his second world championship gold medal, and he beat Gushue 7-6 in the first Page Playoff game. Gushue then lost 7-6 to Ontario's Glenn Howard in the semifinal before bouncing back to beat the great Kevin Martin of Alberta 10-5 in the first-ever bronze medal game at the Brier.

It was the second career bronze medal for Fry and a nice feather in his cap, but it was nowhere close to enough for him, and there were signs that there were happy feet inside those curling shoes. The vagabond never stays in one place too long before moving on to find a more exciting location. Fry decided to give it one more go with the Gushue team, though the following season he played third and the team recruited a new front end in Geoff Walker and Adam Casey. They made it back to the Brier one more time, but this time the magic just wasn't there. While Fry curled 84 percent in the tournament, third among all vice-skips, they compiled a disappointing 5-6 record and failed to make the playoffs for the first time in five years.

The Gushue team was in flux and the skip no longer felt the optimism he had developed in the previous seasons. Only a few weeks later, it was all over for Gushue and Fry. Despite admitting Fry was his team's best player at the 2012 Brier, Gushue decided to cut his third after four seasons, four trips to the national championship and three playoff berths. Fry simply wasn't on the same page as the rest of the team, especially with two new players who were just learning to play the game at a high level.

"On our team, I had no problem with the intensity and everything he brought to the team," Gushue said in 2014. "It just didn't match up with the couple of guys that we had. You just have to find four personalities that match and blend well together.

"Ryan and I are good friends and I'd love to curl with him again at some point in the future. We were kind of going through a change and brought in two guys that really hadn't learned the game and we were somewhat in the development stage and I don't think Ryan was ready for that or as committed to that as I was. It wasn't necessarily a good fit. He wanted to win right now and wasn't as willing to sacrifice to get those guys to the level we needed to get them to."

It was a shocking development for Fry and one that set the curling world abuzz. Had the ultra-intense Fry, the player with the nerve to call out the great Randy Ferbey, the "little young puke" with the fiery temper on the ice, finally worn out his welcome on the competitive curling scene? Some thought so, but they were sorely mistaken. It only took a couple of weeks for Fry to find a new home, and this time it had the potential to be the mix he had always been looking for. The vagabond was on the move again.

On April 9, 2012, promising skip Brad Jacobs of Sault Ste. Marie, Ontario, announced Fry would join his team as the third. Scott Seabrook, the team's lead, was leaving the team and Jacobs had asked his cousins, E.J. and Ryan Harnden, to move down to the front end. This was their golden opportunity to bring in not only an experienced curler, but one who was very like-minded and shared their passion for athleticism.

"We've known Fry for quite a few years now and we get along, so he was a perfect addition to our team," Jacobs told the *Sault Star*. "In terms of talent and skill, ability and experience, as well as having four really similar guys, I think this is probably the strongest team we've had."

Fry quit his job in St. John's, sold a bunch of his stuff, packed up the rest and made the move to Sault Ste. Marie. Although he was not headed to a curling hotbed, he was joining the best team in the region and a squad with a great chance of getting to the Brier and beyond each and every year. At least one curling analyst loved the move by both Fry and Jacobs the minute it was announced.

"To escape his reputation in Manitoba [Fry] decided to go out to Newfoundland

and play with Brad Gushue, and I think in many ways he brought some life to Brad's team," Cathy Gauthier explained. "It didn't settle him down but just gave him a little more perspective. At that point in time I noticed that his personality started to mature and change and yet he still had that spark that maybe didn't fit with that team.

"When I found out that he was playing with Brad Jacobs, I thought he definitely should fit in there, but what I never, ever envisioned was that he would become sort of the senior statesman."

Few people envisioned that, but it was there as plain as day. Jacobs and the Harnden brothers were notoriously temperamental and had pissed off more than their share of curlers and fans over the years. They liked to "go hard" off the ice and loved to work out in the gym — "Some of that fitness definitely helps them and some of it just makes them look good in shirts," Brad Gushue laughed — and Fry fit in like a pair of old, perfectly worn curling gloves. But he also brought a new dynamic immediately. He was a talented curler and he had mellowed a bit over the years. With the volatile Jacobs crew, Fry was described in a way few people would have ever imagined: As a calming influence.

"He learned, back with myself and with Gushue, [about] being able to control his emotions and being able to know how to make your skip better and how to make your front end better and that's what all good teammates do," Jeff Stoughton said. "They bring everyone up to a better level and he's been able to do that with the Jacobs team.

"He doesn't have to be the fiery guy out there. He can be the calm head and remind everyone that this is probably the best option, this is the best shot, and it worked out great for them. Brothers and a cousin can be pretty tough on each other, and it's great to see Ryan play the role of the calming person out there. It's good to see that maturity from him. It's all happened over the last 10 years and it's pretty phenomenal."

Fry obviously saw the potential of the team immediately and knew it would be partly on him to help them grow into a perennial contender. "We knew we had something special right off the hop," he said. "These guys are basically three brothers and, for me, I felt like I fit in right away. We're all very much the same personality. We take things pretty lightly and we have a lot of fun along the way.

"I knew the team had the capability to compete for the Olympic Trials. For me it was a pretty obvious decision, and I think, for the guys, it was as well. We're younger. Brad, as a skip, is still coming into his own, but he's catching up very quickly. But the team, in itself, we have a little bit stronger personalities than I would say some of the teams on tour do. For us, it's keeping a lot of our successes and failure internal, keeping our emotions in check and keeping supportive of one another and not sort of getting into the aggressive side of the sport. I think the potential of this team is higher than the teams I've played for in the past."

If nothing else, he was certainly correct in that assessment.

CHAPTER FIVE

A FATHER'S INSPIRATION

Her first memory of curling — or perhaps it was just something she saw in a picture — was of sliding down the ice on a curling rock at the age of two, with her father Keith guiding the way. Kaitlyn Lawes was born to be a curler and it had been a huge part of her life since she was old enough to take her first nervous steps onto the pebbled surface. Born in Winnipeg in 1988, Lawes curled for the first time at the age of four and spent so many hours of her formative years around the curling rink. Her father was a curling enthusiast — perhaps "curling nut" would be more apropos — and as long as anyone can remember, he had his youngest daughter with him.

"I can remember looking out on the ice and there'd be Keith and this tiny little girl — she couldn't have been much more than five years old at the time — out there throwing rocks together," longtime Manitoba curler Vic Peters, who was the ice-maker at the Fort Garry Curling Club at the time, told the *Winnipeg Free Press* in 2008.

Keith Lawes was born in 1937 in Montreal and lived in three provinces before finally settling down in Manitoba in the 1980s. He had five children, the oldest born in 1962, and he introduced them all to curling, his true passion, as soon as he could. His eldest, Andrea Lawes, was born in Toronto and grew up to be a competitive curler in Ontario, playing on five teams that won provincial championships. In 1990, when her half-sister Kaitlyn was just two years old, Andrea won the Scotties Tournament of Hearts with skip Alison Goring and went on to the world championship, where she won a bronze medal. Not only was Kaitlyn exposed to curling by a loving father at a very young age, but she had a sibling who was a Canadian champion to look up to.

With her father and older sister as inspiration, it was no surprise that Kaitlyn began curling competitively before she was even a teenager. "I played a lot of other sports but as I started to curl more and more I slowly started to quit the other sports," Kaitlyn explained. "Curling has always been my passion and always in the forefront. I always wanted to be an athlete of some sort and curling was that one sport that I stuck with my whole life."

Unlike her sister, she liked to throw skip rocks and entered her first big bonspiel in 2002 at age 13. With her dad coaching, Lawes skipped a team to the 13-and-under championship at the Manitoba Youth Jamboree. The following year she skipped a team in the provincial junior women's championship at age 14, finishing with a 2-5 record against curlers who were as old as 20, and also played third for Sabrina Neufeld at the Canada Winter Games. That team finished a disappointing eleventh, but never again would Kaitlyn suffer that kind of humbling experience.

In 2004 she skipped a team to a 5-3 record at the provincial junior championship, and in 2005, improved that to 7-3. Then, in 2006, she bumped the record up to 8-2 and lost the final to three-time provincial champion Calleen Neufeld. The 2007 championship was a mirror image — Lawes finished at 8-2 and lost the final to Neufeld again. There was one thing different this time; Lawes was playing with a heavy heart, her mind distracted by a loved one's devastating illness. Her father, Keith, was in the hospital, having surgery for a brain tumour. It was a testament to her father's love of the game and his daughter that he insisted she keep curling while he was in the hospital.

"He was unable to watch but he was up and talking and doing really well after [the surgery]. As soon as he got out of surgery, he said he wanted to call me to wish me luck before my game." The surgery took place on a Friday with Lawes in playoff contention, and the tournament wrapped up on the Sunday.

"[Friday] was a hard day, but I could concentrate on curling while I was on the ice," an emotional Lawes said. "Off the ice, I was pretty worried. But's he's in really good hands. My mom and family are there with him."

Although losing another provincial final in 2007 was crushing for Lawes, it paled in comparison to what she was going through in her personal life. No one in her world meant more to her than her father, and now he was in the fight of his life. Sadly, on November 3, 2007, with his family around him, Keith Lawes passed away. The focal point of Kaitlyn's life had slipped away when she was just 18 years old.

"He was my inspiration, a big part of my journey, my whole life up until then," Kaitlyn said.

Perhaps fittingly, Keith's funeral was delayed because both Kaitlyn and Andrea were curling. "We knew that for curling he wouldn't have minded having his funeral delayed," Kaitlyn said to the *Winnipeg Free Press*. After the funeral, Keith's ashes were placed inside a curling rock, yet another testament to how much the game meant to him. Kaitlyn had mixed feelings about the decision. "It just was so different. And I didn't like the idea that I couldn't see him anymore. I just didn't know how to deal with the idea he was in a curling rock."

Though Keith's death was devastating, it did nothing to quell Kaitlyn's determination to succeed. In fact, it increased her drive, knowing how much her dad would have wanted to see her take the next step in competitive curling. "Curling has helped a lot because he's there with me every step of the way," she said. "I'm sure he'll be watching me. But it's hard . . . the holidays were tough and it's hard to not see him out here."

Regardless of her personal heartbreak, she was getting stronger every year and with five provincial tournaments under her belt at the age of 19, she was ready to stop settling for second place. It didn't hurt that her old nemesis, Calleen Neufeld, graduated from the junior ranks in 2008. Lawes and teammates Jenna Loder, Liz Peters and Sarah Wazney plowed through the competition at the 2008 provincial championship, compiling a 9-0 record and winning their first title. There was no question who Lawes was thinking about as she slid off the ice, eyes filled with tears of both joy and sadness.

"I miss him so much," she said through sobs. "I wish I could share this with him. But he was out there with us all the way. He gives me strength to keep going."

As the foursome prepared to play in the Canadian junior championship for the first time, Kaitlyn's teammates were in awe of their skip. "She's really strong and I admire her for everything she's gone through," Liz Peters said. "She's just been amazing."

The entire team was pretty amazing at the Canadian championship in Sault Ste. Marie, Ontario, following up a perfect provincial with an 11-2 record and a gold medal, Manitoba's first in junior women's play since 1995. While her father wasn't there, Kaitlyn had plenty of family in the stands to cheer her on, including her mother, grandmother, a couple of aunts and her half-sister Andrea. That was when she started the tradition of looking up into the stands, making eye contact with family members and picturing one more person sitting there with them. She would carry that tradition on to the highest heights of curling over the coming years.

The Lawes foursome earned the right to represent Canada at the world junior championship in Ostersund, Sweden, and headed overseas with a large entourage that included her mom, brother, grandmother and an aunt. She also carried a piece of her father with her. Just before Keith died in November 2007, he gave her an early birthday present. "My birthday is in December, but before he passed away he gave me a necklace. Just kind of as a little reminder. It's just a little heart shape, just a cute little necklace."

Lawes and her teammates finished with a 5-4 record and lost their first playoff game in Sweden, but they bounced back to win the bronze medal over Russia. Although it was a disappointing result for Lawes, who admitted to struggling with the straighter ice conditions, she was happy to have brought home a medal from her first taste of international competition. "It's been such an amazing experience. It has been an eye-opener." Interestingly, that year, the world championship was won by Scotland's Eve Muirhead, a junior curling powerhouse, who would loom large in the future for Kaitlyn Lawes.

If the curling world had not noticed Kaitlyn's arrival after the world junior championship bronze medal win, it certainly paid attention the following October when the still junior-aged skip pulled off a major accomplishment at a cash bonspiel in Winnipeg. Lawes, still just 19, made it to the quarter-finals of the Casinos of Winnipeg Classic by defeating, in succession, former world women's champions Kelly Scott, Jan Betker (Sandra Schmirler's third) and Anette Norberg. "It was just three victories, but we're pumped about it," Lawes said. "We didn't let it get to us, who we were playing, but it was kind of satisfying after." No one could have predicted her team would be so successful so early, but when it was all said and done, her competitors were envisioning big things for the young Winnipegger.

"If it means anything to her, she reminds me of me at that age, where you're hungry and there's lots that you want to do in the sport," Kelly Scott said. "She's got a real good future."

In 2009, Lawes took another step forward, playing in her seventh Manitoba junior women's championship (one short of the record held by Scott), winning for the second straight year and then repeating as Canadian champion in Salmon Arm, British Columbia.

Lawes, who beat Ontario's Rachel Homan in the final, became just the third skip in the 40-year history of the junior women's event to repeat as champion, but that was not the only thing that made the win particularly significant. Lawes and her teammates, who now included Jenna Loder, Laryssa Grenkow and Breanne Meakin, earned the right to represent Canada at the 2009 world junior championship, which was slated for Vancouver and would serve as a test event for the 2010 Olympic Winter Games. The curlers would be treated like Olympians for 10 days and that experience proved invaluable down the road.

After winning a bronze medal at the worlds in 2008, Lawes and her teammates were determined to take a step up on the podium and they did just that. Canada made it all the way to the final, where once again Scotland's Eve Muirhead was waiting. It was a dramatic final, and Lawes had a chance for glory with a difficult but makeable shot to upend the Scottish skip who was looking to become the most successful junior curler of all time. It came down to the tenth end and the tension in the Vancouver Olympic venue was palpable; the gold medal was so close the Canadians could taste it. Just 20 years old and facing a moment of immense pressure with her team trailing 7-6, Lawes tried a come-around, tap-back shot that would have given her team two points and the world title. Instead, the rock was slightly heavy, Scotland stole one point and Muirhead won her third of four world junior championships. Lawes was predictably devastated and was barely able to get any words out when reporters approached her after the game.

"It's too soon to talk about," she said through sobs. "It meant a lot to me."

"The whole team's upset," coach Rob Meakin said as Lawes and her teammates consoled one another. "It was a big game, and they had a shot to win, and it hurts. The way it is for us, it's gold or you're disappointed. It was their dream to win the world championship and you never know when you're going to get that chance again. The girls should hold their heads high, but right now, it hurts."

In the big picture, Lawes had improved on her bronze medal from the previous year and had been inches away from the world title, which were both worthy accomplishments. Even more importantly, Lawes had established herself as an up-and-coming skip, the kind of curler who would surely be a contender at the women's level, the kind of young, enthusiastic talent every team wants to add. Just weeks after the world junior championship, she was already in demand and played her first major women's event, the Canada Cup, as the third for Edmonton's Cathy King. After Lawes made the grade in that event, King, the 1998 Canadian women's champion, asked her to play full-time in 2009–10 and the 20-year-old took up the offer, moving to Edmonton that summer.

The reward was immediate, as King had a spot in an Olympic Trials qualifier and Lawes wanted nothing more than a chance to get to the Olympics. "It would be a dream come true. That was one of the reasons I did this — a chance to go to the Olympics." Lawes was a good fit with the King team right away and they won money on the cash bonspiel circuit. King was thrilled with the way Lawes quickly adapted to a new position, after skipping for so many years, and added life to a team that was feeling a bit stale about curling. Still, while the season started well, the Olympic dream was over almost before it began. The King team went to the pre-trials qualifier in Prince George, British Columbia, with high hopes, but managed just two wins against three losses in the triple-knockout and failed to advance to the 2009 Canadian Curling Trials in Edmonton.

The Olympic dream was officially on hold for Lawes, but given that she had not yet reached her twenty-first birthday, it was hard for her to be too disappointed. Surely there would be other chances down the line for a young player with her unique blend of talent, youth and big-game experience. Things did not go particularly well with the King team, but Lawes had tasted the women's game and the Olympic qualifying process and was hungry for much more.

As she watched the Vancouver Olympics on television in February 2010, a team of well-known curlers in her home province had set their sights on her. Her father's inspiration was about to take her places she never dreamed of going.

Just one day after Cathy Overton-Clapham was unceremoniously jettisoned from Team Canada, Jennifer Jones and her remaining teammates announced Kaitlyn Lawes as the replacement at third. One full season removed from her glorious junior career, Lawes was named to the three-time defending Canadian champion women's team, and it was like winning the lottery. She would have a chance to wear the Team Canada colours at the Scotties Tournament of Hearts and play on a team that was deadly serious about its pursuit of a place in the Olympics four years down the road. Twenty years younger than Overton-Clapham, Lawes came from a different curling generation, saw the game differently and brought a refreshing attitude that Jones hoped would rejuvenate her team.

"We felt that we might be getting a little bit stale and needed to be rejuvenated and especially if we are looking four years down the line," Jones said. "You look at teams and they seem to have their success and then they get a little bit stale and we're just looking to the future." The move made sense for Jones on so many levels, not the least of which was bringing one of curling's rising stars, and a potential future rival for an Olympic berth, into the fold. Jones knew Overton-Clapham was an amazing player, perhaps the best third of all time in the women's game, and a huge part of her team's success. At that moment in time though, they were contemplating retirement and were in a lull. They needed to either retire or make a significant change, one that would recharge them for the gruelling four-year Olympic cycle. "Cutting [Cathy O] was one of the hardest things we've ever had to do. But Kaitlyn just brought this energy to the team and gave us that kick in the butt to really want to go for it," Jones said.

It all made sense, and in the end nobody could argue Jones made the right decision, but in the immediate aftermath of the split, her popularity hit an all-time low.

"They, particularly Jen, went through a lot with the separation with Cathy O," Cathy Gauthier said. "They just felt the weight of the world, whether it was in social media or the regular media or just people stopping her. I remember that year in Charlottetown [at the Scotties in 2011], she was clearly not the favourite with the crowd and those things take their toll, so you withdraw into yourself. After that I think she realized there were also a lot of people who were vocally in support of her and her choice to make whatever decisions she needed to make."

Although Jones separated from her husband in early 2011, it was not nearly as volatile as her split with Cathy O. Because the Jones team was already Team Canada for the 2011 season, they didn't have to compete in the Manitoba provincial championship that season. However, their spurned teammate, Overton-Clapham, did compete in the provincials and had a large, razor-sharp axe to grind. Overton-Clapham decided to skip her own team that season and took the motivation of getting blindsided by her former teammates into the event. By the time it was over, Overton-Clapham had yet another provincial championship to her name and a large throng of local curling fans in her corner. Immediately after Cathy O won the Manitoba title, a fan at the Sunflower Gardens in Altona, Manitoba, yelled out an encouraging message: "Watch out Jenny!" Cathy O heard it and admitted it made her smile.

"It was nice to hear something like that," she said. "It was funny and it lightened the mood. What's happened the last eight months has been tough to take." It was quickly pointed out that Overton-Clapham's Team Manitoba would meet Jones's Team Canada in Charlottetown, Prince Edward Island, at the national Scotties on February 23. This time Overton-Clapham took the high road — "It has nothing to do with them . . . it's done . . . it's been a long eight months" — but long before that national championship started, it already had the juiciest of storylines, with Jennifer Jones cast as the villain.

The support for Overton-Clapham from the curling world was phenomenal. She received emails from all over the world, including from Scottish phenom Eve Muirhead, Sweden's two-time Olympic gold medallist Anette Norberg and six-time Canadian champion Colleen Jones. It seemed everyone believed she got a raw deal from the Jennifer Jones team and wanted to see her land on her feet. As the Scotties in Charlottetown approached, the grudge match between Jones and Overton-Clapham was all anyone wanted to talk about. Well, anyone but Jennifer Jones. "What game is that?" she said glibly, when asked if she was ready for the "big one." "I'm not just saying that. It really is just another game in the round robin and we're going to treat it like any other game."

It wasn't just any other game though. With the amount of press the game was receiving, the Tournament of Hearts was suddenly a hot ticket. TSN was expecting an increase in viewership on February 23, with even non-curling fans across the country likely to tune in, wanting to see a potential catfight. It all could have been terribly disconcerting for the newest member of the Jones team, the now 22-year-old Lawes, who was thrown into the middle of public squabble and was under pressure to replace one of the best curlers in the history of the women's game. She took it all in stride however, a quality that had to bode well for the future of the team. "I don't feel like I've replaced Cathy," Lawes said. "That's one thing I can't do. I can't fill her shoes. She's a great curler, so I really obviously haven't felt that pressure on myself because it's a brand new team this year."

"Kaitlyn has dealt with everything really well and obviously, she had nothing to do with our tough decision," Jill Officer said on the eve of the 2011 Tournament of Hearts. "She's a very mature 22-year-old, and sometimes I forget she's that young. She's brought some youthful energy, great shot-making and she's a fantastic sweeper. She's a really positive person, very supportive and she's been great all around."

Overton-Clapham was adopted as the fan favourite in Charlottetown, while Jones heard jeers and derision from the crowd. Even the other curlers were caught up in the hysteria. "Everyone's talking about it," B.C. skip Kelly Scott said. "It's great. People thrive on these kinds of rivalries. It won't go away either. They're going to battle one another out until one of them decides not to play anymore. It's just the start I'm sure."

"I'm just happy Cathy is here," Saskatchewan skip Amber Holland said. "She deserves to be here and I was pretty happy she ended up winning Manitoba. I feel for her because I've been in that position where you feel a little bit blindsided, when you get cut from a team."

"I mean, come on, all of Canada's interested," Kerry Galusha of the Northwest Territories chimed in. "Even I'm waiting for it. The drama of it all overshadowed a lot of the other teams coming here. I feel so bad for Cathy. I'm sure she has a bit of sweet revenge on them in mind."

Amid all the hype about the big game, Overton-Clapham got off to a terrible start in the tournament, losing four of the first five games and sitting at 2-6 and out of the tournament by the time the grudge match arrived. Jones was sitting at 6-2 at the time and contending for top spot. While all eyes were on the former teammates about to do battle on national television, all tongues wagging about the soap opera, Jones continued to downplay the game. "I can honestly say I have not lost any sleep over it. I have not had one person come up to me and say anything negative, outside of the media."

It was impressive that Jones was able to block out the anger fans and curlers felt toward her over the Overton-Clapham saga. In reality there were plenty of negative feelings toward her — justified or not — and the *Winnipeg Sun*'s Paul Friesen summed up just how much of a villain Jones had become after speaking to a taxi driver on his ride home from the rink. "You are from Winnipeg, home of those two curlers," the affable driver started. "All of Canada will be cheering against Jennifer Jones." How odd it was to hear people talking like that about a skip who was wearing Team Canada colours in the tournament. The anger ran deeper than Jones could have ever imagined.

In the end there was no hair pulling or eye gouging or even name calling when *Jones versus Overton-Clapham: The Grudge Match* finally came about. The game was played before a big crowd in Charlottetown and drew a TV audience on

TSN of roughly 647,000 viewers, considerably more than the NHL game between Colorado and Edmonton that followed it (492,000). From the get-go, the crowd was on Cathy O's side and so were the curling gods. She curled her finest game of the tournament, while Jones struggled mightily, and rode the wave of support to an 8-5 victory that was celebrated across the country. "I imagined the crowd being as great as it was," a jubilant Overton-Clapham said. "I didn't imagine all my peers being as excited and rooting for us. Kelly Scott was giving the pump-fist. That was fun! I guess you could say that was my final, because I'm not going to be in the final. I had a fire under my ass."

Predictably, Jones refused to admit the loss held any special significance and, in the big picture, she was right. Her team was still headed to the playoffs and the grudge match that people couldn't stop talking about was finally out of the way. The Jones team finished with an 8-3 record and made it all the way to the final once again. One more win and they would capture a fourth-straight Canadian championship, a feat accomplished only once before — by Colleen Jones — in the history of women's curling. It was clear that the nastiness of the Overton-Clapham split had not affected Jones, Lawes, Officer and Askin. In fact, Lawes handled the pressure and the situation beautifully, leading all thirds in curling percentage in the tournament. You could argue with the timing and the harshness of the Overton-Clapham firing, but you couldn't debate the choice of Lawes as her replacement. "We knew she was a great player," Jones said. "It was more just trying to find that whole team dynamic, and it was the easiest thing in the world. She's got a good head on her shoulders and lots of experience playing in big games at the junior level. She's a pretty calm individual."

A funny thing happened during that fourth straight Canadian championship final — the Jones team lost. Saskatchewan's Amber Holland upset Jones 8-7 with Team Canada skip missing an angle-double-raise that would have clinched the win. Jones was sure she had the shot made and was ready to celebrate another Canadian title. Most observers expected her to make it as well — after all, she always made the big shot — but it wasn't meant to be. The Jones team had lost the right to wear the Team Canada colours and it would be a few years and many life changes before they would get it back.

CHAPTER SIX

THE BUFF BOYS

One of the greatest 16-month runs in the history of Canadian curling started in the gym, where four men in Sault Ste. Marie believed they could find success. They lifted weights, ran on the track and worked the cardio machines till sweat poured from their skin and their muscles ached. It was a daily routine that earned the curlers a nickname: The Buff Boys.

When curling became part of the Olympics in 1998, curlers began to take athleticism more seriously and nobody more so than Brad Jacobs and his teammates. There was funding from the World Curling Federation and the Canadian Curling Association that teams could use for training as they worked toward Olympic qualification, and the Buff Boys took full advantage. They all worked with personal trainers and also developed their own system in the fall of 2012. "Our team is very committed to it," third Ryan Fry said. "I think you can tell by the appearance of us.

We're committed to the weight training and being as strong a team as there is on tour. Not only do we feel it increases our chances of lasting through some gruelling events — days when you have three games — but we want to be known as one of the fittest teams, so that down the road, if there are corporations looking to sponsor a team, we're hoping they're going to want to sponsor a fit team that really cares about that side of the sport as well."

Physically, they were unlike anything curling had ever seen; nobody had put in that kind of effort in the gym before. "We've seen people become athletic and we've seen people work out and be fit, but nobody has the physique that the Jacobs team does," TSN analyst Cathy Gauthier said. "It is intimidating. It's a layer unto this sport that we have not seen before."

They matched time spent in the gym with time spent at the curling rink, throwing rocks in practice or heading out on the road to compete for cash. They didn't have the time or the sponsorship to spend every weekend on the road competing on the World Curling Tour — they all had day jobs and couldn't afford to travel every weekend. When they did enter their first bonspiel, an Ontario Curling Tour event in Oakville, Ontario, Fry and his new teammates didn't click immediately and Jacobs admits there was some frustration early on.

The team held a meeting to make sure everyone was on the same page. "It was almost like we had a honeymoon 'spiel with a few bumps in the road along the way," Jacobs said. "Then everyone just kinda figured out in their own minds what we have to do in order to win." But a few hiccups were to be expected, of course. E.J. and Ryan Harnden were being asked to play new positions and the team had a new third who brought a new set of skills and ideas.

The team started to click in November when they competed in the Grand Slam of Curling's Masters tournament in Brantford, Ontario. They ran off five straight wins to qualify for the playoff round but lost in the quarter-finals, and though they made some money, it was immediately clear that they would not be satisfied with merely contending. "Personally I'm not happy with finishing out of the quarters," Fry said. "We're better than that and I think we should be competing to win championships. It's going to be about learning from our mistakes and being able to put stronger performances together."

While Fry wanted more out of the team right away, Jacobs was thrilled with how things were working out. The Harnden brothers had adjusted beautifully to their new positions and talked about wanting to be the best front end in Canada. He had a team with four players who all wanted to win desperately and were willing to do anything to make it happen. "I'm not saying we weren't in the past, but we really are four super-hungry guys," said Jacobs at the time.

If this new team had not already served notice to the curling world, it did in December at the Canadian Open of Curling Grand Slam event in Kelowna, British Columbia. There, they went 6-1 in the round robin against a who's who of Canadian men's curling and made it all the way to the final against four-time world champion Glenn Howard of Coldwater, Ontario. Along the way they defeated top-ranked teams skipped by Jeff Stoughton, Mike McEwen and Kevin Koe. In the final, Jacobs had a shot to win the game but misjudged the line call and wound up missing the shot by a half-inch to lose 3-1. While hating to lose, Jacobs was getting more and more excited about his team and its ability to run with the big dogs. "We leave it all out there every game," the skip said. "It's just blood, sweat and tears all the time. All four of us want to win so badly and you can just feel it every time we step out on the ice." When the World Curling Tour rankings came out later that month, the Jacobs team was eighth, its first time cracking the top 10.

Jacobs qualified for the quarter-finals at the next Grand Slam, the National, in late January 2013, before bowing out to Stoughton, but once again they were in the money and pushing toward their goal of winning a major tournament. More importantly, they were playing well at a high level, with the Northern Ontario championship right around the corner. Jacobs entered the Northerns as the three-time defending champion and another win would give him the provincial record, breaking the mark set by the great Al Hackner in 1980–82. Fry had a chance to do something only one person had ever done before — qualify for the Brier with three different provinces (Manitoba, Newfoundland and Northern Ontario). If he could win the Northerns, he'd be heading to the Brier for the fifth straight year and sixth time in seven years.

To no one's surprise, the Jacobs team was the class of the field at the Northerns in Nipigon, Ontario, and they beat Sudbury's Robbie Gordon 6-5 in the final. For all the history they had made by winning, there was absolutely no question they were no longer satisfied by merely qualifying for the Brier. "It's been a lifelong dream to win the Brier," Jacobs said. "We've had a pretty successful year to this point and I feel like we're doing everything we need to do to potentially win the Brier."

"We've put in a lot of time and effort in practice," Ryan Harnden chimed in. "We're capable of winning the Brier. We've played the top teams this year and we've beaten them on a regular basis."

After finding success on the World Curling Tour (fifth on the money list), the Jacobs foursome entered the Brier on March 2 in Edmonton with a different mentality and more confidence than ever. They had lost just five games in three Grand Slam events and had picked up wins over many of the top teams in the world along the way. More than anything, they were having fun and were putting far less pressure on themselves than in the past. Whether that was the result of Fry's calming influence and experience or simply something they learned from past trips to the Brier, it was clear the Jacobs foursome planned to enjoy their time in Edmonton while settling for nothing less than a Canadian championship. "We're not happy just to be here anymore," Jacobs said. "The goal is to win the Brier, and that's where our heads are at."

Their Brier could not possibly have gotten off to a better start. Like body builders picking on 98-pound weaklings, the Buff Boys pummelled their first three opponents — winning 9-3 over British Columbia, 11-6 over the Northwest Territories and 10-4 over Prince Edward Island. Given, those were all games they were expected to win, but Jacobs and his teammates did it with authority and curled with the goal of being as close to 100 percent as possible at all times. In their next game, they did something no one expected, continuing to pound on an opponent who was anything but a weakling. Kevin Martin was a heavyweight in every sense of the word, having won Briers, world championships and gold and silver medals at the Olympics. Jacobs destroyed Martin 8-1 in only seven ends. This team was showing its teeth.

On the very next draw they were reminded that winning any game at the Brier is a tough task, after an encounter with an old friend. Brad Gushue's Newfoundland team was next up and it was a huge game for Fry, who was cut by the former Olympic gold medallist just a few months earlier. Though there seemed to be no hard feelings between Gushue and Fry, and the latter was very much enjoying his new team, it's always special for an athlete to play his former team. This time, Gushue emerged with a hard-fought 9-8 victory in an extra end, handing Jacobs and Fry their first loss of the Brier. They got whipped 8-2 by four-time world champion Glenn Howard on the next draw, and things were suddenly looking a lot less promising for the team from Northern Ontario. Once again, however, a newfound perspective shone through, and Jacobs was able to take the losses in stride, a trait many suggested was not his strong suit in previous years. "We ran into a team that's curling amazing. We lost. We move on. We're in a good spot . . . we've been here before."

They bounced back right away, beating former Brier champion Jean-Michel Menard of Quebec 6-4 to improve to 5-2 before dropping a surprising 7-6 loss to unheralded Brock Virtue of Saskatchewan. That set up a big game against perennial contender and old foe Jeff Stoughton, another former teammate of Fry's. Sitting at 5-3, Jacobs knew his team could not afford another loss and they needed to put together one of the finest games of their careers. They got it, and that game proved to be a turning point in their lives as well. From that moment forward, the Jacobs team was known for being at their best when things looked the bleakest "I can't even explain how big this was," Jacobs said after a 9-4 victory over Stoughton. "We went out with our game faces on and I'm proud of how we played.

"By midweek it was starting to look like we might be out of it," Jacobs said, reflecting on that Brier experience. "We had a lot of ups and downs. But then we had that game against Jeff. That was the turning point of the whole Brier."

Still not able to afford a loss, they closed out the round robin with a 7-4 win over New Brunswick and a 5-2 win over Nova Scotia to finish at 8-3. It was enough to put them in the playoffs and earned them a date with Gushue, of all people, in the Page Playoff third versus fourth game. The winner would move on to the semifinals, the loser would be eliminated. Of course the game had to be against Gushue, as if the storyline were scripted from the very beginning. And of course, it came down to an extra end where Jacobs had to draw the four-foot for a 6-5 win. On this night in Edmonton, it was no problem for the skip, who curled an astounding 99 percent in the game. "Amazing to be a part of that game," an elated Jacobs told Sun Media. "It was a thrill to be out there and I'm pumped to be able to continue this little roll that we're on."

It never gets any easier when you are playing in the Brier against some of the best teams in the world. The semifinal was up next, and standing in the way this time was Howard, one of the greatest players in the history of the game. Howard, who had former Brier-winning skip Wayne Middaugh as his third, had gone 10-1 in the round robin, but lost the Page Playoff first versus second game to Jeff Stoughton. And by the time the game with Jacobs came around, Howard had lost the magic. The teams traded deuces for the first four ends until Jacobs turned the tide with a steal of two in the fifth, then opened up an insurmountable 9-5 lead with another steal in the eighth. The final score was 9-7 and Jacobs was finally off to his first Brier final. This was exactly what his team was built for, exactly why it added Fry at the beginning of the season, exactly why it worked harder than everyone else to get in shape. "We've never had a whole lot of success on the Tour until this year," Jacobs said. "I'll give Fry a lot of credit. Since we brought him on, look what we've done. We seem to be playing a lot more consistent. He brings a lot of confidence, a lot of calmness. He brings a good attitude. He's a total package. He wants to win, he's super competitive and he wants to be the best."

As if to emphasize to the world that the time had come for Team Jacobs, the Brier final was never even close. It was supposed to be that way, of course, except almost everyone expected Jeff Stoughton to be the crusher, not the crushee. Jacobs and his teammates were outrageously good in the biggest game of their lives. Ryan Harnden curled 100 percent, E.J. Harnden 99 percent, Fry 94 percent and Jacobs 88 percent, every one of them outshining his counterpart. It was 6-2 after four ends and Stoughton knew already that he was defeated because the Jacobs curlers were such good hitters. It wound up 11-4 and Jacobs, at age 27, was a Brier-winning skip — the youngest to win since Kevin Martin at age 24 in 1991 — and was named the winner of the Brier's Hec Gervais Most Valuable Player Award. It was the first national men's championship in 28 years for Northern Ontario, an area that was almost voted out of the Brier at one point because of its non-province status. Amazingly, none of the Jacobs team members were named to the tournament's all-star team, likely because the writers who vote on such things never expected to see them in the final after finishing fourth in the round robin. It seems Jacobs and Co. stunned absolutely everybody, except themselves.

"Oh, my God," Jacobs blurted out to reporters after the epic victory. "I don't even know how to feel. It's overwhelming. It's really overwhelming what's going on. I'm so proud of the guys for curling the way that they did. Phenomenal. We're Brier champs. This is a dream come true. This is what we've wanted ever since we were kids. It's been too long since Northern Ontario has held that Tankard. To bring it back to Northern Ontario, to Sault Ste. Marie, means a lot to us."

So there they were, four men who had flown slightly under the radar their whole curling lives, standing on top of the Brier podium, leaving former world champions in their wake. They were four regular guys with day jobs — Jacobs a bank accounts manager (curling success had taken him away from his dream of becoming a police officer), Fry a general contractor, E.J. Harnden an Ontario Lottery brand manager and Ryan Harnden a real estate appraiser — not professional curlers like some of the others in the field. They showed what hard work, determination and desire could do. The win might have been most gratifying for Fry, who had dedicated his life to the pursuit of this moment, travelling across the country in hopes of realizing a dream. Fry, who had made such a difference to this team, hopped the boards and headed straight for his dad right after the win.

"It's an unreal feeling," Fry said, fighting the emotion. "We've been working our asses off all year to get to this point. We've actually accomplished this goal and this dream and it feels unreal.

"My dad never really cast a shadow. My dad's been one of my biggest supporters along with my mom, and I'm lucky to have two parents that are willing to sacrifice probably retirement to follow me around curling. I love them to death and I'm very lucky."

Perhaps the most incredible thing about the Brier win was that it came just a few months after the new team was formed, and it was just in its infancy in terms of success. They didn't know it at the time, but a year later this Brier win would seem like small potatoes. Still, at that moment, it was the highlight of their sporting lives and the realization of their lifelong dreams. "We started curling because of what the Brier meant to our families," Jacobs said. "Once we became good curlers, it's always been about the Brier. We reached the pinnacle in winning it."

When they arrived home in Sault Ste. Marie, they were conquering heroes, greeted by a large throng of fans, family and friends at the airport and feted by the city in the coming weeks. Jacobs had more than 200 messages on his phone when he turned it on after the championship game. They were sports stars in a city that had watched them grow up and develop into elite curlers.

"They were just so focused, so intent all week. They wanted it. You could tell they wanted it," said Sault Ste. Marie mayor Debbie Amaroso, who later held a reception for the team at City Hall. Meanwhile, at the curling club where Jacobs spent so many of his formative years and worked as an ice boy, they were planning to hang a national championship banner from the rafters for the first time in history. "Brad was determined at that time he worked here that he was going to go to the Brier and he was going to win the Brier, and he's done it," club president Peter Zultek said to the *Sault Star*.

Along with their physical fitness and the addition of Fry, the Jacobs team also showed a tremendous amount of mental strength in reaching the top of Canadian curling. They were able to put their emotions aside, forget about bad shots quickly and keep focus in trying times. "Very little of this game is your slide, your delivery, that stuff," Jacobs said. "The physical part of the game is the sweeping, the rest of it is all mental. Really, we were able to stay within ourselves, stay within our team. We really wanted this, and it comes down to when you want something that bad, I think the mental focus just kicks in. We were in a place where we were almost in the zone."

To many observers, it was all about the newfound level-headedness. You certainly might still see the occasional broom slam from any of the four curlers, and they could still bicker like relatives are wont to do, but they refused to let frustration get to them and curled their best with their backs against the wall. "One of the best things about Brad Jacobs and his team is they are angry a lot of the time," TSN's Cathy Gauthier said. "They came into the Canadians and they got angry but they found a way to not be angry at each other and that was the biggest difference between that year and other years. In the past they would get mad at each other or themselves and they weren't able to shake it.

"I've known Ryan Fry since he was really young and in juniors and I would never have predicted what he has done. He has just stepped up. Not only is his curling ability brilliant — he's got the soft shot, the big shot — but he became the guy that manages to balance their emotions, stop the bickering and help them focus on stuff. I don't think anyone would have seen that coming 10 years ago. It's beyond phenomenal."

With the Brier win came the Jacobs team's first taste of major international competition with a berth in the 2013 world men's curling championship in Victoria. The worlds are a different beast from the Brier, arguably the overall level of the teams not quite as high, but many Canadians have underestimated the competition. A few days before the worlds were set to begin, it seemed Brad Jacobs could be counted among that number. "The Brier, to any Canadian curler, is bigger than the worlds," Jacobs told the *Sault Star*. "It's more difficult to win. Winning the Brier is what you aim for as a kid, but the world championships are also extremely important. We're going there to represent Canada. We're going there to win and anything less will be a disappointment."

Accompanying the Jacobs foursome to the worlds were fifth player Matt Dumontelle, a former rival from the junior days, and coach Tom Coulterman, the retired teacher and veteran curler who survived pancreatic cancer in 2006 and was now a big part of the team. Coulterman had been watching Jacobs and the Harndens curl since they were old enough to wear a slider and had seen them grow through the high school and junior ranks into some of the finest curlers in the country.

"When they were in high school you could see that they had so much potential," said the 67-year-old Coulterman in an interview with Mike Verdone of the *Sault*

Star. While he was obviously impressed with Jacobs's shooting ability and Fry's leadership, what struck Coulterman about the team was the way every player knew his role and was willing to adjust to find success. "With E.J. and Ryan moving down and just playing front end, that is one of the strongest front ends in all of curling right now," he said. "Ryan [Harnden] is quiet and physically a very strong individual and very tough mentally, and so is E.J. They're playing their positions with a lot of pride. They know the game very, very well. They would like to be maybe calling shots, but they know when to step back a little bit and let Fry and Brad make the calls in the house."

Coulterman certainly knew curling and was very familiar with the Jacobs team, so he was a great fit to coach the team. A science teacher by trade, Coulterman ran a high school curling league for more than 20 years and spent 13 years as the team leader with the Canadian Junior National Men's Team. His international experience would come in handy as the Jacobs team prepared for the world championship. He knew it wouldn't be as easy as some Canadians might think, but he loved the team's attitude. "I've got to give Ryan Fry a lot of credit," Coulterman said. "He said right from the beginning of the season, 'We're going to win the Brier.' And he kept emphasizing this until we won it." Now Fry was pumping up his teammates about the world championship. With a taste of victory on his tongue, Fry was now craving more.

"Once you win the Brier you realize there's one more event to finish off what becomes a remarkable feat, to win a Brier and a world," Fry said. "If you don't go and win the worlds, it'll leave a little bit of a bad taste in your mouth.

"We've done what we had to do, and we collected all the accolades and we've reflected a bit and looked back. But for us now, it's focusing on what's ahead. If you rest on your laurels, and you're happy with the successes you've had in the past, you don't make room for succeeding in the future."

From the minute they won the Brier, life changed for the Buff Boys. It had been an incredible ride and it seemed all 75,000 inhabitants of their home city recognized their success. Even though so many people in the Soo had been following them for years, the newfound fame that came with the Brier win was difficult for the Jacobs team to take in. More than 500 people turned up for a world championship sendoff reception at the Soo Curlers Association, so many that organizers had to turn people away. They dropped the puck at a Soo Greyhounds junior hockey game and received a standing ovation. Now it was time to put the celebration in the background and focus on the new task at hand.

The world men's curling championship began on March 30, 2013, at the Save-On-Foods Memorial Centre in Victoria. Several of the teams in attendance had already punched tickets to the 2014 Olympics in Sochi and were hungry to prove themselves at the worlds. Among those who were destined for Sochi the next year were Niklas Edin of Sweden, Liu Rui of China, Andrey Drozdov of Russia, David Murdoch of Scotland, Rasmus Stjerne of Denmark, Sven Michel of Switzerland and Thomas Ulsrud of Norway. This would by no means be an easy field.

The Canadians were up at 6 a.m. each day working out. It was the routine they established at the Brier in Edmonton, and they were not about to change a thing. "We don't go in there and lift weights or anything," Jacobs explained. "We go in there, get the blood flowing, ride the bike. We do all the stretching in the gym and get a nice little sweat on, get the blood flowing, get the heart rate up and kind of wake up. We were ready to go, all stretched, and that's a great routine that we have going. The routine is all mental, and when you get into that good routine, and you keep winning games, it becomes like a ritual almost. It puts everyone into the right mindset going into every game."

Whatever they were doing, it seemed to work wonderfully. Canada got off to a great start with five straight wins over China, Finland, Scotland, Switzerland and the United States. Looking down from the stands were their fathers, including Barry Fry and Eric Harnden, both highly competitive curlers in their day. Sun Media's Terry Jones caught up with the Snake, who was beaming with pride after his son won the same event he captured in 1979 to get to the worlds. "I remember real early in the year when Ryan told me 'Dad, this is it . . . this is the team. We have something special here.'"

Their first blemish came on draw 9, when they lost 6-4 to the Czech Republic, and the reality set in that it wasn't going to be as easy as it seemed. After a win over Norway, they lost 10-8 to Japan, a team, like the Czechs, that was not expected to contend for a medal, but the Jacobs team improved to a 7-2 record with an 8-5 win over Russia. It looked like Canada had a good shot at first place and a berth in the Page Playoff first versus second game, but the wheels fell off in the final two games of the round robin. First the Canadians lost 5-3 to Denmark to fall to 7-3, and then they got obliterated 11-7 by Sweden. Fortunately, their 7-4 record was still good enough to get them into the playoffs in fourth place.

The entire round robin had been a wake-up call. The Jacobs boys were realizing just how much of a grind it was to represent Canada at the worlds. Firstly, everyone wants to beat you, whether they are contenders or not, simply because Canada is the measuring stick for success. Secondly, there's a different kind of pressure when you are Team Canada. "When you lose a game representing Canada, it's a lot different than just being a team, losing a game and it's just your own little thing," national team coach Rick Lang said. At this world championship, every team was equipped with four strong players and a vastly improved strategy that came with increased coaching. In past world championships, there would be four or five teams that could contend and the rest were also-rans — the countries still developing their curling programs that had technically weaker players and got lost in the strategy. Those days were gone.

Jacobs and his teammates had no delusions now after entering the world championship thinking it would be easier to win than the Brier. They were in a similar position as they had been in the Brier, however, having squeaked into the playoffs and needing to win out. They seemed to relish playing in those must-win situations . . . and they would prove that to be true once again. They got off to a great start with an 8-6 win over Denmark in the Page Playoff third versus fourth game and then doubled up on Scotland 6-3 in the semifinal. "It goes to show you that getting to that one-two game isn't everything," E.J. Harnden said. "You don't win a championship by winning in the round robin. You do it by winning in the playoffs."

"I think that do-or-die situation really brings out the best in our team," Jacobs added. It certainly seemed that way, but there was one more game to go and it was against a formidable opponent. Niklas Edin of Sweden was the European champion and had won nine games already at the worlds, including an 11-7 win over Canada. Still, somehow it seemed impossible that this Canadian team of destiny, these Buff Boys from blue collar Sault Ste. Marie, could possibly fall short on home soil after coming so far. But in the end, the impossible happened. Sweden took full advantage of having the hammer to start the game, got off to a 4-1 lead through three ends and never looked back. The final score was 8-6 and the stunned Canadians found themselves standing on a podium with the wrong colour of medals around their necks.

When it was all over — the handshakes, the medal presentations, the speeches — the demoralized Canadians remained in disbelief. E.J. Harnden stood outside the team dressing room, leaning against a wall, sobbing. "It's tough," he said. "We played so well these last five weeks, but at the same time we missed an opportunity. I'm sure we'll be back some day . . . I hope we'll be back some day. I think we should be proud of each other."

They had represented Canada proudly in their first taste of international competition and this loss was only going to make them hungrier. Only a few months earlier they were just another bunch of curlers who were good enough to make it to the Brier out of a relatively easy region, and now they were world silver medallists. It was an incredible accomplishment for two brothers, their cousin and a curling vagabond they all called a best friend. "When you try your hardest, you can't feel too bad," Fry said. "We gave it everything we had."

Jeff Stoughton, who lost to Jacobs in the Brier final, saw what happened at the world championship and thought at the time it was the best thing for the Jacobs team. Things never come that easily in curling, and this would be a great learning experience for the four young men from Sault Ste. Marie. "Having the chance to play on the world level in 2013 was huge," Stoughton said. "They needed that opportunity to understand how difficult it is at that level, where every team plays their best against Canada. It was a great learning process for them to be able to play in Victoria."

Jacobs, still just 27 and the second-youngest man ever to skip Canada at a world championship, had his head up and chin forward as he came off the ice. He knew his team had accomplished a great deal — they were Brier champions, which was something they had dreamed of all their lives, and they very nearly were on top of the world as an added bonus. It was a strange time for the skip to be looking at the big picture, especially since Jacobs had a reputation for living in the moment too much, but he was full of perspective just moments after the devastating loss.

"We're young," he said. "We won the Brier young, we came to the worlds pretty young. Hopefully, as long as everybody's health is good, we've got another 20 years of curling left. We'd love to get back to an event like this or make it to an Olympics."

He had absolutely no idea how soon one of those dreams would come true.

CHAPTER SEVEN

ISABELLA'S INFLUENCE
AND HOMETOWN GLORY

Jennifer Jones and Jill Officer had achieved just about everything possible in women's curling — save a trip to the Olympics — but there were still things they wanted off the ice, most notably to start families. Friends and teammates since they were teenagers — Jones was now 36, Officer, 35 — both had always wanted to have children. Officer was the first to do so, becoming pregnant shortly after the Tournament of Hearts in 2011. That meant the Jones team had to start the 2011–12 season with a new player at second while Officer prepared to have a baby in December. They recruited Joelle Sabourin, a former teammate of Dawn Askin's when she played with Jenn Hanna, and picked up where they'd left off on the pebble. Even without its steady second, the team had a solid season on the cash bonspiel circuit and in December, just a week before Officer gave birth to a baby girl, they gave themselves an early Christmas present. The Jones team went to Cranbrook, British Columbia, and won the Canada Cup, which came with a very special prize on top of the $26,000 payday — a berth in the 2013 Olympic Curling Trials in Winnipeg. It was still two full years away, but the Jones team was already starting down what it hoped would be the road to Sochi. "We weren't really looking that far ahead," Jones said. "But now that we're in, it's great. To play at home in Winnipeg at the Trials is going to be amazing." Not only did Jones have a berth in the Trials, but the organizers of the Winnipeg event had a pretty significant name to put on the marquee.

Officer and her husband, Devlin Hinchey, became parents to Camryn on December 12, 2011, but that wasn't the only big news for the team that month. Dawn Askin's boyfriend, Winnipeg curler Mike McEwen, decided to pop the question at Christmas in Ottawa that year as well, and the answer was yes. "She was very surprised," McEwen said. "I caught her off guard. The ring is shinier than the Scotties ring."

After the holidays, the Jones team convened in Portage La Prairie for the Manitoba women's championship, the first time they had been required to play in a provincial since 2008. Just one month after the birth of her daughter, Officer was back in the fold, ready to start the long road back to the top. "I did my best to keep in shape during pregnancy, but I think stamina and being able to sweep will probably be the biggest challenge." Just in case Officer was unable to handle the rigours of the tournament, the team kept Sabourin around. "At this point, we have five people getting ready to play," Officer said.

It wasn't as easy as it had been in the past — they had to come from behind to beat an up-and-comer named Chelsea Carey — but, to no one's surprise, the Jones team claimed yet another Manitoba title. They were off to the national championship for the eighth consecutive year, looking to improve on their seven podium finishes. In seven years, the Jones team had finished no worse than third in the country and had clearly established itself as one of the greatest in Canadian history. However, 2012 was easily one of the most challenging of their lives, particularly for Jones, and there were times when the skip was certain her curling career was over.

Jones filed for divorce from Labonte on February 10, 2012, citing "no possibility of reconciliation." Though Jones did her best to keep her personal life private, her new relationship with Ontario's Brent Laing, a world champion curler as Glenn Howard's second, was a hot topic. It was not public knowledge at the time, and Jones was sensitive about the subject, bristling at any questions from the media related to her personal life and keeping the focus on curling. It was at the Canadian championship that rumours emerged that Jones had been living with Laing in Ontario for more than a year and perhaps should not have been allowed to play for Manitoba. She was peppered with questions about her residency and her relationship with Laing, to a point where she was clearly annoyed and had tears in her eyes. CurlManitoba, the organization that oversees the sport in the province, assured everyone that Jones met the residency requirements, but there were still questions about Laing, which Jones refused to answer.

The Canadian championship was business as usual for the most part — the Jones team was in contention from the get-go and sailed to first place in the round robin with a 9-2 record. If questions about personal relationships and residency were bothering Jennifer, or if Officer's recent pregnancy was affecting her, there were no signs of it on the ice. At least, that is, until the playoffs arrived. There, the Jones team lost 7-5 to old foe Kelly Scott and dropped into the semifinal, where they shockingly fell 6-5 to Alberta's Heather Nedohin. That game came down to a last-rock measurement after Nedohin threw her final brick, and Alberta won, even though they had already shaken hands, thinking they had lost. The Jones team was out of contention after two straight losses and would have to settle for a bronze medal, thanks to an 8-6 win over Quebec's Marie-France Larouche.

As soon as it was over, Jones was once again asked if she had played her last game for Manitoba, as she was now spending much of her professional life in Montreal and Toronto, working as in-house counsel for National Bank Financial and dating a man from Ontario. Perhaps those asking the questions didn't understand just how much curling meant to Jones and how much qualifying for the Olympics was on her mind. She'd put this team together for an Olympic run and had no intention of breaking it up, especially when an Olympic Trials spot was already guaranteed. "In my mind, there's no doubt. I just think they're terrific teammates, terrific human beings and amazing players. The plan is to play to the Trials."

Despite those good intentions, that plan was very nearly derailed by circumstances off the ice. During that off-season, Jones was hurting. Her knee was in bad shape and she knew she was going to need surgery in order to continue with curling. Before she could get to that point, something much more pressing came into her life — she found out she was pregnant with Laing's child. At age 37, Jones was about to become a mother for the first time and was hobbling on a bum knee. At that moment, the notion of going through the grind of Olympic qualifying over the next couple of years seemed almost absurd. The first thing she needed to do was have reconstructive surgery on her anterior cruciate ligament (ACL) and do it without drugs because she was pregnant at the time. "The knee surgery was way more painful than labour, so it really prepared me for giving birth. When I hurt my knee I was thinking I might never play again."

While the pain was bad, the timing was excellent for Jones to have a baby. She was going to be off the ice until early 2013 because of her knee anyway, and she had seen her great friend and teammate Jill Officer have a baby just one season earlier and still recover in time to curl at a high level. "Brent and I couldn't be happier," Jones told Al Cameron of Postmedia in July 2012, acknowledging for the first time that she did, indeed, have a relationship with Laing. Though she was already pregnant, Jones's divorce from Labonte was not final until August 2012. Her relationship with Labonte had long been over, and she was fully prepared for the long-distance partnership she had forged with Laing. "It will be a challenge, of course, but we feel ready for it. We really are thrilled." Jones made it clear that she intended to continue to curl in Manitoba, as long as her knee would allow and, so far, she was recovering nicely. "There's no question in our minds," she told Cameron just a few days after her 38th birthday. "It will be challenging to have parents in two locations, but Winnipeg is my hometown, my team is in Winnipeg, and I want to compete to represent Manitoba in the Scotties."

To that end, Jones was working hard at physiotherapy to get her knee ready for a return to curling. Just a month after the surgery, her doctors were already telling her she was ahead in her progress and she was starting to feel much more optimistic about returning to the ice. As that summer turned to fall, the Jones team was preparing to soldier on without the skip, but it seemed there was no doubt she'd be back. "She's always wanted a family, and we're all really happy for her," Officer said. "But every pregnancy and every labour's different. Jen's a pretty determined girl and, like me, it will be pretty hard for her not to curl. But this is a bigger deal than curling. It's life changing." In the case of Jennifer Jones, no truer words were ever spoken.

The team announced that Lawes, who had attended the 2012 Summer Olympics in London as an athlete representative for the Canadian Olympic Committee, would take over as skip for the first half of that season, while Kirsten Wall, who formerly was the vice-skip for Ontario's Sherry Middaugh, would fill in at third. They got off to a rollicking start, winning their very first bonspiel, a cash tournament in Edmonton, with Lawes handling the skipping duties like a pro. Jones was feeling so much better already after her surgery that she accompanied the team on the cash circuit for much of the fall just so she could keep her head in the game and stay in shape for the second half of the season. "It's going way better than I even hoped for," she said. "I don't find there's any adjustment right now. I don't even feel like I'm pregnant when I'm out there curling."

The big day came far sooner than expected. Jones was planning to have the baby in Winnipeg in mid-December, but she went into labour a month early and gave birth to little Isabella on November 13 in Barrie, Ontario, where she was visiting Laing. Despite being four weeks premature, Isabella Laing was healthy, weighing in at seven pounds, six ounces, and Jones felt like a new person. "Honestly, she's the best thing that's ever happened to me," she said. Over the next 15 months, Jones was a changed person, a woman who'd realized yet another lifelong dream and an athlete who knew there was much more to the world than sports. Her baby was happy and healthy, eating and sleeping well, making life easy on the new mother. As far as her athletic career went, having Isabella early was a blessing in disguise — just two months after the baby was born, Jones was back on the ice and hungry for yet another provincial and Canadian title.

On January 28, 2013, the team took the first step, winning the Manitoba championship in Stonewall, playing one of the best tournaments of their careers despite all the adversity they had faced over the past year. "It's probably the most emotional win I've ever had," Jones said while fighting back tears. "It's not different because I'm a mom. We worked so hard to make sure we played well in this provincial and I thought it was our best provincial from start to finish. Considering all the obstacles we went through this year, I can't say enough about how proud I am of the team."

Everything seemed right with the world. Jones was happy in her personal relationship and had experienced motherhood, Officer too was mother to a young daughter, Askin was due to get married to Mike McEwen and Lawes was proving to be an excellent addition in so many ways. "It's very exciting," Askin said. "It's awesome, with Jen overcoming her surgery and having Isabella a few months ago and it all coming together. I think it far exceeded the expectation of everybody. I'm so proud of her. She really worked hard to get back to where she needs to be."

"I think every obstacle thrown at us is kind of a good thing," Lawes said. "We can only learn from them and get stronger as a team."

For the ninth straight year, the Jennifer Jones team was heading to the Canadian women's championship, and despite team personnel changes, surgeries, pregnancies and future uncertainty, it remained one of the favourites. There was a new kid on the block though — Ontario's Rachel Homan was beating every team in sight that season — and some observers believed the time had come and gone for Jones.

"I don't see them winning the tournament," two-time world champion Marilyn Bodogh said on the eve of the 2013 Scotties in Kingston, Ont. Bodogh was picking Homan to win it all and described her as the skip of the best women's team in the country. It wasn't meant as a slight toward Jones, but it was clear that, at age 38, her window of opportunity was closing. Still, Bodogh wasn't about to discount the chances of a four-time Canadian champion completely. "They're just so good. They'll be in the playoffs. Jennifer has amazing timing. She had a baby, came out, had hardly curled at all and won her province. She played phenomenal. Everyone was saying, 'I don't know if Lawes can make it, she's so young.' But she has really filled that position and given Jennifer a new bloodline. There's good balance."

When the tournament got underway in Kingston, it was business as usual for Jones and Co. both on the ice and in the media mixed zone after the game. Everyone wanted to know what the future held for Jones, given that she was a new mother who lived in Winnipeg, and the father lived in a different province. Many people still found her residency claim suspicious and were certain this would be the last season for her team. "I'm still Manitoban," she told reporters after the opening draw in Kingston. "Winnipeg is my home and I live there. Brent and I have agreed not to talk about [who will move where] until after the [Olympic] Trials. We've managed pretty well. Isabella's a frequent flyer. She flies really well and so far, it's good."

The Jones team looked better than ever during the round robin of the 2013 Scotties. Manitoba went 11-0 and outscored its opponents 95-45. Old foes Kelly Scott and Heather Nedohin, the defending champion, also made the playoffs, as did the Next One, 24-year-old Rachel Homan, who went 10-1 to take second place, her only loss coming against Jones. Jones and Homan would meet twice more in the playoffs, a living legend of curling squaring off against the future of the game in two epic battles. This time, the future prevailed. Homan beat Jones 8-5 in the Page Playoff first versus second game, and after Jones beat Nedohin in the semifinal, Homan laid down the hammer again in the final. The final score was 9-6 and Homan, with such a massive expanse of potential in front of her, was already a Canadian champion. For Jones, she had to face the very real possibility that she had been usurped as the Queen of Canadian Curling.

There was one thing very different about this tournament for Jones, however — when the skip wasn't at the rink she was spending time with her three-month-old baby. Isabella was there every time the Jones team stepped off the ice, including after the final, and that brought about a major change in the mindset of the skip.

"I remember losing the Canadian championship final, and it's a pretty big loss and it's something you want to win, but Isabella came to see me after the game and she just looked at me and snuggled in there and it just made me melt," Jones told CBC. "You just realize there are so many bigger things in life than sport. Maybe I've become more vulnerable because you want her to see that vulnerability."

Jones saw a change in herself and others saw it as well. She had always been stoic in defeat, at least outwardly, but those who knew her best knew she took losing hard — at least up until the moment she became a mother. "Jennifer was so driven that she would beat herself up after losses and you can't obsess about this game," Cathy Gauthier said. "It doesn't make you any better. It can make you too edgy and I think that might have led to struggles in the past. Having a child and coming off the ice to somebody who doesn't really know or care what happened has brought that perspective to her life and it has made her so much better."

That off-season was one of the most enjoyable of their lives, with all the curlers in their happy places. Askin and McEwen were married in July at the Ottawa Golf and Hunt Club, Askin having grown up in the capital region. They quickly returned to Winnipeg and settled down, but very little changed. They were still both dedicated to curling and both had berths in the Olympic Trials in Winnipeg that December. "It's all we know, really," Dawn McEwen said. "That's how we met was through curling. He's on the road a lot with his team and I'm on the road a lot with mine. And it's kind of just the way it is. That's what our lifestyle is. We're big fans of one another." In fact, they were not the only curling couple trying to qualify for the Olympics in Sochi. Jennifer Jones's boyfriend, Brent Laing, was scheduled to play in the Trials as the second for Glenn Howard's Ontario team. Meanwhile, both Wayne and Sherry Middaugh of Ontario were slated to play in the Trials as well, and Heather Nedohin and her husband, Dave, the third for Kevin Martin, were in the field as well.

"To compete at Sochi together with my husband would be phenomenal," Dawn McEwen said as the Trials approached. "We'd be head-over-heels. It would be a once-in-a-lifetime experience, especially to go together." Of course, the possibility existed that Mike McEwen and Laing would play against each other for the right to go to Sochi, which would have pitted Jennifer and Dawn against one another in terms of allegiances. "Not at all," Jones assured. "Dawn and I are such great friends, and Brent and Mike are great friends. We both want the best for each other. If Mike's team won — even if he beat Brent in the final — I'd be right there to give him a hug. I know the same would hold true for Dawn."

As the 2013 Olympic Trials approached, it was evident that this was the big one for Jones and her teammates. Jones, Officer and McEwen had been through this grind before, with very poor results. Lawes was a newcomer to the Trials but had already handled every stressful situation that came her way and was clearly capable of taking on this next challenge. With the Trials in their hometown, the team members were feeling a kind of excitement they had not experienced in Halifax (2005) or Edmonton (2009). There was also a sense that this might be their last hurrah. Jones was 39 and had an infant daughter to look after, as well as a partner who lived in a different province. Officer was 38 with a two-year-old at home. If these Olympic Trials went as badly as the previous two, there was a good chance the team would split up. "We would always say, 'Let's see what happens at the Trials, and then we'll make some decisions.'" Jones said. "So, I guess some decisions will be made soon."

The Canadian Curling Trials are packed with more pressure than any other curling event on the planet. The top teams in Canada, many of them among the top ranked in the world, spend four years putting everything they have into qualifying for the Trials and then have to be almost perfect for a week to have any chance of realizing the Olympic dream. Great teams have wilted, no-names have risen to the top, seemingly minor head colds or sore knees have taken their toll. That said, the Jones team entered the Olympic Trials with an air of confidence and, if they were experiencing that familiar flutter in their stomachs, that extra pressure that came with an all-important, every-four-years tournament, they certainly weren't showing it. "Right now, just knowing that we prepared over the last three years to get to where we are is just a great feeling," Lawes said. "Right now, I don't feel nervous. I just want to go out and play."

For Jones, the most important factor heading into the Trials was her health. Her knee was clean, she had recovered beautifully from her pregnancy, and for the first time in her Olympic Trials career, she wasn't sick. In 2005 it was kidney stones that put her in the hospital, in 2009 a nagging bug that sapped her of her energy. "The biggest thing is we want to make sure we're healthy. And, knock on wood, so far we are. It does take a lot of energy. It's a long week, and the competition is so tight you just want to make sure you have every ounce to put into curling."

Jill Officer was heading into her third Trials and had been extremely frustrated by the first two, unable to explain why the same team that could win world championships and Canadian titles could not show up to the most important of all events. As part of their preparation in recent years, the team consulted with noted sports psychologist Dr. Cal Botterill, father to Olympic women's hockey player Jennifer Botterill and NHL player Jason Botterill. The doctor's influence seemed to be taking hold with the Jones team as they prepared for yet another run at the Olympics. "It's just that sometimes you can over-think the plans around the event and all of the things that are happening off the ice, and you have to remember to focus on your game," Officer said. "I don't know, maybe we lost sight of that at one point. This time, we just really want to stay focused on what we're there to do and that's to curl and perform."

The Olympic Trials began on December 1 at MTS Centre in Winnipeg and featured a mix of former Canadian champions and up-and-comers. Among those in the field were Rachel Homan and Heather Nedohin, who'd both eliminated Jones in the previous two Canadian championships, as well as veteran Sherry Middaugh, Chelsea Carey, Val Sweeting, Stefanie Lawton and Renee Sonnenberg. It was not exactly a who's who of women's curling, with notable names like Kelly Scott and Amber Holland missing from the list, but everyone was capable of winning, even if they didn't come close to Jones in terms of experience. Many of the skips were first-timers and had their entire curling careers ahead of them, but they approached the event with the same kind of desperation as everyone else. "Because you don't know how many chances you've got," 24-year-old Rachel Homan said. "So we're going to take this like it's our only opportunity. It doesn't matter your age or how much experience you have. You just have to seize the moment right now."

Perhaps the most interesting appearance at the Roar of the Rings Olympic Trials came from American comedian Will Ferrell, who brought his Ron Burgundy character to Winnipeg to promote his upcoming movie *Anchorman 2*. No one seemed to pay any attention to the curling that took place during the first day of the Trials, with Ferrell doing his shtick and the curlers and fans soaking it all up. Burgundy took part in TSN's broadcast of the event, cracking some of his classic jokes, and, while it was all designed to boost ticket sales and TV ratings for the Roar of the

Rings, it also seemed to loosen the curlers up. "I think it's fantastic," Jill Officer said, and Jones added, "It's awesome for curling. To have Will Ferrell come to our city, for one, and to put curling in a spotlight like that."

Perhaps the levity brought on by Ferrell's appearance set the tone for the Jones team, which looked relaxed and razor sharp as the tournament got underway. The trials started with a game against fellow Manitoban Chelsea Carey, who had been a bridesmaid for many years with Jones dominating the province. It wasn't even close. Jones pummelled Carey 10-2, scoring an almost unheard-of six points in the sixth end. Jones also won her second game, stealing two in the tenth end to beat Middaugh 9-7, before hitting a bump that threatened to send the team careening off course. In the third game, against Alberta up-and-comer Val Sweeting, Jones gave up a ridiculous seven stolen points on the way to a 9-6 loss. Jones felt like her team let one slip away with some bad misses in the game against Sweeting, but vowed to come back stronger and was true to her word. The next two games were blowout wins, 7-2 over Sonnenberg and 8-3 over Lawton, which gave Jones a 4-1 record and set up an ultra-important match with the number one challenger, Rachel Homan.

Despite being Canadian champion and a co-favourite at the Trials, Homan was struggling, particularly with her draw weight, and at an event like this, there simply was no room for error. Homan actually had Jones right where she wanted her in the round-robin game and headed into an extra end with the hammer and the score knotted at 6-6. Jones knew her counterpart was struggling with draw weight and played the end perfectly, forcing Homan into playing a draw to the four-foot for one point and the win. The draw was heavy and Jones walked away with a stunning 7-6 victory. She didn't even know it as she walked off the ice, but her team had just clinched first place and a berth in the Olympic Trials final. They were one win from Sochi.

Jones and her teammates refused to get caught up in the excitement of reaching the final, knowing there was still one more game to go and they could well face the talented and hungry Homan once again. They could taste it though. For the first time in several years, the team was playing its absolute best at exactly the right time. All four women were at the top of their game and were playing with precision and confidence. They had been dreaming of this since they were little girls and there was a sense that nothing could take it away from them now.

In the last draw of the round robin, Jones beat Nedohin 6-5 and eliminated the former Canadian champion from contention. That left Homan, Middaugh and Carey all tied at 4-3, with only two playoff spots available. Homan was awarded second place because she beat the other two teams in the round robin and Middaugh beat Carey 6-3 in a tiebreaker. The real shocker came later that evening, when Middaugh pulled off a huge upset, hammering the struggling Homan 10-4 in the semifinal and earning a date with Jones in the final. Everyone expected another showdown between Jones and Homan with the Olympic berth on the line, but Middaugh had thrown a major wrench into things. Jones's new concern would be losing to a team she would normally beat. It turned out to be a completely unnecessary concern.

Jones cracked three points in the second end of the final and three more in the seventh, cruising to an 8-4 victory. The skip curled 91 percent, Lawes 90 percent, Officer an ungodly 99 percent and McEwen 88 percent. They were absolutely on fire and no team in the world could have stopped them that day. Finally, after almost 20 years of competitive women's curling, Jennifer Jones was going to the Olympics and taking her three best friends along for the ride.

"This is one of the best, if not *the* best, moments of our curling career," Jones said over the P.A. to the crowd moments after the victory. "You guys are unbelievable. We played one of the best games of our lives in front of this amazing crowd. It's very surreal. When you work so hard for three years and it's one game and to come down to a couple of shots here and there, and today, we made them. And it's hard to believe but my team played outstanding. I'm so proud to be a part of this team. They're amazing people."

Jill Officer had been there almost since the beginning for Jones and always had the skip's back when things looked the bleakest. In the Trials final, when the Jones juggernaut was in full force, Officer was at her absolute best. Her triple kill that got the team out of a sticky situation in the first end was one of the most memorable shots of the tournament, and her curling percentage was the best recorded by any player in any game during the week. "It's probably pretty close to my best game ever," Officer said through tears of joy. "I felt like I couldn't wait to play today, and I just wanted to get out here and throw. I'm not sure it's really, totally sunk in that we're going to the Olympics. We're really happy, we worked really hard to get to this point and we're just so happy."

McEwen, who had been with the team for six years and had experienced so many highs, so many near misses and a few lows, had her eyes fill with tears just from the sight of the Team Canada jackets being presented to the team. "Given the circumstance and what was at stake, we played amazing, and we kept our composure, and it was awesome," McEwen said. "Going to Russia is gonna be amazing and I can't wait to go. It's an opportunity of a lifetime, and I'm so excited."

McEwen's effect on the team could not be ignored. She had developed into one of the best leads in the world and in six years on the team had won six medals at the Scotties (three gold, two silver, one bronze) and an Olympic Trials title. "I don't think Dawn gets enough credit for that team," Cathy Overton-Clapham said in 2014. "I don't think that team would be as successful as they are if they didn't have Dawn. She's a great player and the best lead out there, the most consistent player. She sets that end up every single game, every single end. I think if there's ever a moment where Dawn struggles, that team struggles. She's just a phenomenal player. I think having Dawn throw before Jill out there makes Jill that much better of a player."

Motherhood was a big theme for the Jones team as they celebrated the biggest win of their lives. Little Isabella Laing was sick for much of the week and Jones was not able to be with her as often as she would have liked. Carol Jones, Jennifer's ultra-supportive mother, made sure everything was fine with the baby. "I'm going to see my daughter," Jones said, wiping away tears, as the festivities started to quiet down. "I miss her like crazy. My Mom — I'm gonna cry — she's looked after my baby girl all week, and Isabella was sick all week, and my Mom had to miss some games to take care of her, and I didn't have to worry about her. I knew she was in great hands, and I can't really thank them enough for helping make my dreams come true."

Kaitlyn Lawes, as she always did, looked up in the stands at the end of the game to find her mother, Cheryl, and saw her dancing in the aisles, completely wrapped in a Canadian flag. Of course, her mind drifted to thoughts of her father, but her heart was uplifted by the sight of her mother's moment of pure joy. At least for a few moments, there was no time for sadness. At age 24, Kaitlyn had qualified for the Olympics, a feat that was beyond her wildest dreams, or her father's.

"I don't really want to take this jacket off," a beaming Lawes said. "To have an opportunity to hopefully win that gold medal for Canada, we're doing it for the country. It's going to be such an amazing feeling."

In less than two months, the Jones team would be heading to Russia for the Olympics, fulfilling a dream that had been cultivated since childhood. Their lives were a whirlwind, with family, friends, national Olympic executives, media and even complete strangers all wanting a piece of their time. They all went out for a big family dinner, told a few stories, shed a few tears, hugged, laughed and celebrated until it was time to focus on the next goal. Only two days after winning the Trials, the Olympics were already front and centre in their minds. This team had always taken curling seriously and it wasn't about to lose focus now. "It's a once-in-a-lifetime opportunity, and you don't want to let it pass you by," Jones said.

They were introduced at a Canadian Olympic Committee press conference at the Winnipeg Art Gallery on December 9 and received their official Team Canada jackets, the ones all Olympians would wear in Sochi. "I don't know if I'll take it off," Jones beamed. "I may sleep with it tonight. Not many people can say their dreams have come true, and ours have come true over and over again with the biggest one on the weekend at the Trials."

There was one more dream they all shared but it was one they were always apprehensive to think could come true. Lying there that night, still wearing that red and white jacket with "Canada" emblazoned on the front, Jennifer, Kaitlyn, Jill and Dawn could finally dare to believe.

CHAPTER EIGHT

THE PERFECT STORM

They always seemed to do things the hard way. They came through the Page Playoff third versus fourth game in both the Brier and the world championship, winning one gold and one silver medal. Time and time again, they proved that they played their best when everything seemed to be going against them. This time, they really wanted to make life easier on themselves. Brad Jacobs and his teammates entered the Players Championship at the old Maple Leaf Gardens in Toronto — the last Grand Slam event of the season — knowing they could lock up a spot in the 2013 Olympic Trials by making the final. It wasn't particularly pleasing to Jacobs to know that his team had won the Brier and finished second in the world but still didn't have enough Canadian Team Ranking System points to get one of six direct berths into the Olympic Trials, which were slated for Winnipeg in December 2013. They wanted that direct berth badly, so they could avoid having to play in a pre-trials event in the fall, where only two of 12 teams would advance to the Trials.

They made it to the semifinal at the Players Championship, but that was as far as they could get, stopped in their tracks by four-time world champion Glenn Howard. They had fallen just short in the tournament and in their quest for the automatic trials berth. While Jacobs and his teammates shrugged it off, behind the scenes they were seething about having to go through the pre-trials. "They were pissed about having to play them," CBC's Mike Harris said.

It was still a remarkable season, of course. They won the Brier, finished second in the world, qualified for the playoffs in all four of the Grand Slams. It was success beyond their wildest dreams, and they had some time — a whole summer, in fact — to get over missing out on the Trials berth and start preparing to play those pre-trials. There were still plenty of accolades coming their way as well. They were honoured with a leaf on the Sault Ste. Marie Walk of Fame in May and named to the Sault Ste. Marie Sports Hall of Fame in June. Not bad for a team of men in their twenties or early thirties. Also, on June 11, Jacobs's 28th birthday, they were awarded with the H.P. Broughton Trophy as Sault Ste. Marie's Sportspeople of the Year.

It was on July 4 that the Jacobs team members faced perhaps more adversity than they had in their lives. On July 3, it was announced that a member of the Jacobs team had tested positive for an anabolic steroid at the world championship in Victoria. The player tested positive for Methandienone Metabolites after the gold medal game against Sweden, but it was not announced until July, when the World Anti-Doping Agency (WADA) handed down a two-year ban. The player was Matt Dumontelle, the team's fifth, who had not played a single game at the world championship. Fortunately that meant his positive test would not affect the team's silver medal. But it definitely cast suspicion on the Buff Boys, a team of curlers who had unusually large arms and chests and were known for their dedication to fitness.

"We have been tested in the past and we will be tested in the future and we will continue to post negative results," Jacobs said in a team statement. While vowing to remain friends with Dumontelle, the rest of the team in no way condoned his actions and did their best to distance themselves from the banned curler. Dumontelle acknowledged his misdeed publicly and waived his right to appeal the finding. He said he was taking a workout supplement that he believed was safe. "Clearly, it was not and I regret that decision," he said. "I had no intentions of trying to beat the system. At the end of the day I accept that it was, and is, my responsibility to make sure that I am playing by the rules."

The uproar over the Dumontelle suspension died down over the rest of the summer as the Jacobs team played in charity golf tournaments, acted as parade marshals and generally basked in the glow of their finest season. Jacobs also got married to his longtime girlfriend, Shawna Pozzebon, on July 27. When they hit the pebble again in September, they picked up right where they left off. The very first event of the season was the World Curling Tour's Shorty Jenkins Classic in Brockville, Ontario, and Jacobs won it, beating Jeff Stoughton, yet again, 7-5 in the final. Not only did they take home some cash, but the win lifted them to the number one ranking in the world for the first time. "That's crazy," Jacobs said. "It's mind-boggling."

There was more adversity on the way for Jacobs however. His mother, Cindy, was in a legal bind, having been arrested for fraud in December 2012. An employee of Algoma University, Cindy Jacobs, 54, confessed to stealing almost $400,000 from the post-secondary institution to fuel a gambling addiction. She appeared in front of an Ontario Court of Justice in Sault Ste. Marie on October 1, 2013, and pleaded guilty to the charge. Brad Jacobs was an alumnus of Algoma University, where his mother worked for 34 years as a student accounts officer. Prosecutor Dana Peterson said that between April 2006 and October 2012, Cindy had defrauded the university of money that was provided by various organizations to be used for tuition. Her sentencing date was set for April 2014. So much would change in Brad Jacobs's life before then, but it was always a weight on his mind over the coming months.

In October 2013, with the pre-trials still a month away, the first-ever Men of Curling Calendar came out and two members of the Jacobs team were featured prominently. Jacobs appeared in the calendar, wearing only a towel and standing in the doorway of a sauna, while E.J. Harnden appeared with his shirt off, doing a chin-up. If any men's team in the world was going to be asked to show off their fit and trim bodies, it would be the Jacobs team — but they certainly didn't consider themselves to be models. "I'm very well aware of where I rank as far as being a model goes," Jacobs laughed in an interview with Mike Verdone of the *Sault Star*. "I'm far, far from that." Produced by *The Curling News*, the calendars have been coming out for a few years, normally featuring the women of the sport but always raising money for charity. Most of the pictures are tasteful and highlight the athleticism of the curlers, but some are more risqué than others. Married for only a few months to Shawna, Jacobs was careful about how he appeared in the calendar. "Mine's pretty tame compared to some of them," he said. "If I wasn't married, if I was a single man, I probably would have been a little bit more risqué with my photo. [Shawna] didn't want me going completely nude, obviously. She wanted me doing something in the sauna, as long as I was covered up and it was tasteful. That's what I ultimately went with."

The team welcomed back old friend Caleb Flaxey, who had curled with them since they were preteens, to replace Dumontelle as their fifth player. He was almost like another family member, having been with them for so many years, and he was certainly like a son to E.J. and Ryan's father, Eric Harnden. Fifth players rarely have much of an effect on a team, other than helping with decisions and being ready to step in if someone gets ill or injured, but there was just something right about having Flaxey on board as the team began the pursuit of an Olympic dream.

While all of 2013 was an incredible ride for the Jacobs team, the most spectacular part was still to come, and it all started at the Kitchener Memorial Auditorium on November 5. The Road to the Roar Olympic pre-trials featured 12 teams in a modified triple-knockout format, with only two teams advancing to the Olympic Trials in Winnipeg. Among those in the field were 2006 Olympic gold medallist Brad Gushue, 2010 Olympic gold medallist John Morris and former Brier champion Jean-Michel Menard. After losing their first game of the pre-trials to Greg Baldson of Toronto, Jacobs ran off four straight wins — 7-4 over Rob Rumfeldt of Guelph, Ontario, 8-7 over Mark Kean of Toronto, 9-3 over Gushue and 9-6 over Steve Laycock of Saskatchewan — to capture the B-event of the triple-knockout draw. That put the team into the playoffs, where they played Morris for the first berth in the Trials. Morris won that game 5-4, but Jacobs still had a chance to qualify with another game against Gushue. This time Jacobs won 7-5, and finally, after trying for so many months, they had their hands on a berth in the Olympic Trials. They were going to Winnipeg.

"They were pissed about being there, but the fact that they were able to go through those pre-trials and win was huge," former Olympic silver medallist Mike Harris said. "I half expected them to roll over at the pre-trials and not make it, but all the credit to them for getting it done. What they did was so impressive."

As always, they had done things the hard way. Only when they were down to their last possible hope did they qualify for the Olympic Trials. There was no question they belonged in the field in Winnipeg, and now they were going to be there. It was bad news for the rest of the field because the hottest team in the world was bringing it, and the skip had a chip on his shoulder.

"At the pre-trials, Brad Jacobs was really angry," TSN analyst Cathy Gauthier said. "He was angry that he had to play it. He was mad and he really felt that because he won the Brier, he should have at least been given a shot to get into the Trials. They played the pre-trials mad.

"Then they won and then they get to the Trials, and they're still mad because they had to play a step before that. Those guys are all about emotion, and the biggest difference is they have learned how to convert that into something positive. They're not directing the emotion at each other but at the game or the sport and just have this massive desire. They're a huge crowd favourite because of all that energy they bring."

Jacobs, the Harnden brothers and Fry had all grown up dreaming of playing in the Brier, and the Olympics was never really on their radar, but now that they were heading to Winnipeg, the new reality of the curling world was setting in. The Olympics had become everything and this team had as good a chance as any of getting there. "This feels amazing," Jacobs said. "It feels even better than I thought it would. We had to do this the hard way, but being the Brier champ, it wouldn't have been right if we weren't there." It had been a grinding week of curling, and the team came through in a big way and now had a chance to carry that momentum into the Olympic Trials. "This team never ceases to amaze me," Fry said. "This week is so typical of our team — we'll do whatever it takes to get the job done."

They had secured the very last available spot in the Olympic Trials but headed to Winnipeg as one of the hottest teams in the world. In an eight-team field that included world champions and Olympic medallists like Jeff Stoughton, Glenn Howard, Kevin Martin, John Morris and Kevin Koe, Jacobs was certainly not the favourite but his team was hardly a great unknown. They arrived in Winnipeg brimming with confidence and expressing an all-business attitude. Even Fry, once considered a party boy by many curlers, had little interest in socializing on the eve of the biggest bonspiel of his life. "Our team's not that jovial to begin with," Fry said. "It's high competition and it's definitely going to be intense. I like it that way. I like the fact curling is so social, but in an event like this there's no need to make friends. Everyone's out here to win."

While sporting their usual intensity and a bit of lingering anger over having to play in the pre-trials, the four Sault curlers were trying their best not to look too seriously at the gravity of the event. It would be easy to get eaten up by the magnitude of a once-in-four-years tournament that offered such a tantalizing prize to the winners. While Stoughton, Martin, Howard, Morris and Koe had all been through the rigorous Olympic qualifying process before, this was the first time for the Jacobs team, and they almost viewed it as a stepping-stone more than an opportunity to qualify for Sochi. Realistically they hoped to be big-time contenders in 2018 and thought the Winnipeg tournament would be a valuable learning experience.

The Olympic Trials started on December 1 at Winnipeg's MTS Centre, and Jacobs served notice immediately that his team was going to be a contender. A 7-4 win over Jeff Stoughton, who Jacobs had been dominating since the Brier in March, got the Buff Boys off on the right foot. "That's almost as good as we can play," Jacobs said. "From lead to skip, we played really well." It was truly a sign of things to come. Jacobs needed to make an ultra-precise tap-back to the button with his last rock in the second game and came through for a 7-5 victory against Mike McEwen of Winnipeg. Jacobs had played two games against hometown teams and came away with two wins, which was no small feat in itself. Jacobs and John Morris of British Columbia were the only two skips with unbeaten teams, while some of the favourites, including Stoughton and McEwen, were 0-2. Four-time world champion Glenn Howard was struggling and so was Koe. Even the best teams could falter on such an intense stage, but Jacobs seemed to be thriving.

Jacobs beat Howard in the morning draw on Day 3, scoring an early three points and holding on for a 6-5 win, and pummelled Koe 9-4 in the evening draw. The Olympic Trials were half over already, and Jacobs was plowing through the field, each of his teammates at or near the top of the leaderboard in curling percentage at his position. "I'm feeling awesome about 4-0 right now," Jacobs said. "I think that's a big number right now. What can I say? We're perfect right now on the leader-board. It's a beauty start." Jacobs and his teammates were playing the best they had since forming a year earlier, and that was really saying something. You could sense the momentum in their voices, their swagger as they came off the ice. The youngest team in the tournament was showing all the others who was boss. "There's no taking our foot off the pedal now," Jacobs said. Actually, they put the pedal to the floor.

The next game was against John Morris, who'd won an Olympic gold medal as Kevin Martin's third in 2010 and was throwing third stones for Jim Cotter in the Trials. Jacobs kept the pressure up and cracked a four in the fourth end, putting Morris in a big hole he could never emerge from. The Jacobs team was so good at hitting — E.J. Harnden was one of the best in the world and Fry and Jacobs were no slouches — that it made it almost impossible for a team to come back. The final score was 8-6 and Jacobs had improved to 5-0. Three sheets over at the MTS Centre, Kevin Martin, known as the Old Bear in curling circles, was hammering John Epping of Toronto 9-5 to improve his record to 5-0 as well. It set up the most intriguing matchup of the Trials — Jacobs and Martin would meet on the next draw and the winner would get a berth in the final. Jacobs and his teammates, practically unknown a year earlier anywhere outside Northern Ontario, were two wins away from qualifying for Sochi.

Winning the Brier had been no fluke, nor had the world championship silver medal, the Grand Slam playoff appearances and the cash tour success. These guys were for real and they were ready to show the old guard of the sport that they were the future of men's curling. The Jacobs foursome were the modern rock stars, the physically fit young men in tight shirts who brought so much fire and intensity, fist-pumping and broom shaking, yelling and screaming to the game. They were something curlers and fans had never seen before, and the paying customers were eating it up. "For sure they would not be an easy team to play against," Cathy Gauthier said. "It's one of those things that when you miss a shot, you're hoping to see no emotion from the other team. Most of the time you don't get it, but when they make a great shot and they let everybody know it, it's just different from everyone else and other teams find them really hard to play."

Meanwhile, the classic rock stars were starting to fade. Martin was 47 and only a few months away from retirement, while Stoughton was 50 and Howard was 51. This was likely their last chance to qualify for an Olympics and the youngest team in the field was making it harder and harder. Howard was already out of it and Stoughton was on his last legs. It was up to Martin to bring Jacobs back down to Earth, but he couldn't make it happen. He almost did, but Brad Jacobs was simply too good when his team needed him most.

The game came down to the tenth end. Martin led 4-3 but Jacobs had the hammer and something special in his skill set. Facing two Martin counters with his last rock, Jacobs used control weight to attempt a runback double takeout that would give him two points and the win. When all the rocks came to rest, there were two Jacobs rocks counting. They could scarcely believe it themselves, but they were off to the final and were just one win away from qualifying for the Olympics. "I definitely think that is the best shot we've been associated with to win a curling game," a breathless Jacobs said. "We're so pumped to have won that game. The adrenalin is still coming out of us. We're ecstatic that we have a chance to go to the Olympics. It sounds pretty cool."

"It's insane," Fry added. "It's a hell of a shot. I'm pretty speechless."

It was the signature moment of the Olympic Trials but not just because of the precision and significance of the shot. It almost seemed to trumpet in a new era of curling, where this brash, emotionally wild skip was taking over from the old guard. The celebration after Jacobs made his spectacular shot was equally memorable, with the skip, as Paul Friesen wrote in the *Winnipeg Sun*, "Looking like a linebacker, who'd just taken the head off the quarterback, exhorting the crowd with both arms and a Roar of the Rings, full-throated yell." No doubt there were curlers and fans in attendance and many more watching on TV who thought the celebration was a bit over the top for the staid old sport of curling. Jacobs had heard it all many times before and was making no apologies. "That's unsportsmanlike, or that's going to come back at you," Jacobs said of a refrain he sometimes heard about his behaviour on the ice. "Whatever. When you think about every other sport that's played at the highest level — tennis, golf, hockey, football — I mean, football players are celebrating after every play. It's only natural.

"And unless you compete at this level in something, I guess it's hard for the general public to know what it feels like. Especially when you have 14,000, 15,000 people out there and they all go nuts at the same time you do. Almost all of the curlers said that was amazing, that the celebration was awesome. If anything, people are saying we need more of that."

The Buff Boys knew they weren't going to please everyone. They play a very traditional sport, and there would always be detractors, but they were in the process of revolutionizing the game. From their physiques to their emotional outbursts to their ability to intimidate opponents, they were a very unique crew and seemed to have the formula for success. "We're trying to play to our strengths," E.J. Harnden said. "When we play our best, it's showing some emotion. Curling needs more energy, it needs more excitement, it needs more of a personality. Our team's bringing that."

Another one of the younger skips in the tournament, Winnipeg's Mike McEwen, 33, was all in favour of the on-ice histrionics, especially if it helped draw a younger audience to curling. "It's fun to watch those guys play," he said. "They're a great image for our sport and what a curling athlete can be. I love it. I wouldn't change their formula."

While the shot was something incredible to behold and held so much significance, credit was always due to the rest of the team as well, and on this day, lead Ryan Harnden deserved special kudos. He'd injured his knee the previous night while swimming at the Fairmont Hotel pool. When he arrived at the rink he could barely even bend down to get in the hack. The knee was swollen and stiff, and he could hardly move it. There was no way he was going to admit it to his teammates though, and he toughed it out, playing one of his best games of the tournament. "I won't be off the sheet unless I'm in the hospital," he said.

The round robin wasn't even over yet, and the Jacobs team was already looking ahead to the final, but there was one more piece of business to take care of. With a win over John Epping in the last draw, Jacobs could become the only skip to ever lead his team to a perfect round robin record at the Olympic Trials — men or women. Jacobs won that game 7-4 and pulled off the perfect round robin, but this time there was no celebrating. The win meant very little to Jacobs, who had his eyes squarely focused on the championship game, the game that could send his team to Sochi, the game that would come two days later.

It was a long, agonizing wait between games for Jacobs and his teammates. They had to sit back and wait for an opponent in the final, had to watch as Jennifer Jones booked a ticket to Sochi, had to try to corral all of their nervous energy and put it to good use. Sure, they were in the final, but the Old Bear was still looming and would be eager to take another swipe at the young guns. The Old Bear, however, never got the chance. In a complete shocker, John Morris upset his former skip Kevin Martin 7-5 in the semifinal. Martin had finished the round robin 6-1, with his only loss coming against Jacobs, while Morris was just 4-3 and barely squeaked into the play-offs. But it was Morris, not Martin, who would provide the opposition for Jacobs in the final — a strange twist of fate since both teams had to play in the pre-trials in Kitchener just to get into the big event. Now one of them would be going to Sochi.

There probably was never a question as to which team it would be. Certainly when the two teams were piped onto the ice and started throwing rocks, there was no doubt. The Jacobs team curled 92 percent as a group and outplayed the Morris team at every position. Jacobs, who was nearing superstar status in the sport, curled 93 percent in the final and made a brilliant double in the ninth end that helped his team score two points and clinch a 7-4 win. The entire curling world was in awe, including the four men who had just booked tickets to the Russian Riviera. If anyone thought the Jacobs foursome winning the Brier was a fluke, those thoughts were now put to rest. This was not just a mere hot streak, but a run of success of epic proportion. "When everything goes good, they annihilate people, and that's the way it went in Winnipeg . . . there was no bump in the road there," longtime friend and mentor Ian Fisher said. These may not have been the best four players in Canada, but they were certainly the best team, with the best dynamics and four curlers who clearly believed in one another.

"They came out of nowhere," curling analyst Mike Harris said. "Going into the Brier a year and a half ago, nobody was even talking about these guys. They've had an amazing 12 months. It was well deserved. Nobody worked harder than those guys the last two years. They could have rolled over and gone away after the Brier, but they came back and had a plan and just killed it. The whole year, they were awesome."

As the victory celebrations commenced and the curlers were presented with their red and white team jackets and medals, Jacobs was given a chance to speak to the crowd and knew exactly what he wanted to say. "This is a special group of guys. Love you all."

To have done this at all was something incredibly special, but to have done it with two of his cousins, brothers who cared so much for each other, and a curling nomad who fit in perfectly with the group, was truly remarkable. "I wouldn't say that we were any better, talent-wise, than some of the top teams," E.J. Harnden said. "What we have is chemistry. We're best friends off the ice, not just teammates. I see these guys every day, by choice, not just because I have to curl with them."

They hugged their wives and girlfriends, families and friends, posed for pictures, shed a few tears as they donned their Team Canada jackets for the first time and tried to come to grips with the fact that they were going to the Olympics. It wasn't easy. "This is incredible," Jacobs said. "I never thought this would happen for a second. To go through this field undefeated is just mind-boggling to all of us. I'm just really happy this is over with to be honest with you. It's a relief. It was a long wait between games, and it was really hard on us. Our guts were just turning."

"It's crazy . . . it's boggling my mind," E.J. Harnden said. "I can't believe it. We won the Brier, and we were a little short at the worlds, and now we're going to the Olympics!"

As angry as they were about having to play in the pre-trials in Kitchener, the extra games clearly worked in their favour. The Jacobs team came in on fire and there was no team in the Trials field that could put it out. "It was a little bit disappointing when we didn't make it directly into the Trials, but we quickly accepted it, and we were able to win it the hard way," Jacobs said proudly. "I think coming through the pre-trials really gave us momentum going into the Trials. It was almost a blessing in disguise."

For one member of the team, this victory held a little bit of extra significance. Fry had grown up in Winnipeg and had a last name that was synonymous with curling. He had persevered through troubled times, been thrown off teams, quit other teams and had made great sacrifices to find the right mix. He would never be described as the most popular curler in Winnipeg, but he was now among the most successful. His dad, Barry, the 1979 Brier champion, was sitting in the crowd along with Ryan's mom, Judy, and that simply added to the excitement for the Small Fry.

"Being that my dad won the Brier, it was always for me to get that Brier so he could stop holding it over my head," Ryan said with a smile. "Now that I got that last year and now got a step above him, now he can't do anything!

"If I could write a perfect script to win the Olympic Trials, it would be to win it in the MTS Centre in my hometown. It's an unbelievable feeling. I was willing to move to find the right guys. I thought in my career I would find those three right guys to play with. It took a few years to find them, but they're three of my best buddies. You're playing with three family members, so when I fit in, it almost becomes family right away. I feel like I'm part of their family. Being an only child and you get three brothers out of it . . . that's pretty cool."

The hardest thing now for the Jacobs team would be waiting two months to play their first game at the Olympics. There would be plenty to do in between, but the four curlers wished they could start the Olympics the very next day. When you are as hot as they were, you never want to cool off. They were introduced as Team Canada the very next day at the Winnipeg Art Gallery and returned home to another hero's welcome in Sault Ste. Marie. Mayor Debbie Amaroso was waiting for them at the airport with a throng of fans, and a police escort took them through a parade route to the Soo Curlers Association Club for a celebration. For curlers from a small city, it felt like they had won the Stanley Cup.

"Everyone was decked out in Canada colours," E.J. Harnden said. "There were hundreds of people, even almost thousands of people, between the airport, on the way from the airport and at the curling rink, just to welcome us. We rode in a limo and it was awesome, amazing."

"It's not easy getting out of Canada," Ryan Harnden said. "It's probably the toughest country in the world to be able to represent at the Olympics. We played all the best teams in the world there, the top 8 teams on the world rankings, and we came through on top. That feels pretty amazing."

They wanted to play right away, but there were other things to look after first. They had to spend time with their over-the-moon families — they all came from rich curling backgrounds — get through the Christmas season and, most of all, stay fit, trim and sharp. Jacobs and his new bride, Shawna, took a honeymoon trip to Grenada in the Caribbean at Christmas. Like everyone else they kept a nervous eye on the goings on in Russia, where terrorists were threatening to mar the Olympics. Suicide attacks in Volgograd did nothing to allay everyone's fears, but the curlers were assured by the Canadian and International Olympic Committees that everything would be fine. They certainly didn't want anything to ruin their experience, so they had no real choice but to believe.

They took part in a Skins Game, complete with a draft of curlers, in Banff and then the craziest of all curling bonspiels — the Continental Cup — in Las Vegas of all places. They played golf, took in a show at Caesar's Palace and enjoyed the Vegas lifestyle, and they curled in a Ryder Cup–style tournament, including North American and International teams, before surprisingly large crowds. It was a massive moment for curling and the perfect tune-up for Jacobs and his teammates, who got to try out all of their shots in the Continental Cup just a few weeks before the start of the Olympics in Sochi. They also played against a handful of the curlers they were due to face in Sochi, like Great Britain's David Murdoch and Sweden's Niklas Edin, who'd beaten them in the world championship final a year earlier. Now, almost a year later, with some time to reflect on it, Jacobs saw that loss to Edin as a major turning point for his team.

"That world championship was important in so many different ways," he said.

"Obviously to get the experience of playing against other countries — because it is a bit of a different game than we're used to in Canada — was huge and helped prepare us for something like the Olympics. Losing the final has only made us more hungry for the Olympics."

The Continental Cup ended on January 20 and the curlers were due to leave for Switzerland and an Olympic training camp on January 30. They still had their regular jobs to tend to, as well as daily practice and, of course, rarely would a day go by when the Buff Boys were not seen working on their bodies. Their physical fitness played a huge role in getting them this far. Now, they wanted it to carry them to new heights.

"We're definitely in Olympic mode now," Jacobs said, excitement in his voice. "It's all about staying healthy and staying loose, getting a little bit of rest and relaxation and getting some good competition at the same time.

"And we'll be in the gym every day."

How could it be any other way?

CHAPTER NINE

THE GOLDEN ROAD

The skip that arrived in the picturesque Black Sea city of Sochi was very different from the one anyone in the curling world had encountered before. Over the years the TV cameras and fans had become accustomed to a businesslike Jennifer Jones, one who spoke every word carefully, had a reputation for being ruthless and at times looked like she would be hard-pressed to have any fun — in other words, a lawyer. Whoever this person was who landed in Sochi, decked out in Team Canada colours, sporting a broad smile, giggling like a schoolgirl and looking like she was having the time of her life, it certainly wasn't the old Jennifer Jones.

She had tears in her eyes every time she even spoke about being an Olympian, about having a chance to play on the world's biggest stage and about the possibility of standing on the podium. Just looking at her Team Canada jacket, which she vowed she had not taken off since the Olympic Trials, was enough to bring on the emotion. There was immense pride in not only getting a chance to curl in the Olympics but also being part of the larger Canadian team, living in the Athletes' Village and proudly displaying the Maple Leaf everywhere she went. From Day 1, there was a sense that Jones and her teammates were not feeling an abundance of pressure, that they were legitimately happy just to be there and that they were going to enjoy the experience no matter what. That attitude would not change a bit over the next two weeks and played a huge role in their success.

"Absolutely, this is one of the high points of my life," Jones said. "It's different from a world championship for sure. You're part of this bigger Team Canada, and just to see all the other athletes was incredible. And then we got our HBC clothes and honestly, I get goosebumps even just talking about it. We got them and it was Christmas. It was one of the best moments of my life. To put these clothes on and be part of the Olympic Games is unbelievable.

"Our biggest thing coming to the Olympics is to enjoy it. We've waited a lifetime for this moment, and we wanted to soak up every moment we possibly could."

Although the Sochi Olympics received a lot of bad press prior to the Opening Ceremonies — with threats of terrorism, criticisms of overindulgent spending by President Vladimir Putin's government, housing problems for the media and a purported but unproven mass cull of the region's stray dogs — the Olympic villages in the towns of Adler and Krasnaya Polyana were spectacular. The curlers were awestruck by the beauty of the coastal region, with its six tightly clustered venues — including the Ice Cube Curling Center — nestled by the serene Black Sea beaches and its views of the jagged peaks of the Caucasus Mountains. Tightly organized and efficiently run, the Sochi Games overcame some early scathing reviews to become a star of the Olympic movement.

From the minute she arrived in Russia, Jones was also a star. The oldest member of Team Canada at age 39 but still a first-time Olympian, Jones was selected by the Canadian Olympic Committee to be the only athlete involved in its opening press conference. Sitting on a dais in the Main Press Center with COC president Marcel Aubut, chef de mission Steve Podborski and assistant chefs Jean-Luc Brassard and France St. Louis, Jones was presented as the kind of athlete Canada could really get behind, one who'd worked for the better part of two decades to arrive at that point and was now basking in the glow of the Olympic spotlight. She was there for another reason as well: Aubut and Podborski had been talking for months about Canada finishing on top of the table in Sochi, with as many as 35 medals, and Jones was one of the athletes they were counting on to mine gold.

"It's pretty crazy," Jones said. "To have a curler at the opening press conference for the Olympics is amazing. To be asked is a pretty big honour, and I was thrilled to do it and thrilled to be a part of it. It was a big moment for the Canadian team, and to have curling showcased and represented like that is amazing for our sport. We just want the sport to grow, and we're still a pretty young sport for the Olympic Games but it just keeps getting more and more popular, and that's amazing to be a part of."

If the COC's bravado brought added pressure to Jones, who at that point had not even seen the Ice Cube Curling Center where she would soon go to work, she didn't show it in the slightest. She continued to suggest she'd be happy with a podium finish of any kind because she was lucky enough to be an Olympian, had no idea if she'd ever get such an opportunity again and was determined to enjoy the experience.

"Being a part of the village and looking into all of the Canadian athletes' eyes you can see that we're all here to try to win gold and try to win for each other," she said. "You just feel like it's your family instantaneously. It's different than being alone at a world championship where you're the sole team there representing Canada. Being in the village with all the other Canadian athletes, you feel like you're at home. You feel like you're just in your own little community that's part of Canada, and it really is incredible."

"It just feels like we're at home but a million times better," Kaitlyn Lawes chimed in.

The Athletes' Village was, like everything else in Sochi, ultra convenient. Built a curling stone's throw from the Black Sea, many of the rooms had a bird's-eye view of the Olympic Village and the sporting venues in the coastal cluster. When Jones and her teammates arrived in their rooms, they looked out and could see the Ice Cube Curling Center, just a short walk away. Jones loved the fact that she could wake up every morning and look out on the curling rink. What better place to stay for a woman who had devoted the last 30 years of her life to curling?

This entire adventure had been so long in the making for Jones, longer than for any other Canadian athlete. In fact, Canada's first medal-winner of the Games, slopestyle snowboarder Mark McMorris, was just 20 and had not even been born when Jones first started working toward this Olympic dream. Jones felt like she and her teammates had a big advantage over someone like McMorris, who competed on the very first day of the Olympics and was on his way home soon after.

"We get to experience the Olympics for longer," she said. "It's the best moment of our lives and we don't want it to end. Our Games go on for a really long time and we're really happy to be playing almost the whole time and to really soak everything up."

Though rookies at the Olympics, the Jones team felt well prepared for what lay ahead. The team had been a part of the COC's Own the Podium program for eight years and had learned a great deal from that experience. Jones also had the luxury of having been at Vancouver 2010 as a member of the media, which gave her an opportunity to learn what the Olympics were all about. There would be a tendency to place too much importance on the event because of the magnitude of the Olympics, but deep down Jones knew this was just another bonspiel, and she had won many of those before.

As Jones was preparing to leave to check out the curling venue for the first time, an astute reporter, Gary Lawless of the Winnipeg Free Press, noticed she was wearing an interesting and perhaps fitting shade of eye shadow. "Is that gold?" he asked.

"No, actually," she replied. "The girls were still sleeping so I got ready kind of in the dark. So no, it's not on purpose." Still, gold eye shadow kept reappearing throughout the Olympics.

A major difference between the Jennifer Jones of years past and the one who was ready to take on the world in Sochi was her openness with the media. For many years the media would seek out another member of her team in order to get an answer that was more real and heartfelt, knowing how guarded Jones could be. In Sochi, she was an open book from the very beginning and talked freely about her emotions, her love for her daughter Isabella, and her appreciation for her family, boyfriend Brent Laing and teammates. As the beginning of the Games approached, with the excitement of the Opening Ceremony surrounding the Canadian curlers, there was a feeling that Jones just might provide one of the best stories of the Olympics.

On Friday, February 7, the lifelong dream finally came true when the Jones team marched into the Fisht Olympic Stadium for the lavish Opening Ceremony. It was what they had all been waiting for, that goosebump-producing moment when you follow the Canadian flag into the most coveted position in the world among athletes, waving and grinning, decked out in Canadian colours, pride oozing from your very pores. No matter what happened over the next 16 days, all 220 of the Canadian athletes were gold medal winners at that moment, and nobody could ever take that amazing feeling away from them.

If there was anything weighing on Jones's mind in the days between the Opening Ceremony and the beginning of the curling tournament, she wasn't showing it. However, she did repeatedly take time to caution Canadians that this was not going to be easy. Canadian curlers had won eight medals in eight Olympic events prior to 2014 and everyone back home expected nothing less than a podium finish in Sochi. Jones warned that it was no slam dunk, not with a field full of former world champions and Olympic medallists. Her team had played in four world championships between 2005 and 2010 and only won one of them, so she knew first-hand how hard this was going to be.

"It is the most amazing field and I believe it's the best ever assembled for an Olympic Games," Jones said. "You have so many world champions, European champions and it's going to be tough from start to finish. Honestly, every single team out there could be standing on the podium and they've all been working as hard as we have, so we're going have to be at our very best to be on the podium at the end."

Among those in that "amazing field" were defending world champion Eve Muirhead of Great Britain, 2012 world champion Mirjam Ott of Switzerland, 2009 champion Bingyu Wang of China and 2003 champion Debbie McCormick of the United States (third for Erika Brown). Sweden's Margaretha Sigfridsson had won back-to-back silver medals at the worlds, while Ott was a two-time Olympic silver medallist and Wang won a bronze in 2010.

Despite all that, there was a sense among the Canadian players that this was their time. "This opportunity only comes around every four years, and it's hard to win in Canada," Jill Officer said on the eve of the tournament. "There's only one team every four years that gets to go, and you think about the depth that we have in Canada. To have this opportunity is a once-in-a-lifetime experience. We're all really excited, and we're going take it all in."

They were a loose, happy bunch. They were having fun and it was evident to anyone paying attention. Photo bombs and video bombs were their thing. The photo bomb is a modern custom of jumping into a picture as it is being taken and making a goofy face. Lawes had mastered the art. Video bombs are the same thing, except of course it's done when a teammate is being interviewed on camera. The practice continued throughout the Olympics, a sign of just how much these women were enjoying the entire experience.

It was about to get even better.

The curling tournament started on Monday, February 10, and Canada had a seemingly tough test right off the bat. Bingyu Wang of China, called Betty by many, was the only non–North American or European skip to win a world championship. Her team spent much of its time training in Canada and was a regular on the World Curling Tour cash circuit. Just 29 heading into the Olympics, Wang had already represented her country at nine world championships. There was no way Jones was going to take the Chinese team lightly and that was bad news for Wang and her teammates. Jones was a wrecking ball in the tournament opener, curling 96 percent, scoring at will and cruising to a 9-2 victory in just seven ends.

Jones was immensely proud of the start, considering it was her team's first Olympics and they played seven almost-flawless ends against a great opponent. The highlight of the day for the skip was not the beatdown of China, but rather simply the act of walking into the Ice Cube Curling Center, behind the bagpipes, knowing she was about to play a game in the Olympics.

"Amazing . . . it makes me emotional just thinking about it," Jones said. "Coming over here we were super, super excited, and we just wanted to get on the ice and it lived up to our expectations and then some. To be piped out and you see the Olympic rings and you get to slide over the rings, it's unbelievable.

"But from the moment practice started and we shook hands and the game was going, it felt like just another big event for us, which is exactly what we wanted to feel."

It was not just another big event, however, because this one had a different atmosphere than all others. This one had the loudest, most unusual group of curling fans in the history of the game. Their attention was focused almost entirely on the Russian team, skipped by Anna Sidorova, and they cheered after every single shot taken by the home side. It made life difficult for the curlers on the other three sheets, but the Canadians didn't allow it to become a distraction.

"It was nuts when I was in hack," Lawes explained. "They were screaming like crazy, and as soon as I made a shot, it was crickets. It's not what we're used to but it's giving us a little chuckle."

As always, the Jones team was prepared. They watched some of the men's draw that morning and had a good sense of what the atmosphere in the building would be like. They used hand signals to combat the noise and seemed to deal with it as well as any team on the ice, certainly more effectively than the Canadian men's team, which was clearly distracted by the overly exuberant crowd.

"It was so fun," Jones said. "You can't ask for anything better. When you come to the Olympics, you want people to be watching the sport you are playing and the crowd was loud and exciting and energetic. It was just different from what we're used to, but it was amazing to be a part of. It's just that you can't really hear very well, but we'll come up with some solutions to that. I thought we did a good job of managing it."

The big win and the wild atmosphere made the opening draw of the Olympics special for the Canadians, as did the sight of their families, decked out in red and white, sitting in the stands. Jennifer's parents, Larry and Carol Jones, were up there with her boyfriend, Brent Laing. Dawn McEwen's husband, Mike, was there too, along with her parents, Jane and Wayne Askin, and Jill Officer's mom and dad, John and Leslie. Kaitlyn Lawes's mom, Cheryl, was there too.

"They're all so excited," Jennifer Jones said. "They've waited for a lifetime for this too, and to have them all cheering us on is so fantastic. It means a lot to us to have them here.

"To have Brent and Mike here, with our parents — they've sacrificed as much as we have so we can play in this event. With Brent, I can talk to him and get his opinion on things after the game and he's definitely helped me be the player that I am today."

As emotional as the players were about competing in their first Olympic game, the pride and joy in the stands was just as prevalent.

"I'm so impressed with her," Carol Jones said. "She's poised and has grace. I can't put into words how proud we are of her."

"This is quite thrilling really," Larry Jones added. "This is a long time coming for her and a dream she's always had and I'm quite pleased for her."

For two of the observers from the family group, the moment was even a bit more surreal. Laing and Mike McEwen are both highly accomplished curlers and both took part in the Olympic Trials in Winnipeg. McEwen skipped his own team in his hometown, while Laing played second for four-time world champion Glenn Howard of Coldwater, Ontario. Both players shared the Olympic dream with their spouses, both came up short, but here they were sporting Canadian colours in Sochi just the same.

"It's a surreal experience just even being a spectator for the Olympics, let alone watching your spouse playing," Mike McEwen said as he watched the opening game. "That just adds another dimension. It's a little tough watching and not playing. The environment in here is very entertaining, and it kind of distracts you from agonizing over what's going on, on the ice."

For Laing, having the opportunity to experience the Olympics, even if not from the side of the boards he wanted to be on, was a good consolation prize for falling short at the Trials. Still, he wasn't exactly enjoying himself when the opening game was on.

"I hate it," he said. "It's really hard to watch because you have no control, and you just want the best for her out there, and you want her to make every shot and win every game, and that just doesn't happen. It's much harder to watch than it is to play. When you're playing, you're in the heat of the moment, and you're in control. I guess it's probably a man thing. The lack of control really sucks."

Back home in Ontario, a little girl too young to understand what was going on was staying with Laing's mother while her mom and dad took part in the Olympics. Little Isabella, now 14 months old, would occasionally run to the TV screen when she saw her mommy and do a little dance. She was never far from her mom's mind though, bringing the usual combination of inspiration and perspective to the first-time Olympian.

"I'm trying to keep notes every day of things that I want to tell her, just special moments, so that when she's old enough to understand, I can tell her that she was a huge part of this for me," Jones said. "I wear a necklace that says her name on it so she's here with me all the time."

The Jones team spent the rest of Day 1 with their families at Canada Olympic House, where they could all eat, drink and socialize with other Canadian athletes and stay out of the glare of the TV cameras and photographers. For the families, it was a chance to feel like part of the Canadian team, which was especially gratifying for Mike and Brent. What all the Canadian contingent saw on Day 2 would be even more uplifting.

Canada's second game of the tournament was against another gold medal contender — Sweden. In fact, Sweden's Anette Norberg, who retired at age 46 in 2013, won the gold medals in both Turin in 2006 and Vancouver in 2010, her team the only one in Olympic curling history to repeat as champion. This team, however, was skipped by Margaretha Sigfridsson, who threw lead stones while Maria Prytz threw fourth. The team was runner-up at the previous two world championships and brought the typical Swedish consistency to the pebble. Despite all that, the Swedes were badly over-matched against Canada on Day 2 of the Olympics.

Jones curled a statistically perfect game, her teammates were brilliant as well and Canada cruised to a 9-3 victory in only eight ends. Canada had now played two games and a total of only 15 ends while outscoring the opponents, both medal contenders, 18-5. Anyone who knows Jones is aware she'd never separate a shoulder patting herself on the back, but her teammates were in awe of her 100 percent performance.

"Yeah, Jen's pretty good," Lawes marvelled. "She just had that fire in her eyes. She was going after it all. It's a great start against two really strong teams."

Jones never looks at the stats. She knows when she and her teammates have curled a great game or a bad one. Still, the smile on her face gave her away.

"I couldn't ask for better teammates, and we're just having the time of our lives out there. We're having so much fun. We're playing consistent and we're getting more comfortable. It's exactly where we want to be after Day 2, and we just have to keep it going." They would do just that, though Day 3 would be anything but easy.

Eve Muirhead of Great Britain was just 23 years old but was already a highly accomplished and decorated curler. She won an unprecedented four world junior curling championship gold medals between 2007 and 2011. At the age of 19, while she was still a junior-age player, she was selected to skip Great Britain at the 2010 Olympics in Vancouver. Though her team didn't make the playoffs that year, she bounced back to win a silver medal at the world championship that season in Swift Current, Saskatchewan, and won her first world women's title in Riga, Latvia, in 2013. Muirhead was unquestionably a force to be reckoned with, and Jones knew it.

Muirhead's reputation in the world of curling is for being uber-aggressive, putting all kinds of pressure on the opposing team to make big shots. She's also a bit of a risk taker, and both those factors played into the game with Canada. In the fifth end with the score tied 3-3, Jones made one of her best shots of the entire tournament. With Great Britain lying one in the four-foot, and Canada holding second and third stones, Jones attempted an all-or-nothing angle-raise of her own stone that was outside the rings. The thinking was if it missed, the worst that would happen would be Great Britain getting a steal of one. If Jones could hit it and make her raised stone stick in the four-foot, she'd score three and take full control. That's exactly what happened, and it was just another indication of how hot of a hand Jones had at that moment. Canada led 6-3, but it was nowhere near enough to put away the tenacious Muirhead.

After an entertaining but somewhat sloppy second half of the game in which both skips had to make some big shots, Jones led 8-6 heading into the final end, but everything set up beautifully for the Scottish skip in the tenth. Lawes whiffed on a takeout attempt with her second shot in the end, putting Canada into a world of trouble with Great Britain lying two and holding the hammer. "It was not looking pretty," Officer said.

Jones made another huge shot with her first one in the end, a double takeout that took away some of Muirhead's momentum. Still, Muirhead had a golden opportunity to throw a draw with her last stone to tie the game at 8-8 and send it to an extra. Muirhead had one big problem though. The 75-minute shot clock that ticks away during a curling game was down to 30 seconds, and she needed to get into the hack and release her rock quickly. If the clock were to run out, she would automatically lose. She made a snap decision not to go for the draw that would tie the game, but to try a much more difficult triple takeout that would have allowed her to score three and win the game outright. The shot went awry and Canada stole one point for a 9-6 victory. As she left the ice, Jones drew her hand across her brow and gave a silent "Phew" to the camera. She knew she had narrowly avoided a potentially tournament-changing loss.

Though Jones would not have tried the shot herself, she expected nothing less from Muirhead, who clearly thought she had a better chance of winning the game that way than going into an extra end against Jones without the hammer. "There was no time, so I really didn't have a chance to look at the angle," said Jones. "It looked tough to me but she's such a great player. If she sees it, obviously it was there, and she makes them a lot of the time."

For her part, Muirhead said she'd go for the big shot and the win every time in the same position. "It was a gamble, but I wouldn't have gone for it if I didn't think it was there. These shots are always going to be a gamble. That's the skip — they get the glory if they make them and all the slack if they miss them, and that was one of those shots. We're an aggressive team and we like to call an aggressive game. I'm not one of those glory hunters that would just go for it. I thought it was there, I just didn't quite get out to it enough."

For the first time, Canada had encountered some pressure and adversity at the Olympics. Also for the first time, the Jones team had been pushed to the full 10 ends. "We certainly weren't quite as sharp, and we got away with one," Officer said. Still, the perfect run continued thanks to some good fortune and some fantastic shot-making. This would not be the only bump in the road for Canada, and Jones knew those types of games were much better indicators of what the playoffs would be like than her team's first two blowout wins.

"It was a nail-biter, but that's what you want," a relieved Jones said. "We've had a couple of games end early, so to come out and really grind one out when we weren't really our sharpest says a lot about our team and gives us a great feeling going forward."

The following day produced two more wins by identical 8-5 scores, over Denmark and Switzerland. The win over Switzerland's Mirjam Ott meant Jones had beaten four former world champions in her first five games while going undefeated. It was a sign of big things to come for this team. Sitting at 5-0 and having the time of their lives, the Canadians now had the added luxury of a day off. And it just happened to be Valentine's Day.

"It was the best Valentine's Day ever," Jones said, letting her emotions show once again.

"I went and hung out with Brent for a bit and then we had Curling Day at Canada House, we had practice, we went to CBC, got to sit on the couch and fulfill that dream, which was pretty cool. You know, the Olympian kind of moment. All around it was a fabulous day."

The Olympic curling tournament was much more forgiving than anything the Canadians were used to. At most Canadian and international events, the teams play two games per day, every day, with very little downtime in between. At the Olympics, Canada had several days with only one game and one day off. The schedule allowed for members of the Jones team to spend a lot less time than usual obsessing about curling and just enjoy the Olympic experience. It also gave them a chance to rub shoulders with some of Canada's most famous athletes, either at Canada House or back in the Athletes' Village. One day, Officer and Lawes got into a mixed doubles ping pong game with Canadian hockey stars Patrice Bergeron and Shea Weber. When it came time for a second game, Bergeron stepped aside and was replaced by none other than Sidney Crosby.

"That's a pretty cool moment," Officer said. "It was neat to be a part of that. Meeting some of the hockey guys was cool. The chance to chill out with them was super sweet. [Silver medallist figure skaters] Tessa Virtue and Scott Moir and Patrick Chan were here at the rink cheering us on too, which was super awesome to see."

When they returned to the ice on Saturday, February 15, the Canadians had not lost an iota of their enthusiasm or sharpness, which was bad news for the rest of the field. They had a fairly tough morning game against Japan's Ayumi Ogasawara, winning 8-6. In the afternoon, they had a date with Russia, which brought a whole new set of challenges. If the Canadians were the stars of the tournament because of their play on the ice, the Russians were darlings of the crowd and many curling fans around the world. The Ice Cube Curling Center was rocking with Russian fans putting everything they had into supporting the home country, and the Russian curlers were clearly buoyed by the overwhelming support.

The Russians were skipped by Anna Sidorova, a 23-year-old from Moscow, who'd turned heads in the curling world by posing in lingerie, holding a curling rock and broom, in a Russian magazine. Lead Ekaterina Galkina had also appeared in curling-themed photos in the Russian version of *Maxim* magazine. Some of the lingerie photos were of the not-safe-for-work variety. As a team of four attractive women, two who had posed in sexy photos, the Russians encountered some unwelcome attitudes early in the Olympics.

"We want more serious attitudes toward us," Galkina told the *Toronto Star.* "Even today there were a couple of comments from the stands like 'You look good girls.' Okay, so what. I mean, this has nothing to do with the game or with the athletes or sportsmanship at all. First of all, [Sidorova] is an athlete. That's what we're trying to bring to the people. You're a nice girl, but first of all you're an athlete."

Online pictures of the Russians circulating around the arena certainly caused a stir and fired up an old discussion amongst the curlers about the value of sex appeal in their game. Jill Officer was one of many curlers from around the world to have posed in an annual curling calendar and was a big believer in accentuating the athleticism of the curlers. In her calendar picture, she appears holding a 40-pound curling rock and looking particularly muscular. The picture could not really be compared to the ones featuring the scantily clad Russian curlers, but it gave Officer a certain perspective on the debate.

"It was an opportunity to promote the athletic side of our sport," Officer said. "People who maybe don't know a lot about curling think that it's easy or don't think there's athleticism involved in it, so for me it was an opportunity to show some of the athletic bodies that people have in our sport. It was a fun way to do it and a good opportunity. That was the purpose of the pose that I chose to do."

Officer was careful not to condemn the Russian curlers for their choices.

"I don't think it's necessarily a bad thing if it's classy, to have a little bit of sex appeal in it. I certainly don't think that it's hurting the sport and as long as it's done in a classy, respectful way, I think it's fine. The minute that it starts demeaning our sport or making us look ridiculous then I don't think it's fine."

With so much talk about lingerie photos, some people overlooked the fact that Russia was an emerging curling nation, and these women could actually play. Sidorova, who was a figure skater until a leg injury forced her to give up the sport at age 12, had represented her country at four world championships after being named skip of the Russian team during the 2010 Olympics in Vancouver. Just 19 at the time, Sidorova was a late addition to the Russian team and was called on to replace skip Ludmila Privivkova in the fifth game of the Olympics. With four years of women's curling experience now under her belt, Sidorova had earned respect from her peers.

"They're awesome," Jennifer Jones said. "They're just a great bunch of girls, great curlers, and they really have a lot of fight in them."

Russia actually gave the unbeaten Canadians a pretty good test, making one big mistake in the third end that allowed Jones to score three. The Canadians simply wouldn't allow Sidorova and her teammates to get back in the game from there, and that kept the huge Russian crowd subdued. "I thought they played really well but every time they gave us a bit of an out, we made it tonight," Jones analyzed. Canada wound up winning 5-3 to improve to 7-0. Jones didn't know it until she walked off the ice and was told by a reporter, but her team had just clinched first place in the Olympic curling tournament — with two days still to go in the round robin.

Jennifer Jones (left) and Kelly MacKenzie chat after the Manitoba junior women's final in 1995. MacKenzie won that game and went on to Canadian and world junior championships, while Jones was robbed of a chance to represent her country because of a Canadian Curling Association decision.
SHAUN BEST/*WINNIPEG SUN*/QMI AGENCY

Kaitlyn Lawes was one of the most promising young curlers in Manitoba in 2007 and she found success despite dealing with her father Keith's illness and death that year.
JASON HALSTEAD

(TOP LEFT) Jennifer Jones (bottom) at age 17 in 1992. She skipped a team to the Manitoba final that year but lost to former teammate Tracey Lavery (top). SHAUN BEST/*WINNIPEG SUN*/QMI AGENCY

(TOP RIGHT) Even back when they were pre-teens, Brad Jacobs (left) and Ryan Harnden (front right) were already turning heads in the curling world. Their first team included Matt Premo (middle, back) and Scott Seabrook (right, back) along with coach Eric Harnden. R.J. FROST/*SAULT STAR*/QMI AGENCY

(BOTTOM) Ryan Fry at age 15 in 1993. He won two Manitoba junior championships but never found a home with a team in his province, so he went looking for one elsewhere. *WINNIPEG SUN* ARCHIVES/QMI AGENCY

(OPPOSITE) Jennifer Jones (centre) and Jill Officer (left) had already won a Scotties championship but the team really took off when it added Dawn Askin (right) as lead for the 2007-08 season. JASON HALSTEAD

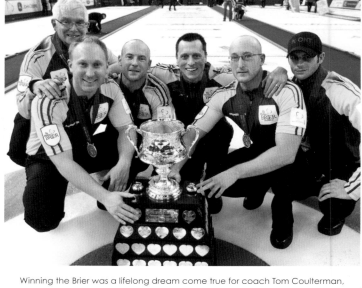

Brothers and best friends, E.J. (right) and Ryan Harnden followed in their dad Eric's footsteps and started curling together as teenagers.

IAN MACALPINE/*KINGSTON WHIG-STANDARD*/QMI AGENCY

Winning the Brier was a lifelong dream come true for coach Tom Coulterman, Brad Jacobs, Ryan Fry, E.J. Harnden, Ryan Harnden and fifth player Matt Dumontelle.

CODIE MCLACHLAN/*EDMONTON SUN*/QMI AGENCY

Among the giants of curling Brad Jacobs had to beat to win the 2013 Brier in Edmonton was four-time world champion Glenn Howard (right). Jacobs beat Howard 9-7 in the semifinal and has been impressing ever since. CODIE MCLACHLAN/*EDMONTON SUN*/QMI AGENCY

While they won four Canadian championships and one world title together, things weren't always perfect between Cathy Overton-Clapham (left) and Jennifer Jones, and despite being one of the best thirds in the world, Overton-Clapham was unceremoniously dumped after the 2010 season. REUTERS/ANDY CLARK

Janet Arnott (centre) was a fifth player and lead with the Jones team before settling into the role of coach. Eventually she became Jennifer Jones's go-to person. IAN MACALPINE/KINGSTON WHIG-STANDARD/QMI AGENCY

The Jones team won the Manitoba title in 2012, clinching an eighth straight appearance in the national Scotties Tournament of Hearts, where they were perennial contenders. JASON HALSTEAD/WINNIPEG SUN/QMI AGENCY

(LEFT) Fist bumps, broom slams and full-throated belly roars are the signatures of the Jacobs team and they were on full display at the Olympic Trials in Winnipeg. E.J. Harnden reacts to a score of two in the ninth end of the final against John Morris. KEVIN KING/*WINNIPEG SUN*/QMI AGENCY

(OPPOSITE, TOP) Dawn McEwen (right) and Jill Officer sweep a rock during the 2013 Olympic Trials in Winnipeg. KEVIN KING/*WINNIPEG SUN*/QMI AGENCY

(OPPOSITE, BOTTOM LEFT) The addition of Ryan Fry to the lineup in 2012-13 helped propel the Jacobs foursome to its first Brier title in March of 2013 in Edmonton and to a perfect record at the Olympic Trials in his hometown of Winnipeg. BRIAN DONOGH/*WINNIPEG SUN*/QMI AGENCY

(OPPOSITE, BOTTOM RIGHT) Kaitlyn Lawes proved to be the perfect third for Jennifer Jones — loyal and not apt to disagree with her leader. KEVIN KING/*WINNIPEG SUN*/QMI AGENCY

(TOP) Young and unapologetically enthusiastic, (left to right) Brad Jacobs, Ryan Fry, E.J. Harnden and Ryan Harnden plowed through the Olympic Trials in Winnipeg, becoming the first men's team to win it with a perfect record. KEVIN KING/ *WINNIPEG SUN*/QMI AGENCY

(BOTTOM) The Jones team beat Sherry Middaugh 8-4 in the final of the Roar of the Rings Olympic Trials in Winnipeg, and a lifelong dream of qualifying for the Olympics was finally realized. KEVIN KING/*WINNIPEG SUN*/QMI AGENCY

(OPPOSITE) Less than a month before they were due to compete in Sochi, the Jacobs and Jones teams converged in Las Vegas for the Continental Cup, a Ryder Cup–style international event that drew surprisingly large crowds. CHRIS HOLLOMAN/KATIPO CREATIVE

(OPPOSITE, TOP) Canadian fans, some sporting Team Jacobs "rock head" hats, make noise for the boys from Sault Ste. Marie. BEN PELOSSE/*JOURNAL DE MONTRÉAL/QMI AGENCY*

(OPPOSITE, BOTTOM) After a rough start, the Jacobs foursome found its collective focus and started reeling off wins at the Olympics in Sochi. AP PHOTO/ROBERT F. BUKATY

(LEFT) Jennifer Jones was in the zone from the minute she stepped on the ice in Sochi until she stepped onto the medal podium. AL CHAREST/ *CALGARY SUN/QMI AGENCY*

Jill Officer, Jennifer Jones's trusted lieutenant for decades, throws a stone during the Olympic semifinal win over Great Britain's Eve Muirhead in Sochi, with Kaitlyn Lawes (left) and Dawn McEwen sweeping. BEN PELOSSE/*JOURNAL DE MONTRÉAL/QMI AGENCY*

(OPPOSITE, TOP) After starting off the tournament with a 1-2 record and feeling the heat, Jacobs needed a big boost and got it with a win over Russia that started his team rolling all the way to the gold medal. AL CHAREST/*CALGARY SUN*/ QMI AGENCY

(OPPOSITE, BOTTOM) Ryan Fry's calming influence was a big part of the success of the Jacobs team in Sochi. He served as a buffer between the Harnden brothers and their cousin Brad, who had been known to bicker on occasion. BEN PELOSSE/*JOURNAL DE MONTRÉAL*/QMI AGENCY

(RIGHT) Jennifer Jones dreamed of this moment since she was a little kid and she didn't disappoint. When she scored the point that clinched the gold medal, all she could think was "We did it, we did it!" AL CHAREST/*CALGARY SUN*/ QMI AGENCY

The golden moment in Sochi. Jones celebrates with her teammates after a 6-3 win over Sweden that clinched the gold medal for Canada. AL CHAREST/CALGARY SUN/QMI AGENCY

(left to right) Kirsten Wall, Dawn McEwen, Jill Officer, Kaitlyn Lawes and Jennifer Jones step onto the podium for the flower ceremony after winning gold in Sochi. AFP PHOTO/JUNG YEON-JE

The Harnden brothers, Ryan and E.J., couldn't think of anything greater than winning a gold medal together in Sochi, along with their cousin Brad and best friend Ryan Fry. BEN PELOSSE/*JOURNAL DE MONTRÉAL*/QMI AGENCY

(left to right) Caleb Flaxey, Ryan Harnden, E.J. Harnden, Ryan Fry and Brad Jacobs had something special in mind for their podium appearance at the Ice Cube Curling Center in Sochi — they jumped up in unison. AP PHOTO/ROBERT F. BUKATY

On March 30, 2014, the ladies traded their curling outfits for evening wear and walked the red carpet at the Juno Awards in Winnipeg. They even presented an award that went to the absent Justin Bieber. BROOK JONES/QMI AGENCY

Life was a whirlwind for Team Jacobs upon returning from Sochi with appearances all over the country. On March 18, 2013, they dropped the puck at Rexall Place in Edmonton before an NHL game. IAN KUCERAK/EDMONTON SUN/QMI AGENCY

"It's amazing," she said, repeating a word she had used so many times already regarding her Sochi experience. "Our goal at the beginning of the week was to make the semis in such a tough field, and we know we're in. We know we'll have a chance to be on that podium, and I get goosebumps talking about it."

There were two essentially meaningless games remaining for Canada, and some worried Jones and her teammates might have a letdown. But they were having so much fun embracing every moment of the experience at the Olympics that there was no way they'd take their feet off the gas pedal. "I can't believe how fast it has gone by. We've played seven games, we're loving it, and we're in the playoffs at the Olympics. It's more than you could have ever dreamed of in your entire life. It's not hard to keep it going." Jones had been in big situations like this and knew the worst thing possible would be to look too far ahead. She even took umbrage with a reporter suggesting her team had been dominant to that point. "I don't know if we've been dominant. It feels like there have been really close games to me."

As much as she relished knowing she was now just one win away from being guaranteed a podium finish and two away from a gold medal, Jones flashed some of that perspective that seemed to have come into her psyche in the last year. "We haven't been nervous. It's a lifetime of waiting for this moment and it's sports. At the end of the day, Isabella is still going to be there, we have our families and we've made it to the Olympics, so we just want to leave our best on the ice. I feel like we've come to the Olympics and we've performed really well on the world's biggest stage and I'm really proud of us."

For the second time, Jones was asked about the colour of her eye shadow and if it held any significance. Again she deflected the question.

"It's a little different today," she said with a laugh, admitting that the eye shadow had a "gold hue to it.

"Maybe I'll bring it out for the playoffs. I don't even know the name of it. You're asking a girl that knows nothing about makeup."

What she seemingly knew everything about was curling, and right then her team was on a roll like none it had ever been on before. The playoffs were clinched, and the Canadians were just waiting to see who their opponent would be in the semifinals. Their last two games were against non-contending teams, but Jones would not even consider letting up in the slightest. The Canadians pondered letting fifth player Kirsten Wall get into action in one of the two meaningless games but chose to stay the course, with an opportunity to get an even better feel for the ice and the rocks and simply stay sharp for the most important games of their lives that would come a few days later in the playoffs.

The first game was against the United States, skipped by Erika Brown of Madison, Wisconsin. The Americans were having a terrible time in the tournament, with only one win despite having 2003 world women's champion Debbie McCormick at third. Brown, 41, is also an accomplished curler, who had two world championship silver medals to her name along with seven United States championships. She also has a strong connection to the Canadian game as she is married to three-time world champion Ian Tetley (with Al Hackner in 1985, Ed Werenich in 1990 and Wayne Middaugh in 1998) and lives in Oakville, Ontario. Brown's team would have very little to say in this particular Olympic tournament (her second) but did help the Canadians by showing up with an A-game on that Sunday.

It was just what Jones and Co. needed — a close, hard-fought game that tested their mettle, a game they legitimately could have lost but found a way to win. Jones had, by far, her worst game of the tournament statistically, at just 74 percent, as the teams traded points throughout the first nine ends and the Americans stole one in the tenth to force an extra end. The steal came on a rare miss by Jones, who was heavy on a draw attempt with her last rock. She didn't make the same mistake when she had the opportunity again in the extra end though, and Canada walked off with a 7-6 win.

"The quality and calibre of teams here is so tremendous that you're going to have battles out there," Jones said, tipping her hat to a strong effort by the down-and-out Americans. "We're finding a way to be in control of our own game and holding our fate in our own hands. We had a plan coming in here and it worked out perfectly so far. We couldn't have asked for anything to go any better. Now it's just a matter of trying to figure out a way to play well in the playoffs."

The only thing left for the Jones team to do in the round robin was put their names into the history books. One more win and they would be the first women's team in history to go through the Olympic round robin with a perfect 9-0 record. All week, Jones downplayed that possibility, knowing it really wouldn't matter what their round-robin record was if they didn't win in the playoffs. When it came right down to it though, it was obvious the Canadians wanted perfection. The last game of the round robin came on Monday, February 17, against Korea and it wasn't even close as Canada cruised to a 9-4 victory in nine ends. It's not often you will get Jones to admit she's done something special, and it's usually not until the last rock of the last end of the last game has been thrown, and she's the last skip standing. In this case though, she couldn't hold back.

"It feels unbelievable," Jones admitted, finally. "In my opinion this is one of the toughest fields that has ever been assembled for women's curling. To go through undefeated, and to go into the Olympic record books, is pretty awesome. At the end of the day we will take that one, but the goal is to be on the podium."

The round robin was over, and the semifinals were set. Despite their brilliant run, Canada drew a decidedly unfavourable matchup against the fourth place team in the round robin, which just happened to be defending world champion Eve Muirhead of Great Britain. Switzerland (Mirjam Ott) was set to face Sweden (Margaretha Sigfridsson) in the other semifinal, and many observers believed first-place Canada had drawn the tougher assignment. Though Great Britain finished with just a 5-4 record and squeezed into the semifinal, Muirhead was not the slightest bit afraid of the powerful Canadians. The team's coach, David Hay, even had a warning for the semifinal opponent.

"We're definitely better at knockout than round-robin curling, for certain," he said. "Eve's won the world junior championship four times, seniors and Europeans. She can handle the big day."

Before the semifinals got underway, there was an off-day for the curlers, which they used to practise and relax. It was a series of emails from home that were the highlight of the day for Jones. Back in Ontario, family members had prepared a special surprise for the skip. They had taken her daughter Isabella to a studio, decked in Canadian colours, flags and other paraphernalia and sent the photos to Jones as inspiration. As she showed some of the pictures to media members after practice that Tuesday, Jones had tears in her eyes and a lump in her throat. Her favourite picture was of Isabella draped in the flag, holding a sign that said "Go Mommy Go."

"It just melts me," Jones said. "It makes me so happy. I'm just so happy in life and curling is just something I love to do. I feel like I'm living this dream. I've got this amazing little girl, my life is wonderful and I'm at the Olympics curling with the best bunch of girls in the world. And we're 9-0. Life really couldn't get any better for me. We're playing great. We came to the biggest stage for sport, and we've played our best and you can't, as an athlete, ask for anything more than that."

Once again, it was apparent that Jones had a different kind of perspective on life than she had before she became a mother, though she argued that her team had always been ahead of others in that area.

"It doesn't hurt for sure," she said. "I've always thought that we've had a really good perspective on curling. I think we've handled losses better than any team I've ever seen. It's just part of the game. If you couldn't lose on any given day then why play? That's the excitement of sport."

As much as just getting to the Olympics was the realization of a lifelong fantasy, knowing they were just two wins away from a gold medal was almost too hard to digest. Lawes, the youngest player on the team at age 25, had been visualizing this day in her mind for 16 years and was having a hard time believing it was actually happening.

"You dream about it but it's hard to put into perspective that we're living that dream right now," she said. "I remember watching Sandra Schmirler in Nagano when I was 10 and thinking how amazing it was that the sport I play is in the Olympics. You hope one day you can have that opportunity, but you never know if it will come. It's amazing to know that a lot of hard work has paid off, and we're just so thrilled to be a part of this playoff situation."

Jones was also having somewhat of a pinch-me moment. Her mind harkened back to four years earlier, when she was pretty much done with curling and was ready to quit, to 18 months prior to the Olympics, when she had surgery and didn't know if she'd ever be able to play again, to 14 months earlier, when she had Isabella. There were many times she thought this day would never come.

"With all the things our team has gone through over the years, it feels pretty great to be at this point," Jones said. "Eighteen months ago I tore my ACL, then I had a baby and didn't know what the future was going to be for us, and here we are getting ready to play in a semifinal at the Olympics. So it's pretty cool."

While obviously thrilled to be at that point, Jones and her teammates were fully aware of how difficult the road ahead was. Muirhead, Sigfridsson and Ott were all capable of winning the gold medal and Canada was starting from scratch just like the rest of them. Jones had an immense amount of respect for the other teams and the feeling was mutual. The Canadians were excited to play: They had always relished the big games, the adrenalin rush, that feeling of nervousness and anticipation in the stomach. They had worked so hard to reach this point and weren't about to let it pass them by. They would certainly not take an opponent like Eve Muirhead lightly.

"They're a tremendous team," Jones said. "A couple of shots here and there and their record could have been better in the round robin. We expect great things from them. They are one of the best teams in the world, one of the best teams to ever play. They make a ton of big shots, and we just can't leave those for them. We're going to have to be at the top of our game." And, indeed they were.

The semifinal against Great Britain was unusual in the sense that Canada was in control from the very beginning but still had to make a very difficult last shot to win the game. Canada scored two with the hammer in the first end after Muirhead's last rock picked up some debris and sailed through the house and stole one in the second to open up a 3-0 lead it would never relinquish. However, Jones only managed to score a pair of singles in the fourth and sixth ends to keep Muirhead at bay and led 5-3 going into the pivotal eighth end. The turning point in the game came in the eighth when Jones made a long cross-house double with her last rock that took away any chance of Great Britain scoring two to tie the game. Instead, Muirhead blanked the end and then scored just one with the hammer in the ninth to send the game to the tenth with Canada leading 5-4.

"It's huge," Jones said of the double, after which she celebrated exuberantly. "The eighth end is always a big turning point in a curling game, and when we made that double we knew that we were going to force or blank, and we were totally happy to blank. Then even if we give up the deuce in nine, we still have the hammer coming home. That was a huge turning point in the game, so yeah, I was pretty excited about it."

In the final end, Canada had the hammer and a skip who had been waiting all her life to make the big shot. Muirhead did a fine job of putting pressure on the Canadians, and Jones eventually had to make a draw to the button against three Great Britain counters to win the game. There were some tense moments as the rock slid down the ice. Jones yelled out "Gotta go" to her sweepers as the rock neared the house, but Officer and McEwen brushed it to perfection, dragging it onto the button for the clinching point. The Canadians won 6-4, were guaranteed a medal and would have a chance to win their country's first gold in women's curling since Schmirler won in Nagano in 1998.

"Absolutely I was nervous," Jones admitted after her game-clinching draw. "If you don't get that adrenalin rush and it's a guarantee then why play? That's what you train for, and I've had to make a lot of big shots to win games before, so you know what that feeling is all about. You just embrace it. I let it go, and I knew it was close, so that's a great feeling, and the girls just judged it perfectly. I was as excited as I've ever been."

Officer and Lawes both struggled at times during the game, with the second actually flashing two shots that put her team in some trouble. As had been the case throughout their time together however, Jones bailed them out, proving that she has the perfect combination of finesse, savvy and composure when it comes to making big shots at big moments.

"I wouldn't want anyone else throwing that last shot," Lawes said. "Jennifer's an amazing person and an amazing skip, and she's so talented."

Jones gave credit back to her teammates, particularly lead Dawn McEwen, who made two "tick" shots in the tenth end, meaning she bumped opposition guard rocks off the centre line without removing them from play, which would have been a violation of the free guard zone. That left the four-foot open for Jones to hit with her last rock, and the skip had been comfortable with her draw weight all week. As the old adage says, "If you are going to stand in the four-foot, you better be able to hit it," and Jones proved more than capable. True to her word since the Olympic Trials, Jones was thrilled to be assured of a podium finish.

"That was really our goal and we're there," she said. "I'm so proud of us. I thought we came out and played lights out today and had to make a big shot to win the game. The girls swept it perfectly. In the biggest moment, under the most pressure . . . we made a really finesse shot to win the game. I'm proud of us, but we're really going to try to get on top of that podium."

"We're really happy right now that we have a medal," Officer added. "We have to take that into consideration and realize that it's a huge accomplishment."

"It just keeps getting better," Lawes chimed in. "We're right where we want to be, and it's just amazing."

The Canadians went out of their way for weeks to never get their hopes too high, to never talk openly about their desire to win a gold medal, but now there was no way around it. A podium finish would undoubtedly be special, but a loss in the gold-medal game after going 10-0 would be downright devastating. They didn't have to wait long to go for the gold. Their date with destiny came the next day, Thursday, February 20, against Margaretha Sigfridsson and the always steady Swedes.

The morning of the gold medal game started the same way as all others for the Canadian team — with toast and peanut butter. Jones and her teammates are creatures of routine, and they had been starting their day with the same breakfast for years in tournaments all over the world. Normally, they pack their own toaster just in case they can't get what they need. On this day they got their toast and peanut butter fix in the Athletes' Village lounge.

When the curlers rolled into the arena for the gold medal game practice session, the Ice Cube Curling Center was a different place. Gone were the loud, enthusiastic Russian fans — the men's and women's teams from the host country failed to make the playoffs — and in their place were flag-waving, red-and-white-clad Canadians, including other athletes and even well-known NHL coach Mike Babcock. This was much more like what the Canadians were used to at home, and they relished the preamble to the game, waving to fans, friends and family, smiling and laughing as they stretched to get their bodies loose for the biggest game of their lives. Back home in Winnipeg, a few hundred people were gathered for the 6:30 a.m. start at the St. Vital Curling Club and the Manitoba Sports Hall of Fame. Jones could picture them in her mind's eye and wanted badly to do something special for them, indeed for all the people back in Canada who had provided so much support.

Thanks to their perfect record, the Canadians had last rock in the first end but were only able to score one point, a small victory for the Swedes. Canada took back the momentum in the second, forcing Sweden to take one point and tie it up, blanked the third end and then took the lead with a key deuce in the fourth. That set the stage for a pivotal fifth end that could have been disastrous for Canada. Kaitlyn Lawes was struggling, perhaps having one of the worst games of her life. At one point in the third end, Lawes was curling just 18 percent. By the fifth she was up to 48 percent, but her misses were complicating the situation for Jones and, in that end, they opened the door for Sweden to score big and take the lead. In fact, Swedish fourth Maria Prytz had a chance to make a double with her last rock to score four and give Sweden a 5-3 lead. In Jones's mind, the four points were already on the board.

"The thing is, it was early in the game and I said, 'Worst-case scenario, we give up four and we're only down two,'" Jones said. "We're battlers and we're tough and we come back."

Much to Canada's good fortune, Prytz only half-made her shot, removing one Canadian rock but pushing the other one only far enough to score two points instead of four. That tied the game at 3-3 and gave the hammer back to Canada. "Obviously it was huge keeping them to two when it wasn't looking very good that end," Jones said. The Canadians blanked the next two ends and it went into the eighth with the score still tied 3-3. Because of the blank ends, Jones was hitting with most of her rocks and had played only three draws in the entire game heading into the eighth. It came back to haunt her. Canada had a glorious chance to score two and take a critical two-point lead, but Jones came up well light on her draw. Then she had to agonize over a measurement that absolutely could have gone either way. Again, Canada was fortunate to come away with a single point for a 4-3 lead.

It could have been costly, especially with the Swedes taking the hammer into the ninth end, but Jones turned it all around again with one brilliant shot. The ninth was shaping up well for Canada to at least force the Swedes to take one and give back the hammer. By the time it came to skip stones, Jones was lying one behind cover at the back of the four-foot. With her last rock, Jones made a perfect draw — no way it was going to be light this time — to the top of the four-foot, which meant Prytz would have to do something incredible just to avoid giving up a steal of two. "It was one of those shots where I knew if we could put it in the right spot, I didn't think they would be able to score," Jones said. "It was a bit of a gamble, but I felt so good with the speed all week and the girls swept it perfectly. When it stopped it was in a pretty good position, but if it would have been a little bit higher, it would have been a problem. No guts, no glory." The Swedish fourth couldn't pull off the big shot, the Canadians stole two and, with a 6-3 lead, the gold medal was surely theirs.

"When we stole two I almost started to cry," Jones told the CBC's George Stroumboulopoulos after the Olympics. "I knew we had won the gold medal at that very moment. I was shaking and it was all we could do to keep it together in the tenth end. It was like the whole end was in slow motion. I looked at my mom and the tears were streaming down her eyes and my dad . . . I looked at Brent . . . it was all I could do to not start crying in the tenth end of our gold medal game."

They call it running your opponent out of rocks. It's the least dramatic but most enjoyable way to win a curling game. Simply make them go away and your golden moment will arrive. When it came time for the final shot, Jones's first in the tenth end, the skip took plenty of time to compose herself. She sat in the hack much longer than she normally does, flipped her hair a few extra times, checked, double-checked and triple-checked the bottom of the rock for debris. She wanted to not only make sure her shot would be perfect but also make the moment last. She had waited so long for this, worked so hard. There were so many people she wanted to share it with, including her teammates, her family and friends in the building, her infant daughter back in Ontario. But there was more to this. She thought of all the people back home, living and dying with her every Olympic moment. This was for her home province of Manitoba, for her hometown of Winnipeg, for all of Canada.

She rocked back slightly in the hack and sprung forward, released the rock and watched as it slid perfectly toward destiny — a gold medal, an Olympic record 11-0, an eternity of dreams fulfilled. When it made contact, she threw her arms in the air and ran down to greet her beloved teammates, whose lives had been equally devoted to this task. The celebration was on, and it brought tears to the eyes of curlers and Canadian fans alike.

"We did it, we did it!" Jones kept telling herself. That one, almost impossible to believe moment was finally here. They would indeed stand on the podium and they'd be right at the top with gold medals around their necks. After a long celebration on the ice, Jones, Lawes, Officer, McEwen and fifth player Kirsten Wall made their way over to that podium for the flower ceremony. When their names and country were called, they stepped up to the top level and threw their arms in the air in unison, Jones even leaping off her feet. This was the moment she was seemingly born for. She had embraced every last iota of the Olympic experience and was now being rewarded with the ultimate prize.

"We achieved this moment for so many people in our lives," Jones said at a press conference a few minutes later, before being whisked off for doping tests. "We did it for all of our friends and families, the city of Winnipeg, all of Manitoba and Canada and that is priceless really. There's no bigger moment or feeling in the world than that. I couldn't believe it. To have all of Canada behind us, not the pressure of it but the excitement of having all those people cheering us on and people in Winnipeg cheering us on, sitting there on the edge of their seats, and we did it for them too."

Now that they were Olympic champions, curling legends in their own right, the Canadians were able to sit back and reflect on what they had just achieved — a perfect record against one of the toughest fields ever assembled for a women's tournament.

"We're really proud of that," Jones said. "We came out and played consistent from the start of the week to the final and put our best game on the ice, which is exactly what you want to do in the biggest sporting event. We're going to have that little OR, Olympic record, next to our name forever. It's crazy to me. It's one of those records that can only be tied and never broken, so we'll always be remembered for it."

They all had people on their minds. Jones thought of the little girl back home; Officer of her own two-year old daughter, Camryn, whose favourite expression was "Mommy's at the Olympiax"; McEwen of her parents and partner Mike. Lawes, of course, thought of her mother, Cheryl, and the empty space beside her.

"I know my dad would be so proud of me," she said. "I thought about him a lot during the game. I wish that I could share this experience with him. He was my inspiration."

After an evening of celebration with families, friends and other athletes (including the gold-medal-winning women's hockey team) at Canada House, the Canadians were up bright and early the next day for a full media tour. They signed autographs, took phone calls from home, did interview after interview and found out just how big it is to win a gold medal.

"I still get goosebumps every single time someone says the words 'gold medallist,'" Jones said. "When we woke up the day after winning, I actually looked around my room to make sure it wasn't a dream. Then I saw the flowers, and I knew it was real. I haven't stopped smiling. I have barely slept and it's just more from adrenalin than anything. My heart hasn't stopped racing. I wish everyone in the world could experience this because, honestly, it's the best feeling in the world."

They had to two full days before they were scheduled to receive their gold medals at the Olympic Plaza. The men's curling final still needed to be played, and the Canadian girls were in the house that Friday night as Brad Jacobs and his teammates crushed Great Britain to claim another gold medal. Finally, on Saturday, February 22, at 9 p.m. Sochi time, the Canadians received their hardware. It was one of those simply glorious moments that can never be forgotten — five women standing on top of the podium, gold medals around their necks, the Maple Leaf rising up the centre flagpole with the Olympic Torch in the background and "O Canada" playing for all to hear.

"Standing on that podium and seeing that flag being raised . . ." Jones said in a halting voice months later. ". . . I swear there's nothing better in the world than that. We were standing there and we were shaking. We couldn't believe it when they were playing our national anthem for something that *we* did."

"We're gold medallists for life, and nobody can take that away from us," Lawes said.

Jones had tears in her eyes once again. In her wildest dreams, the Olympic experience could not have worked out more perfectly. "We had an absolute blast," she said. "We wanted to leave with no regrets, and it worked out perfectly . . . a perfect fairy-tale story for us."

Now that it was all over, with nothing left to do but go back home to the adoring Canadian fans, Jones finally admitted that her eye shadow did have significance all along. She may have put it on by accident at the beginning, but come playoff time she knew exactly what she was doing.

"It's called Gorgeous Gold," she said with a smile. "It was pretty fitting."

CHAPTER TEN

GUT-CHECKS AND GLORY

The flight that carried the Canadian curlers from Switzerland to Sochi was heavy. It held athletes from several sports, support teams, equipment, personal bags and the weight of great expectations. Brad Jacobs and his teammates arrived in Russia sporting a kind of confidence they had never experienced before: Not only were they first-time Olympians, they were also newcomers to the top of the curling world. Nobody had ever gone through the Canadian Curling Trials undefeated before and nobody, not even the curlers on the Soo Crew, could have envisioned doing so against such a stacked field in Winnipeg. Somewhere in that perfect run to qualify for the Olympics, there was something missing: Adversity. They would find plenty of it, soon enough.

They arrived in Sochi with little fanfare, which was bound to happen since the men's hockey teams from around the world were trickling in at the same time.

Wide-eyed and excited, the curlers settled into the Athletes' Village in rooms with views of both the Black Sea and the Olympic Village. Outwardly, the curlers were their usual selves: Fearless, a bit cocky, ready to take on the world and win. In truth, they were feeling the pressure, believing Canadians expected nothing less than a gold medal from them and knowing in their own hearts that no other colour would do.

"Nothing short of gold," Jacobs proclaimed every time he had the chance between the December Olympic Trials and the Sochi Games in February. "There's only one attitude to have. If we don't win gold, it will be a huge disappointment to all of us and to Canadians."

The attitude differed from the one carried by Canadian women's skip Jennifer Jones. She and her teammates refused to put all the focus on gold, instead suggesting their goal was simply to stand on the podium at the end of the Olympics, wearing a medal of some sort. Jones and her teammates were legitimately thrilled just to be at the Olympics, and if they were feeling any pressure at all, it never showed. The same could not be said for Jacobs and his teammates. An intense bunch to begin with, they were all a collective bundle of nerves and anxiety as the biggest curling event of their lives approached.

There were immense footsteps for the Canadian men to follow. Kevin Martin was undefeated on the way to winning the gold medal in 2010 in Vancouver. Brad Gushue shocked Canada by winning the Trials in 2005 and then brought home the gold from Turin. In fact, Canada's worst showing in men's Olympic curling was silver after both Martin (2002 in Salt Lake City) and Mike Harris (1998 in Nagano) lost gold medal games. That history was not lost on the Jacobs foursome, and they certainly didn't want to be the ones to end their country's remarkable run. As they began practice for the tournament, as the enormity of it all washed over them, the laser-like focus that had brought them this far began to blur. This team was about to find out just how hard it really is to reach Olympic glory.

The lead-up to the curling tournament was uneventful, with Jacobs and his teammates simply carrying on their usual routine of eating, sleeping, working out in the gym and thinking about curling 24/7. Of course, now they were part of a much greater team — 220 Canadian athletes — and they were rubbing shoulders with some of the biggest stars of the NHL in the Athletes' Village. The security concerns that dominated the media prior to the Olympics were largely unfounded due to the huge police and closed-circuit camera presence in Sochi, so the athletes felt safe roaming around the Olympic Village area. Using bicycles provided by the Canadian Olympic Committee, they had a chance to explore the region and unwind a little, but curling rocks and pebbled ice were never far from their minds. Sometimes they had a hard time believing they were actually at the Olympics; Sochi in no way resembled a winter destination, with its moderate temperatures and Black Sea beaches, while the idea of a young team coming this far this quickly seemed almost unfathomable.

"It's crazy," E.J. Harnden said. "We've won a Brier and came second at the world championship and now the very next year we're here at the Olympics. It's been a whirlwind beyond our expectations, even though we set this as our goal and this is what we were working toward. Now for us, it's just completing the puzzle. We're not happy to be here, we're here to compete, and the end dream and the end goal is, obviously, to win that gold, and that's what would truly complete everything.

"That we did this with our family members just goes to show how much chemistry means in our sport and how much impact it has in a team's success. For us it's just been a matter of maturing and now we're at a point where we've always been comfortable but now know how to feed off of each other and help each other. That's why our success has come so quickly, because we found that match. With Ryan Fry coming in it sort of completed the puzzle with four guys who are all on the same page, equally dedicated and at the end of the day are real good friends on and off the ice."

They had a good-size throng of supporters from Sault Ste. Marie in Sochi, including Eric, Sue and Al Harnden, Brad's wife, Shawna, E.J.'s wife, Rachelle, and Fry's girlfriend, Miriam Eslayeh. Curling had been a family affair all their lives and that wasn't about to change now that they were on the cusp of playing for the sport's most lucrative prize. Sue Harnden, for one, was terrified of flying, especially over the ocean, but she knew she couldn't pass up this opportunity. "How could I not go?"

Finally, almost two full months after Jacobs and his teammates qualified for Sochi, the Olympics arrived. On February 7, the Jacobs team marched in the Opening Ceremony at Fisht Olympic Stadium with the rest of their Canadian brothers and sisters. It was a grand spectacle, befitting a Russian organizing committee that spent somewhere in the neighborhood of $51 billion to put on the Olympics and did a remarkable job of allaying terrorism fears with blanket security. For curlers from a Northern Ontario city of 75,000 people, it was awe-inspiring.

"Everybody I talked to says they have a 'Welcome to the Olympics' moment," Jacobs said at the time. "Opening Ceremony was it for me. When we walked out into the stadium, it was unbelievable, it was a spectacle. That was the moment — an awe-filled moment for me and probably for any other athlete who's in his first Olympics."

Another inspiring moment, for at least some of the Canadian curlers, came the following day when the Games opened in earnest. About an hour away from the curling venue, at the Rosa Khutor Extreme Park near Krasnaya Polyana, three sisters from Montreal were writing an amazing story. Justine, Chloe and Maxime Dufour-Lapointe were all skiing in the women's moguls event on the first night of Olympic competition. It was just the fifth time in Olympic history that three siblings competed in the same event and the athletes didn't disappoint. Justine won the gold medal and Chloe the silver. As they stood on the podium together, E.J. Harnden, watching on television back at the coastal Athletes' Village, had tears in his eyes.

"Honestly, I watched that and it was a little bit emotional for me," Harnden said the following day. "That's what I hope to do at the end of the Olympics, stand on top of the podium with my brother and with my cousin Brad. It would be extremely special to me."

That Sunday, the day before the curling tournament was slated to begin, brought some relief to the Canadian curlers, who had been itching to play since the minute the Olympic Trials ended in December and had been allowing pressure to build continuously over that time. They were in Sochi now, had the lay of the land, had been given plenty of opportunity to practise on the ice and test out the rocks and now the wait was finally over. All that was left was to turn up the house music for the warm-ups and start getting pumped up for the games in their customary fashion.

"It's been a long wait between when we won the Trials and getting here," Jacobs said. "To finally be over here and ready to start the Games is awesome. It's almost like a huge weight is lifted off your shoulders just to finally be here at this point."

It would not be long before that weight was back.

The Olympic curling tournament started on Monday, February 10, at the Ice Cube Curling Center. It was a day like no other in the history of the sport. While the playing surface prepared by Canadian ice-makers Hans Wuthrich and Eric Montford, who also made the ice for the Canadian Trials in Winnipeg, was in terrific shape and provided all the curlers an opportunity to be at their best, there was something highly unusual about the building that day. Three thousand seats filled with neophyte Russian fans, who clearly had not spent any time watching curling in the past, the Ice Cube was absolutely rocking on the opening day. The fans were more enthusiastic than those heard anywhere else in the world, but had a singular focus on only the games involving the Russian teams. As a result, they burst into loud cheers and applause after every single shot taken by the Russian team, whether it was a simple guard in front of the house, a draw around cover by the second or a takeout by the skip. The sound was deafening and unexpected to many of the curlers, who are used to polite applause from fans at appropriate times. Jacobs and his teammates were a bit thrown off, unable to communicate the way they normally do because of the noise.

"I've never heard a crowd like that," E.J. Harnden said. "You know what, I think it's great for curling. It's awesome to hear crowds like that and that kind of excitement and atmosphere in a curling arena. You get it in Canada when you make the big shots but here it's every shot. To see that on the international stage is great. It's packed and loud and noisy, and it's incredible."

Jacobs, who seemed to find the crowd distracting, did not necessarily share Harnden's enthusiasm. Not only did the noise make communication difficult, it prevented the Canadians from being themselves. Widely known for being more vocal, emotional and demonstrative than most curlers, the Jacobs team's exuberance was dwarfed by that of the crowd.

"It's just hard to do in that building with it being so loud," he said. "It can almost bring you down, and we want to not let that happen and just play our own game. Big crowds in Canada cheer nice shots on every sheet and then are quiet while the games are going on. Out there is more like a soccer game, a football game or something. There's cheering non-stop and tons of noise."

Perhaps the unusual atmosphere had something to do with what happened on those first two days of the curling tournament. Perhaps it was the Canadian team having difficulty adjusting to the ice and the rocks. Perhaps it was the loss of their usual focus as they looked too far ahead with visions of gold medals in their minds. Whatever it was, the Canadians were nothing like the team that had breezed through the Canadian Trials two months earlier. They looked off from the minute they stepped on the ice for their first game with Germany.

The opener was against John Jahr, a 48-year-old millionaire from Hamburg, who was given no chance of contending for a medal as the tournament began. It was anything but a breeze for a Canadian team that had somehow waltzed through one of the most formidable gatherings of curlers in history at the Olympic Trials. Canada trailed 4-2 through three ends after Germany stole two points and had to claw its way back to take the lead into the late ends. Germany stole another two points in the ninth to make the score 9-8, but Canada eventually prevailed by scoring two in the tenth to walk off with an 11-8 win. It was a sloppy game that was much closer than it needed to be because of Canada's struggles. The Canadians knew they were fortunate to win, given the numbers: Jacobs curled just 82 percent and was the best of the bunch. Fry came in at 79 percent and the two Harnden brothers at 75 percent.

"It was pretty ugly, to be honest," Jacobs said. "It's a different event to any regular event. There are nerves out there."

It got even uglier. Later that day, the Canadians took on Switzerland, skipped by European champion Sven Michel, and this time there would be no reprieve from sloppy play. Though their numbers improved greatly from the earlier game, Canada gave up a pivotal steal of three points in the fifth end, from which they never recovered. Canada started the game with the hammer and blanked the first four ends before disaster struck. For the first time, you could see frustration creeping in as the Canadians tried to fight back from the big deficit. They managed to stay close, and Jacobs even had a chance to tie the game in the tenth and send it to an extra end, but his final shot was a bad one. Trying to hit and stick for two points, his shooter rolled out, and Canada wound up with only one point and a 5-4 loss. Overall, it was certainly not the type of opening day expected from the country that had won the last two Olympic gold medals.

"We're not sharp, not in a rhythm, not making our shots," Ryan Harnden said. "But we will bounce back. We are the type of team that bounces back. Tomorrow's a new day."

The confidence, bravado and momentum the Jacobs team carried into the Olympics were not gone, but they were certainly being tested sooner than expected. An even greater test came the next day when an old nemesis served as the opponent in Canada's lone game. Niklas Edin's team from Sweden was the defending world champion and the very squad that beat Jacobs in the gold medal game at the world championship in Victoria the previous April. Sitting at 1-1 and curling just 80 percent as a team, the Canadians could ill-afford another sloppy game, or worse, another early loss. They tried their best to get a good night's sleep and stuck to their routine in hopes of recouping the magic. They succeeded to an extent, curling their best game of the tournament, but even that was not enough.

Edin, a 28-year-old like Jacobs, was arguably the gold medal favourite after winning his first world championship less than a year earlier. His rock-solid team brought all the shots, setting up a tremendous match with the Canadians. Much like in the gold medal game at the worlds, Edin brought it quickly against Jacobs, scoring a deuce in the second end with the hammer and adding more in the fifth and seventh. Jacobs, who curled an impressive 93 percent in the game, countered with deuces in the fourth, sixth and ninth ends, setting up a dramatic tenth. Edin had to make a draw to the four-foot for the win, and even though his front end over-swept it, the rock stopped just in time. Edin actually had to ask the Canadians who won as they shook hands after the game.

The Canadians had no doubt played a better game than the day before, but there were still some big concerns aside from the unexpected 1-2 record. Fry curled only 76 percent in the loss, E.J. Harnden a woeful 69 percent, and the frustration that was creeping in the previous day was now on full display. Brooms slammed on the ice regularly, and tense words could be heard among the curlers. Even the opposition wondered if the Canadians were starting to unravel under the immense pressure.

"In this game, they kind of struggled a bit," Edin said. "You could tell that on the ice. Smashing their brooms seven or eight times in a row. It was quite hard to miss. Almost all of them were doing it."

Fiery nature was nothing new to these Canadian curlers. When you play with that kind of raw emotion in every game, there are bound to be good times and bad. At their best, when they are pumping fists, letting out shrieks of celebration and shaking their brooms in the air, the Jacobs curlers are entertainers who are perceived as being a bit off the wall by curling purists. At their worst, when the brooms are slamming and the frustration is front and centre, they can appear petulant, normally a no-no in such a traditional game. Nobody on the team wanted to admit that they were getting down on themselves after the loss to Sweden, even if their body language gave them away.

"We're not flat," Fry said. "We're just not making everything. [Playing] against teams that are playing this good against us, you need to make everything."

The Canadians had reached a pivotal point of their Olympics. Another loss would put them in danger of missing the playoffs, a nightmare scenario no one would have ever envisioned. It was the proverbial gut-check time, a time to refocus, re-energize and try to get everything back on track. They had the evening off and planned to visit with their families and maybe have a beer or two at Canada Olympic House. That may have been one of their best decisions of the Olympics.

It was a chance encounter. The Canadian curlers were heading for a little refuge in the Olympic Village known as Canada Olympic House, where athletes and their families could lounge about, eat and drink for free and get away from the rigours of the Games and the glare of the TV cameras and the media. As they were walking in, a familiar face was walking out. It was men's hockey coach Mike Babcock, who had steered Canada to a gold medal four years earlier in Vancouver and was about to do the same thing in Sochi. As coach of the Detroit Red Wings of the NHL, he won the Stanley Cup in 2008 and is one of hockey's most respected individuals. He's also a big curling fan.

Babcock was seen several times watching games at the curling venue in Sochi, as he had in Vancouver four years earlier, so it was no surprise that he recognized members of the Jacobs team as they entered COH. He stopped them, engaged them in conversation and offered some much-appreciated advice.

"We talked to the hockey guys when we were 1-2," Jacobs said. "We talked to Mike Babcock and he said, 'You're 1-2, that doesn't mean anything. It's how you finish. Just go out there and execute.' And that's exactly what we've done. It was nice to take his advice. To have all of these great guys in our corner has really helped us out a lot."

That wasn't the only involvement of the Canadian men's hockey team in the curling tournament. Coaches Rick Lang and Tom Coulterman had lunch with Babcock and his assistants, Claude Julien and Lindy Ruff, one day, and they exchanged ideas as both their teams chased gold medals. On another day, all of the NHL players on Team Canada showed up en masse for a Canadian curling game. It was inspiring for Jacobs and his teammates to look up and see Sidney Crosby, Drew Doughty, Carey Price and Co. sporting their Canadian jackets and cheering them on. Goalie Roberto Luongo, then of the Vancouver Canucks, even donned a foam curling rock on his head as many of the Jacobs supporters did during the Olympics.

While rubbing shoulders with some of Canada's most famous sporting icons was nice, the curlers still had a significant problem on their hands. That 1-2 record was a burden on their fragile psyches, and they knew there couldn't be any more slip-ups. Somehow they needed to regain their focus and needed to elevate their game to the level that had carried them to wins at the Brier and the Olympic Trials. More than anything they needed to channel the energy that made their team distinctive, in a positive manner. Canadian national team coach Rick Lang, himself a five-time Canadian champion representing Northern Ontario, had an idea that he hoped would get things going in the right direction. It was as simple as a little motivation.

"We had a video that had been presented to them after they won the Trials, and it's a spectacular three-minute video of all their highlights with some loud, blaring music," Lang explained. "They didn't want to start something new at the beginning, but we started watching it when they were 1-2. It's a real pump-up. It's a beauty.

"They're funny. They need to be pumped up. Usually curlers, you need to bring them down a bit, but these guys need that energy and fire or they're ordinary. They're just energetic, energized kind of guys. It sometimes doesn't match the mold for our game, but it works for them."

There were meetings, some over food or beer, others in the gym or just back in the rooms in the Athletes' Village. Everyone agreed it was time to get back to basics. Perhaps the enormity of the Olympics had thrown them off their game.

"As much as you train and as much as people have talked to you about what the Olympics have in store for you, it's a different tournament altogether," Fry said. "There are nerves and there's anxiety and doubt, and you've got to wash all of those things out of your head to be able to perform your best."

The biggest key was not getting ahead of themselves. There was more to this whole thing than just winning a gold medal — you had to get there first — and right at that moment they were living dangerously in terms of even making the playoffs.

"The discussion we had when we went 1-2 was, 'Okay guys, let's forget about what this is, the importance of it, the magnitude, the massive stage that the Olympics is, and let's just get back to playing one game at a time, one shot at a time, which got us here,'" E.J. Harnden said. "That's what we did at the Trials."

"Our confidence wasn't lacking. You know these events are going to be a grind. We breezed through the Trials, so to speak, in terms of not having any losses. We were very fortunate going into that event, thinking we were going to pick up at least a couple of losses here or there, to come through without a blemish on our record. But you know going into an event like the Olympics, the same thing is going to happen. We prepared ourselves coming in by knowing it was going to be tough and expecting that we may drop one or two here or there. You have to grind."

In fact, they all viewed themselves as a plugging type of team, much more akin to the New Jersey Devils of the 1990s than the Edmonton Oilers of the 1980s. This was actually their type of tournament, with a little adversity early on to get them into it. The Canadian curlers said their path to success at the Brier, where they squeaked into the playoffs and then won three straight games against favoured opponents, was much more their style than going undefeated at the Olympic Trials.

"There's nothing wrong with a good grind in a week of curling . . . we like it," Jacobs said. "When we lost those two games, we regrouped. We talked a lot. We talked with our coaches, and we discovered what we needed to do in order to be better at this event, and that was to bring a lot more energy to each and every shot, each and every game. Kind of the same energy and intensity we had at the Olympic Trials, throughout the Brier playoffs."

The next day, Wednesday, February 12, brought a significant turning point for the Canadians. Jacobs and his teammates had only one game that day and it was in the evening, which meant they had been off the ice for more than 24 hours. The game was against the host Russian team, skipped by Andrey Drozdov. The Russians were 0-3 already and had been in some wild games, losing 7-4 to Great Britain, 11-10 to Denmark and 9-8 to Norway. One thing they had going for them was massive support, and the Canadians knew the crowd was going to be a factor. However, in this instance, it would not be the same distraction as it had been in other draws. This time the crowd's attention would be entirely focused on the sheet where Canada was playing. Spontaneous cheers at odd times would be a problem for the curlers on other sheets. Given their desire to get more amped up, to make energy and intensity a bigger part of their game plan, the atmosphere in the Ice Cube that night was perfect.

"It got us pumped," Ryan Harnden said. "We just haven't been on our game. We've been struggling with rocks, ice . . . but tonight was normal Team Jacobs."

Canada got off to a great start, stealing two in the first end and then scoring four with the hammer in the fifth to take a commanding lead on the way to a 7-4 victory. This time the lowest curling percentage on the team belonged to Fry at 88 percent. This was the kind of performance Canadians expected from their curlers and the curlers expected from themselves.

"It was nice to take the crowd out of the game with that four-ender," Jacobs said. "It was nice to see all of us with the same intensity that we have had at the Brier, at the worlds and at the Trials."

There was a moment in that game that could be looked back on as a major turning point for the Jacobs team. The Harnden brothers and their cousin were sniping at one another, as family members are wont to do. There was some frustration building after the slow start, and the brothers were questioning some of the skip's decision making.

Fry picked up on the tension and made a quick move to diffuse the situation. "In the fourth game, he basically shut E.J. and Ryan Harnden down," CBC analyst Mike Harris said. "He said, 'You are not to speak to Brad for the rest of this game,' and then Brad kind of calmed down all of a sudden. Ryan [Fry] went back to the coach's bench and told Rick Lang and Tom Coulterman and Caleb [Flaxey], their fifth player, what he was doing. From that moment forward, there was a huge change in the team. Ryan and E.J. were kind of losing their marbles a bit early in the game and Ryan Fry just kind of laid down the law. 'You two guys just shut the hell up and let Brad call the game!' and they did. From that point forward they just got better and better. It was really interesting for me, a great study in team dynamics."

Of course, beating a Russian team that had no chance of qualifying for the playoffs in such a strong field was not much to get excited about. Nor was a 2-2 record for a gold-medal favourite. But feeling more like themselves definitely was. Their next game was against Denmark, skipped by Rasmus Stjerne, and it was far from easy. Jacobs had to make a draw with his last rock in the tenth end to score one and record a 7-6 victory. Before that, some of the old frustration crept back in. A few broom slams and expletives came from a Canadian side that struggled again with poorly matched rocks and tricky ice. Ryan Harnden, in particular, had a rough game, finishing at just 71 percent, but his skip had his back. Jacobs explained that in trying to deal with what they believed to be wonky rocks, the Canadians gave them to Harnden to throw.

"Being the lead, he might get dumped a pig here or there, or a faster or slower, or a curlier or straighter rock." Jacobs said. "It's figuring that out, and then I ice them properly and he adjusts."

Despite some struggles and a sense the Canadians were still nowhere near their best, they had won two in a row and had a winning record overall. It was a good game to build off, and it brought confidence and a bit of swagger back to their game. No one wanted to admit they were scared by what happened the previous two days, but the relief at being back on track was evident.

"I think we're real close now," E.J. Harnden said. "The emotion is there. We're not quite where we want to be, but we're right there, right on the cusp of bringing that Trials game back. Our team has been known for fighting through adversity. The Trials are the only time we've come through and done it the easy way. For us, we kind of laughed it off and said, 'It's par for the course and let's go out and get it done.'"

There was a quick turnaround after the night game against Russia and an early-morning date with Norway, the team with the colourful pants skipped by Thomas Ulsrud. This time Ryan Harnden curled 99 percent, and the Canadians absolutely dominated against a medal contender. A 10-4 win and the rest of the day off was just what the Canadians needed as they could now relax a bit with three straight wins in their pockets and a kind of momentum that had been missing since the end of the Olympic Trials.

The following day, February 16, they got their first look at David Murdoch's team from Great Britain. Murdoch was a long-time veteran of the curling wars and had a stellar resume; among his accomplishments were two world championship gold medals (2006, 2009) to go along with two silver and two bronze, three European championships and two world junior titles. He was competing in his third Olympics and was also a regular fixture on the World Curling Tour cash circuit. Raised in Lockerbie, Scotland, and a witness to the infamous bombing and crash of Pan Am Flight 103 in 1988, the 35-year-old Murdoch had a lifetime of experience to rely on as he pursued his first Olympic medal.

Just 10 years old at the time, Murdoch was in his father's car when pieces of the airplane started to rain down on his hometown. A total of 270 people were killed, including 11 on the ground.

"I was about 300 yards away and I saw it come down," he said. "I was in a car driving back home. I was on an adjacent street. It was just like a bomb going off. They used the rink as a morgue and a lot of troops were using our farm to land on. There were lots of bodies scattered all over Lockerbie, so they were using the farm to put the Chinooks down."

More than a quarter-century later, that day was still on Murdoch's mind, and he was desperately hoping to give something back to Lockerbie, namely an Olympic medal.

"No one can forget what happened. It's a real nice town with a lot of good people in it, and I'd love to walk through there with an Olympic medal."

Murdoch and his mates entered the game with a 5-1 record and looked to be strong medal contenders. A win against Canada would put them in the driver's seat for a playoff spot and put Jacobs and his teammates in a precarious position. It was as crucial a game as you can get in the middle of a round robin, and it turned out to be one of the sloppiest games of the tournament. Both teams were plagued by debris on the ice as rocks picked and went askew before reaching their intended targets, and players from each team, including the skips, missed key shots. Frustration showed throughout the game and was most noticeable in the ninth end when Jacobs had a chance to hit and stick for two points but watched as his shooter rolled out of the house.

"That shouldn't have happened!" Jacobs yelled for all to hear.

The miss left Great Britain down just 6-5 and with the hammer coming home, which was a nerve-wracking scenario for a Canadian team that couldn't seem to do anything easily — the rocks, the ice and their own shot-making all letting them down. The trouble continued in the tenth end with more rocks picking, and Murdoch ending up with a golden opportunity to at least tie the game and perhaps win it outright with his last rock. Indeed, Murdoch attempted a double takeout with his last that would have given him two points and the crucial victory. The rock over-curled just slightly and Canada wound up stealing a point by the narrowest of margins to win the game and improve to 5-2.

"If it had just curled that one millimeter more," Murdoch said. "It was pretty heart-breaking."

As he slid down the ice to shake hands with his opponents and celebrate with his teammates, Jacobs rubbed his face in a fashion that suggested his team got away with one.

"Relief," he said in the mixed zone after the game. "Complete and total relief. We got lucky. That was the most nervous feeling this week."

It was an uncharacteristic game for the Canadians. They had lots of chances to make big shots but were just off the mark. They were in control for the most part but never far from being in trouble.

"When the opportunities presented themselves, we kind of let them off the hook a couple of times, and I think the guys would agree with that assessment," national team coach Rick Lang said. "In the end, David Murdoch had a shot to win and I think we got extremely fortunate there. But, we had two rocks that picked in the tenth end as if it was hairs from a hair brush. It wasn't like they just over-curled. They picked almost off the sheet.

"So kudos to the guys for making David throw his last shot. Nothing's a gimme in this game. It was good that they were able to bear down and not give up in that game even though they were frustrated with their own performance."

Lucky or not, the Canadians were moving up the standings and, at 5-2, were tied with Great Britain for third place behind surprising China and gold-medal contender Sweden, both 6-1, heading into their final day of round-robin play. The next morning Jacobs made it 6-2 with an 8-6 win over the United States, which set up another huge round-robin game against the Chinese, skipped by Rui Liu and coached by Canadian Marcel Rocque. The Chinese coach was no stranger to any Canadian curler. Rocque won four Canadian championships and three world titles while playing lead for Edmonton's Randy Ferbey. Rocque, 42, had done wonders with the Chinese team, turning them into Olympic medal contenders in his first season.

"Coming in I told them I couldn't promise or guarantee any kind of performance, any kind of medal," Rocque said. "You can't promise that stuff. I said I would promise them that I would have them ready to be at the best of their abilities, and they would not have any regrets after this experience."

Rocque took a leave of absence from his job as a school teacher in Edmonton and started working with the Chinese men's and women's teams at the beginning of July 2013. While Chinese women's skip Bingyu (Betty) Wang was the 2009 world champion, the men's team grew immensely under Rocque's tutelage. China was hosting the world championship in Beijing in April 2014, and the hope was Rocque would have a team ready to make some noise. It happened much earlier than expected with the men's team.

"It was a difficult decision to take the job. But I still stick to it," Rocque told the *Toronto Star*. "The reason that I made the decision is that curling needs to be healthy everywhere. And I feel good that hopefully this gives a boost in the arm to curling in China."

Nobody would have anticipated China having a 6-1 record heading into the matchup with Canada, but at least there was no chance the Canadians would underestimate their opponent. Jacobs and his teammates were due an off-day on the final day of the round robin, so there was no way they were going to leave anything to chance. As it turned out, the slugfest that developed with China was the perfect precursor to what was sure to be a laborious playoff round. Canada fell behind 6-3 after giving up three in the fifth end and a steal of one in the sixth but stormed back with a deuce in the seventh, a steal of one in the eighth to tie the game and a steal of two in the ninth to take an 8-6 lead. The Chinese were not to be outdone, however, and they scored a deuce of their own in the tenth to force an extra end and put all kinds of pressure on Jacobs in the eleventh. With two Chinese rocks biting the button, Jacobs needed to prove his mettle with his last rock in the extra, faced with a nail-biting draw to the pin. He coolly let go of the shot, allowed the Harnden brothers to do the work with the brooms and drew full button to give Canada a hard-fought 9-8 victory. If the Opening Ceremony was his "Welcome to the Olympics" moment, this was his coming out party in the curling tournament. It was the kind of high-pressure shot the great skips make at the big moments.

"Brad was able to draw the pin, and that was great for us," Fry said. "We have all the confidence in the world for Brad to be able to make those last shots, and he's got all the confidence in himself. The more opportunities you have to throw those and make them, I think it just seasons you as a skip over the years. We know the type of player he is, and there is no one else that the three of us would want throwing those shots for us."

The round robin was over for Canada, and with a 7-2 record they were destined for the semifinals. First off, they had a glorious two-day break ahead of them. By a quirk of the schedule, Canada's round-robin bye came on the last day, Monday, February 17. Tiebreakers were slated for Tuesday, and the semifinals were scheduled for Wednesday. The Swedes wound up grabbing first place with an 8-1 record, while Canada and China were both 7-2. Great Britain and Norway tied for fourth at 5-4 and had to play a tiebreaker — which Great Britain won — on Tuesday. That meant Canada would face China in one semifinal, while the Swedes would take on Great Britain.

While the other teams were battling it out during that two-day break, the Canadians were unflappable. They had faced so much adversity early in the tournament, but now they were on a six-game winning streak despite having played so many close games that could have gone either way. They kicked back a bit and hung around the Athletes' Village, playing floor hockey, ping pong and video games. They visited with their wives and girlfriends and did some light work in the gym, their usual routine.

"We're pretty loose right now," Fry said on the team's blog during the time off. "I've been trying to shut down and be quiet and relax. We know the intensity's going to start kicking up real high. Right now, it's just about being as relaxed as possible."

"The couple of days off really helped our team," Jacobs added. "We needed the rest, we all needed the rest. We literally didn't do a whole lot other than lie around our room, go to the cafeteria and eat, go to the gym and exercise, and it was so key for our team to get that rest. Everybody came out there rejuvenated and you could tell that the rest paid off."

It was amazing to see the team so relaxed now that they were on the cusp of playing for a medal, when they'd been so tight and out of sorts at the start of the tournament. It was all about mindset, and the curlers admitted theirs was all wrong. They got caught up in the excitement, in the expectations, in the pure adrenalin that powered the wave of momentum they were riding.

"I think coming in, it was a little too much gold, gold, gold," E.J. Harnden said. "That was the expectation not only from the majority of Canada and the curling world, but ourselves as well. So it was just getting that out of our minds."

"Coming here you try to fake it that you're not feeling that pressure," Jacobs chimed in. "But as you go through everything and get closer to the Olympics, you start to feel it, and I think when we got here, we really felt it. So we just had to go back to basics and realized we had to play our guts out, and I think we're in a lot better state mentally, now. We've always been the team that does it the hard way, and we're doing it the hard way again here."

Only China was standing in the way of a guaranteed medal for Canada, a country that had never finished with less than silver in four previous Olympics. It was a most unexpected matchup, but the Canadians knew from their round-robin game that their opponents were no pushovers. The semifinal was on Wednesday, February 19, and started about two hours after Jennifer Jones and her Winnipeg teammates guaranteed themselves a podium finish with a win over Great Britain's Eve Muirhead. The Canadian men looked focused as they came onto the ice, and yet you could sense that much of the tension from the round robin was gone. For the better part of the year, they had been saving their best for the biggest games, and it was obvious they were ready to leave everything out on the ice.

This time the game was not particularly close. Canada was in control from the beginning, leading 4-2 after five ends and cracking a three in the seventh to break it wide open. The Chinese hung in with a deuce in the eighth to make it 7-6, but Canada scored another three in the ninth and ran the opponent out of rocks in the tenth to win 10-6. They curled 90 percent as a team, one of their best marks of the entire tournament. As remarkable as it seemed, the Canadians had gone through an entire round robin and lost only two games without ever putting their best foot forward. That, they saved for the semifinal.

"They finally showed up," Rick Lang said. "That's the team we expected a lot earlier in the week. That's not an insult. I'm just really glad that the A-team showed up at the critical time. If you look back at the last couple of years, in big, big games, they've been the best team and they've beaten everybody."

In the last game of the round robin and the semifinal, the Canadians truly showed what they were made of. Their full arsenal was on display and they made all the shots, from big-weight doubles and triples to finesse draws. It was the kind of curling that made them unbeatable in Canada, the world's most powerful curling nation, and it was making them look unstoppable now that they were rolling at the Olympics. Again, Jacobs attributed the surge to overcoming early hardship and playing in a bunch of close games.

"That adversity helped us out a lot. Going into that last game there, I don't think any of us were nervous at all. That's because of everything we faced this week. We won games by an inch, so it was a different feeling heading into that game. I really thought we'd be a lot more nervous, but nobody was.

"We've got a lot of fight in us, a lot of resilience and perseverance. We're not afraid to be in a close game and have to make our last one to win. I really like that we've had a lot of close games."

The Canadians had guaranteed themselves a medal and kept the country's string of silver-or-better going, and there was some satisfaction in that. They would stand on the podium on Friday and go to a medal ceremony at the Olympic Village plaza a day later. The only question now was which level would they stand on and which colour would they wear around their necks.

"It's great for the sport in Canada that we're guaranteed a medal and Jennifer's team is guaranteed a medal," Jacobs said. "There's a lot of pressure on the Canadian teams to come here and perform well. To get another medal for all of Team Canada is a great feeling. At the same time, we want to come out and get that gold. All I can tell you and promise you is we will be giving it everything we've got and leaving it all out on the ice in the final."

While some members of the team vowed to enjoy the semifinal win for a night and then start focusing on the final the following day, lead Ryan Harnden would have none of it.

"To be honest, I've probably forgotten about the semifinal already," he said, just minutes after the game against China. "We came in here and we want to win the gold medal. We've won at least a silver and we're somewhat satisfied with that but, in the end, we really want the gold. We came here to win the gold."

For Fry, who had been given so much credit for being a calming influence on Jacobs and his two cousins, there was also a strong family connection at the Olympics. His parents, Barry and Judy, were in the stands and he loved visiting with them whenever the opportunity arose. Clearly, by this time, The Snake was simply a fan, knowing that his son could handle himself on the pebble. "My dad lays pretty low when it comes to my curling," Ryan Fry wrote on his blog. "We've had tons of conversations over the years, and when we get together, it's the main focus of our conversations, but we haven't spent a whole lot of time talking about it here because he doesn't like to get too involved in that side of it. But it's definitely nice having both of my parents here because it's a calming influence, and I don't think this would mean as much if I didn't have them here to share it with."

The gold medal game was set for Friday, February 21, against old foe David Murdoch from Great Britain. Murdoch had finished the round robin with a 5-4 record, then beat Norway in a tiebreaker and stunned gold-medal favourite Sweden, a team that entered the game with only one loss, in the semifinal. That meant the day after the semifinal was another day off for the Canadians, while the women's bronze and gold medal games went on at the Ice Cube Curling Center. The schedule was extremely kind to the Jacobs team, with three days off and only two games over five days since their round robin ended. Thursday, February 20, was anything but uneventful, however. It started with some astounding, curious comments from an opposing coach and ended with perhaps the most inspiring moment of the entire Olympics for Canadians.

With the women's games slated for the afternoon and evening, men's practices were scheduled for the early morning at the Ice Cube. The Canadians looked loose as they stepped on the ice and threw stones, matching them as best they could so there would be no surprises in the gold medal game. There was little left to do but go out and play, and now the key was to enjoy the day of rest while keeping focus on the enormous challenge that lay before them. It was after Murdoch's team practiced that things took a surprising turn.

A Swede named Soren Gran, whom Murdoch credited with turning his career around, coached the Great Britain team. Gran had previously been coach of both the Norwegian and Swedish national teams and had joined Great Britain in 2011 with an eye on Sochi 2014. He was a competitive curler himself, who'd won a world junior championship in 1982 and played in the Olympics for Sweden in 1992 and 1994 when curling was a demonstration sport. His timing, however, left something to be desired.

Gran held court with the media that day, most of them British reporters who are always looking for a scandal or an opportunity to ratchet up a controversy. For some reason, the coach chose that day to take a hard swipe at the Canadians for their brash style of curling, everything from their fist pumps to their broom slams to Jacobs's habit of running down the ice after his rock on occasion. Bulletin board material in curling seemed almost unheard of, but here it was, on the day before the gold medal game, coming from a trash-talking coach.

"The aggressive style we have seen from the Canadians here, that's something I don't like about the sport," Gran said. "I don't think it helps anyone. It doesn't help the player and it doesn't help his teammates. I tell my guys to work a different way. If they miss a shot, they've got another 15 to play. You can't be angry with the one you miss. If I see the team we are playing against get aggressive and show anger, I think our guys should be happy because we'd have them exactly where we want them to be."

There's no question the Jacobs team's style is light-years away from the staid Brits, who take purism seriously. Murdoch is as laid back as they come, and the suggestion in the British media was that the Jacobs team was trying to intimidate opponents with their antics. As absurd a notion as it sounded, there's no question the Jacobs team was the most intimidating in the Olympic field, but mostly because they are all deadly hitters who aren't afraid to try any shot. There would be no apologies from Canada for their style.

"I think what works well for us is that we bring a lot of intensity out there," Jacobs said. "That's our style. That's the type of people we all are." Jacobs was also asked if his team's behaviour was designed to bully or intimidate opponents. "You would have to ask other teams that," he replied. "I don't know whether we are bullies or intimidating. I really don't know."

If Jacobs and his teammates were aware of or bothered by Gran's comments at that time, they certainly didn't let on, but at some point that day, they heard about it. Needless to say, it didn't sit well, and it brewed in their stomachs until the following day. As if this team needed a reason to get more fired up for the gold medal game.

They spent the rest of that day doing light work in the gym, resting and relaxing in the Athletes' Village, and finally settling in to watch the women's curling gold medal game on television. While they wanted to go to the game to support Jones and her teammates, the Canadian men didn't want to get too caught up in the moment when they had one of their own coming the next day. They watched as

Jones engaged in a close battle with Sweden's Margaretha Sigfridsson, until the ninth end when Jones made a great draw to steal two and take a 6-3 lead. At the point, Jacobs turned off the TV.

"We watched until we were sure they were going to win," he said. "We didn't want to see the presentation or anything like that before we had the opportunity to do the same thing." The Jacobs boys put on their Team Canada jackets and headed out for the short walk to the Bolshoy Ice Dome, where Canadian history was about to be made.

Canada's women's hockey team entered the Olympic tournament as slight under-dogs to the Americans, even though they were three-time defending gold medallists. The Americans were the more dominant team in 2013 however, and an epic battle for gold was expected between the only true contenders in the women's field. For 56 minutes and 34 seconds the game was all Team USA, which had not won a gold medal since the inaugural women's tournament in 1998. Brianne Jenner got the Canadians on the board with just 3:26 left in the third period and Marie-Philip Poulin, who was also a hero in Vancouver in 2010, tied the game with 55 seconds left. That set the stage for overtime, where Poulin scored again eight minutes in to give Canada an improbable comeback and a fourth straight Olympic gold medal.

"That was absolutely incredible, and that pumped us all up," Jacobs said. "That was so inspiring. To watch them win in that way just fired us all up to go out and get the job done for us as well."

Buoyed by the success of the women's hockey and curling teams, the Jacobs four-some arrived for work on gold-medal Friday feeling as confident as ever and with a bit of anger simmering just below the surface. If history was any indication, a little ire wasn't a bad thing. The British coach's comments were not sitting well, and everyone on the Jacobs side was eager to show some swift Canadian justice. You wouldn't have known that when they took to the ice for their pre-game practice session.

"In practice they were playing waltzes out there," Rick Lang said with a laugh. "And the guys spent more time trying to convince the guy on the sound system to pump some music at them rather than concentrating on practice. They like that house music. They want it on as loud as possible."

Once the game began, the Canadians were all business. In fact, they looked almost uncharacteristically subdued — no fist bumps, no loud exclamations, no broom slams. It looked like a response to the criticism levelled upon them by Soren Gran, but it may have just been that nothing was going to affect their focus and determination. With a gold medal this close to their grasp, the Jacobs foursome that could not be beaten in Canada showed up in Sochi. David Murdoch, with his six world championships and three Olympic appearances, looked like a deer in the headlights.

Murdoch was carrying a heavy load himself. Winter Olympic gold medals are not commonplace for Great Britain and, in fact, they had just one to that point in Sochi, from skeleton racer Elizabeth Yarnold. Murdoch was also playing for the memory of those who lost their lives in the Lockerbie disaster and was dealing with the added stress caused by his coach's ill-timed comments. Added up, his team had no chance against a Canadian team that was curling lights out and had a take-no-prisoners attitude. Canada scored a deuce with the hammer in the first end, added another three in the third and stole one in the fourth for an insurmountable 6-1 lead. No one comes back from a deficit like that while playing a team that can hit like the Jacobs foursome, and especially when the skip curls 95 percent and the team curls 91 percent overall. The rest of the game was purely a coronation, until Jacobs scored one in the eighth to make it 9-3 and Murdoch took away all possible drama by conceding.

After such a beatdown, the Canadian celebration was understated to begin with. They politely shook hands with their opponents, then gathered for a group hug for the ages. Two brothers, their cousin and their best friend, sometimes thought of as another relative, celebrating an almost unthinkable achievement, an Olympic gold medal. They spied their beaming wives and girlfriends lurking at the edge of the ice surface and ran over to share long embraces. They waved to family and friends and supporters in the stands and soaked it all in, not wanting the moment to end.

The Canadians had something special planned for the podium flower ceremony — an in-unison jump up to the gold medal plateau — and just when it looked like the celebration was finally about to wind down, a Canadian flag was thrown their way from the stands. E.J. Harnden grabbed it, looked at his teammates and said, "Do you want to do a victory lap?" Jacobs could think of nothing he'd like to do more. "We can do whatever we want right now. Let's go!" They trotted around the Ice Cube Curling Center like hockey players with the Stanley Cup, letting the euphoria wash over them, knowing they had reached the pinnacle of their sport.

"They were like little kids running around out there," Rick Lang said. "It was amazing."

"The biggest word that comes to mind right now is relief," Jacobs said moments later when meeting the media. "I'm relieved that this is all over with, and we're Olympic gold medallists. Wearing that Maple Leaf, there are a lot of expectations. When we won the semifinal, I felt a huge weight off my shoulders — we all did — and now to go out and win the final and be gold medallists, that weight is completely gone and I feel total relief right now."

The Harnden brothers were feeling much different emotions. This was the moment E.J. and Ryan had been dreaming of since the minute they qualified for the Olympics, perhaps since they were little kids back in Sault Ste. Marie. They now knew that the following day they would be standing together, arm-in-arm on the top of the podium, receiving their gold medals. It was almost surreal.

"Absolutely amazing," E.J. Harnden said. "I watched the Dufour-Lapointe sisters back on the first day of the Olympics and I held back tears. They were standing there on the podium side-by-side and I thought that would mean the absolute world to me, to be able to do that with my brother.

"To do this with a cousin and a best friend in Ryan Fry is absolutely amazing but I'll never, ever, ever, ever, no matter what happens from here on out, forget the moment of standing on the podium with my brother."

"It's a dream come true, to be able to do it with your brother," Ryan Harnden added. "I don't think many people can say they've won an Olympic gold medal with family like that. To be able to do it with my brother — he's my best friend and I love him to death — it's just incredible."

Through all the moments of pure joy and the rush of excitement that came after the anticlimactic final, there was still a bit of an "In-your-face" aspect to the Canadians' performance. Jacobs and the boys had by no means forgotten about Soren Gran, the man who'd suggested just a day earlier that they were bad for the sport.

"We believe in karma, and what you saw out there today, after a comment like that, it's a pretty strange thing," Jacobs said. "I was aware of the comments and I don't think it was necessarily the right thing to say before a big final like that. I think it only gave us more motivation to go out there and win."

It was also a moment of sweet vindication for the team's nomadic third, Ryan Fry. Years of trying to fit in with teams and travelling the country to try to conjure up the right mix had finally paid off. The Winnipegger had devoted his entire life to curling, and now he was receiving the perfect reward.

"This is just one of those things where the stars aligned and it's a fairytale story," Fry said. "I gave everything I had to this sport, and I did it for a lot of years. I've taken a lot of losses and rebounded. I've gotten kicked off teams, I've left teams, and that comes with the territory, but if you commit and give everything you've got to something, eventually good things break for you."

Back home in Sault Ste. Marie, an estimated crowd of 2,500–3,000 was gathered at the Essar Centre, home of the Soo Greyhounds of the Ontario Hockey League, to watch Jacobs and the boys bring home the gold. They exploded into cheers when Jacobs clinched the win with a takeout in the eighth end, and many had tears in their eyes as they watched the Canadians celebrate their triumph on the ice halfway around the world. That kind of support back home was on the minds of the curlers just moments after they won the gold.

"So many emotions," E.J. Harnden said. "I just couldn't be more proud of our team and what we did. We had a rough start, but we stuck with it, we never gave up, we never doubted ourselves and our abilities, and neither did the rest of Canada. This is not just for us, not just for our team, not just for Sault Ste. Marie, it's for all of Canada, and we couldn't have done it without that support. No one doubted us, even when we were 1-2."

The many years of hard work, all the fitness training, the weightlifting, the mental preparation, the time with a sports psychologist, the time on the road away from family, wives, girlfriends and jobs were all designed to bring the team to this exact moment. All the near misses and big losses of their careers seemed worth it now, learning experiences that had helped make them the world's greatest curling team. There was a determination about this team on gold-medal Friday that even the curlers themselves had never before experienced.

"It was a complete, 100 percent belief that this game was ours and that no one was gonna take it from us," E.J. Harnden said. "We had the defeat at the world championship last year and we felt that disappointment, not just for ourselves but for Canada as well. Curling is Canada's game and there was nothing that was going to hold us back, nothing that was going to stop us from winning this game."

"Who knows if we're ever gonna have this opportunity again," Jacobs added. "We wanted to go out, we wanted to attack, we wanted to make all our shots, play a textbook curling game. It all worked out well." The blowout in the gold medal game did a lot to take the edge off for the Canadians, left no room for broom shaking, yelling or any of the customary histrionics. "I'd rather not be like that, to be honest," Jacobs admitted with a broad smile. "Wide open shots for two or three are much better than having to make something and go crazy."

Canada finished with 10 gold medals in Sochi, down four from Vancouver 2010, and with one fewer medal overall, but as always, the curlers did their part. In 10 Olympic tournaments (five men's and five women's), Canada now had 10 medals, including five gold. One thing that had never happened before was double gold, and, thanks to the performance of Jennifer Jones and Brad Jacobs, that was another notch on the country's belt.

"To get double gold for Canada for the first time ever . . . we're very proud of that," Jacobs said. "To see Jen's team go out and win the gold medal for the women and then to come out and repeat as the men is just incredible. It was obviously meant to be."

So now they were Olympic champions, just 16 months after forming as a team, less than a year after winning their first Brier, just a few months after having to go through pre-trials and Olympic Trials against a field of curling superstars. The entire ride was magical, and it culminated with one of those moments that can simply never be forgotten.

"A lot of years from now, I'll look back on Sochi and I know I'll still get the chills," Jacobs said. "From start to finish, this was the experience of a lifetime."

CHAPTER ELEVEN

THE GREATEST OF THEM ALL

Before the Olympics were even over, the legacy of Jennifer Jones was already starting to take shape. The 39-year-old Winnipeg curler had done something only one Canadian woman had ever done before, and that was skip a team to an Olympic gold medal. The curling world was abuzz with talk about Jones and her teammates and, for at very least a few days, they were household names among sports fans across Canada. In a testament to just how meaningful the gold medal win was, Jones's name was bandied about as a potential flag bearer for Canada at the Closing Ceremony, and it would have been a fitting choice. Jones was the oldest athlete on the Canadian Olympic Team and had provided one of the best stories of the Games by reaching the top of the curling podium. All the while, she and her team-mates embodied the Olympic spirit, comporting themselves with equal amounts of wonder and professionalism as they cruised through the curling tournament with a perfect record.

Jones could barely hold in her emotions when she was told she was being considered for the flag-bearer role, which eventually went to two-time gold medal–winning bobsledders Kaillie Humphries and Heather Moyse.

"I can't even begin to describe that," she said. "Just to even be considered is a huge honour. I respect every single one of these athletes so much and to be in that category would be unbelievable. To be able to walk out with the flag in your hand for Canada, for this great country, at the Olympic Games, representing all these great athletes, would be the biggest honour in the world."

While the Canadian Olympic Committee decided to go in another direction with the flag-bearer choice, the kudos were coming in from around the curling world and beyond for the Jones team. The perfect record and gold medal at the Olympics meant Jones had won everything it's possible to win in the sport of curling. She added her greatest achievement to a previous world championship, four Canadian championships, junior titles and cash tour victories. Many people began to wonder where Jones would rank among the all-time greatest skips in women's curling, and at least one legendary Canadian curler placed her right at the top.

Colleen Jones (no relation) had won six Canadian championships of her own, the first in 1982, the last in 2004. She had appeared in the Scotties Tournament of Hearts 21 times, winning six gold medals, two silver and one bronze, and had two world championship gold medals and a silver in six attempts. The Halifax skip, now 54 and a curling analyst for CBC during the Olympics, did not hesitate for a second in anointing Jennifer Jones the best of the best.

"She's the greatest curler of all time," Colleen Jones said. "She's in a league of her own and she played like she was in a league of her own all week. Women's curling keeps evolving year after year. So it's not to take away from any past champions, it's just that right now it's at a terrific level and, with Jennifer, the cream has more than risen to the top, it's foaming."

Few great curling minds would suggest Colleen Jones doesn't know what she's talking about, but she received plenty of hate mail for her assessment. For many people it was almost sacrilegious to suggest any female skip could be greater than the late Sandra Schmirler, who'd won three Canadian championships and three world titles before dying of cancer at the age of 36. The world will never know what Schmirler might have done with a few more years to compete. Other curling fans pointed to the two Olympic gold medals won by Anette Norberg of Sweden and suggested it would be impossible to pick any other skip as the greatest of all time. Colleen Jones, however, was undeterred.

"We always look at Anette Norberg and Sandra Schmirler and they are great curlers but different times, different eras, different competitors," she said. "Jennifer Jones, when you look at the stats and the degree of difficulty of her shots, it's just kind of mind blowing what she did. Jennifer has been around for a long time and she has just consistently, year in, year out, just been one of the greatest players. Add this Olympic gold to her already terrific resume and she's just, for me, taking it to another level."

It's tough to argue against the brilliance of Schmirler, who won more world titles in a shorter time than Jones, but the case against Norberg can be made fairly easily. Though a truly great skip, Norberg never had to deal with trying to play her way out of Canada just to get to the world stage. It is a far easier task to get to the Olympics and world championships through Sweden. Canadian curlers like Jones have to slug it out with dozens of the best teams in the world each year just to get out of their own country.

You could easily make a case for Colleen Jones herself to be in the mix as the greatest of all time, but veteran broadcaster would have none of it. Having just watched Jennifer Jones reel off 11 wins, many of them in dominant fashion, Colleen Jones was convinced.

"She's got a great team in front of her, but the shots she made, game after game, end after end, some of them all you could say was 'Wow,'" Colleen Jones said. "She won in such impressive fashion. Undefeated, pressure shots, she played a highly aggressive game so her degree of difficulty on every shot is super hard. There's no shot she can't make, but it's her ability to do it time and time again under pressure. She's just at a whole other different level."

There's no doubt Jennifer Jones's teammates would agree. Second Jill Officer called her "Absolutely, 100% the best ever," while third Kaitlyn Lawes and lead Dawn McEwen expressed similar sentiments. Jones herself was immensely flattered.

"It's quite surreal to me to have somebody who has won as much as her and somebody that I respect and admire as much as Colleen Jones to say such inspiring comments about myself and our team," Jennifer Jones said. "I think it's very flattering and kind of took my breath away because it came from her and somebody that I respect so much."

Colleen Jones was not the only one to place the Manitoba skip in such elite company. TSN curling analyst Cathy Gauthier, who once played lead for Jennifer Jones and won a Canadian championship, said it's impossible to say there's one clear person who has been the best curler in the world. She would look at three players that would definitely be right up there, for different reasons.

"One of them is certainly Colleen Jones," Gauthier said. "I don't know that anyone will ever win the number of Canadian championships that she did and over the period of time that she did, which is something that's really important. There's longevity to it, and that says consistency and a ton of work.

"I definitely put Sandra Schmirler up there, and we'll never know what Sandra could have done. With her Canadian championships, she managed to always convert them into world championships and won an Olympic gold. The other thing that Sandra did is she changed the face of curling. She was winning in an era where we went to free guard zone and she pushed teams. Sandra just wouldn't let teams be defensive. It forced teams to play the game the way that the rule was intended to have it."

The third team Gauthier would put in the mix is the one skipped by Jennifer Jones.

"Not only has she won a ton — she's owned the Scotties Tournament of Hearts final weekend for a long time — and now winning the gold medal, and the way that she played was so incredible. I was so proud and so happy for her because she just rose above the level that she had played at, which was brilliant in winning Canada, but she's had some struggles with world play over the years.

"She also, in my opinion, does a lot to the game that Sandra did as well, which is she will not let teams run it up and down and play defensive, she just will not. She doesn't care what you do, she'll ignore it and force the free guard zone. I look at the women that are the best we've ever had as not only having longevity and not only having success but also pushing their opponents to do what the game was designed to do — to really demonstrate the abilities of the entire team. I think if Jennifer keeps playing for a few more years, this conversation doesn't even happen, she just surpasses everybody else based on results to date, plus some longevity. Right now I'd say she's absolutely at the top, amongst others."

Two-time world men's curling champion Jeff Stoughton watched the Olympics closely and, being from Winnipeg, had a particular interest in what the Jones team was doing. What impressed him most was the way Jones refused to let anything bother her, blocked out all distractions and simply zeroed in on the gold medal. There were a few games during the Olympics where her teammates weren't performing as well as expected, and Jones never let on that it was a big deal, made sure her team knew it wasn't an issue and showed she would take care of it all with cool game calling and precision shooting.

"To me, during that Olympic run, she was the best curler in the world, men or women," Stoughton said. "It was the best performance I've ever seen . . . it was unbelievable. It's just that self-confidence and knowing that with your abilities, you can do anything and just being so comfortable out on the ice and in that atmosphere, that made her by far the best skip anyone has seen in a long time."

Mike Harris, the CBC curling analyst who'd won a silver medal in curling at the 1998 Winter Olympics in Nagano, Japan, said it wasn't just the fact that people were saying Jennifer Jones was the best women's curler in the world, but who was saying it. He worked in Sochi with Colleen Jones and Joan McCusker, who played second on Schmirler's team at the peak of its greatness, and heard them talking about Jennifer Jones many times. "Both Joan and Colleen Jones said to me that they believe Jennifer is now the best women's skip to ever play the game," Harris said. "Coming from them has a lot more credibility than it does coming from me, but I think that speaks volumes.

"Jen's been around a long time, even though she's still young. She's been winning for a lot of years but she had only won the one world championship prior to 2014. Winning that Olympic gold medal now kind of puts all of that stuff behind her. That gold medal puts her over the top. When you get people like Colleen Jones and Joan McCusker saying it, it kind of solidifies that reputation. There's not a lot left for her to do.

"I admire her a lot for being able to continue to strive to maintain that high level of play. Her legacy is set forever, I would say."

All this talk was extremely humbling for Jones, the shy girl from Winnipeg who was somehow driven to be the best in the world. While she certainly didn't deny that her name belongs in the mix as the all-time best — she obviously recognizes how hard it is to win in today's curling world — she was quick to pass the credit around.

"I do know that I've been on some amazing teams and have achieved some amazing dreams and successes, and it's because of my teammates," she said. As for having her name in the mix with some of the curling legends, Jones said it's tough to make the comparison.

"Sandra Schmirler was tremendous in their run [three world championships, Olympic gold medal], Anette Norberg won two Olympic gold medals," Jennifer Jones said. "Colleen Jones, the longevity of her career is unbelievable. There's so many great players in our game, so I don't know if you can ever pick one. There's so many different eras in curling. To be even considered as one of the best is a true honour for me."

What sets Jones apart from almost any other curler on the planet is singular focus and determination mixed with a deep knowledge of the game's strategy and an ability to execute. Others certainly share those qualities, but with Jones, she is just so smart, it almost looks easy.

"She always has that focus when she's on the ice," Brent Laing said of his girlfriend. "You don't win as many events and Canadian championships as she has without that focus. She's an extreme competitor when she's out there. She's a totally different person off the ice but when it comes time to play, she's always ready. As much or more than anybody I've ever met."

There were so many things going through her mind that it was hard to think about things like where she fit into the grand scheme of things or what the future might hold for her. At that moment, all Jones could think about was that little girl waiting for her back in Canada and the family that had made so many sacrifices for her to get to this point.

"Winning a gold medal at the Olympics takes so much time, so much hard work and so much sacrifice, and so much support from your friends and family," she wrote on the COC blog. "I couldn't wait to hug Brent tonight at Canada Olympic House. The same goes for my parents, Larry and Carol. I threw so many practice rocks with my dad — when I threw my last shot (in the gold medal game), it was almost like he was at the other end holding the broom for me."

They marched in the lavish Closing Ceremony at Fisht Olympic Stadium, alongside Canadian hockey heroes Hayley Wickensheiser and Marie-Philip Poulin, who won an epic gold medal in Sochi. It was a thrill to mingle with the other elite athletes, many of whom approached the curlers to congratulate them and thank them for providing inspiration with their perfect Olympics.

"We're just glad we could help with the medal standings and glad that we can be part of the greater team and greater achievement of the Canadian Olympic Team," Officer said. "We did talk to the hockey girls and the women's hockey coach, who said some of them caught the end of our game just before their warm-up and said it made them ready to go, ready to fight, and that was cool for us to hear that story afterward, after they won the gold medal. It's amazing how much watching the other athletes motivates you to win and to achieve. For us to be a part of that and actually motivate others is quite bizarre but very, very cool."

As much as they wanted to get home to see their children, their families and friends, the Canadians didn't want the Olympics to end. The experience had been so perfect and it would be so difficult to ever get there again.

"It's pretty cool to celebrate with Jonathan Toews and Sidney Crosby and have them tell you how they watched our game and how inspiring it was to them," Jones said. "Now I'm gonna go see my little girl and just enjoy being home in Canada."

The Canadians left Sochi on Monday, February 24, and headed for Winnipeg, where a few hundred supporters were gathering at James Armstrong Richardson International Airport. The Olympic heroes touched down in Winnipeg just after 10 p.m. and were piped down the escalator to the arrivals area, where a red carpet was waiting for them. Fans, young and old, waved flags, held up signs and broke into impromptu choruses of "O Canada."

"We could hear them cheering as soon as we got off the plane, so we knew this was going to be something incredible," Lawes said, above the din in the packed airport. Four Mounties in full uniform escorted them into the greeting area, where Winnipeg Mayor Sam Katz was among the supporters.

"It's so nice to be home," Jones said. "It's incredible to see so many people here and to come back to Winnipeg. We said it was because all of Winnipeg and Canada that we are on top of the podium because the support we received was absolutely phenomenal and we can't thank everybody enough.

"To bring this gold medal back to Winnipeg feels pretty good, I'm not going to lie. Winnipeg is the best place in the world, even though it's minus 30-something outside."

They laughed and cried with family, acquaintances and complete strangers, doled out high fives and videobombed one another's interviews. Nobody wanted to the moment to end.

"It's an overwhelming feeling right now," Jill Officer said after getting a long hug from her brother Rob. "And this unbelievable greeting at the airport is something. This is unbelievable that so many people came out later in the evening to welcome us home and share in this success. We brought this gold medal home to show everybody, and we're just so thrilled."

The thrill was mutual for the fans who showed up just to catch a glimpse of these curling heroes. They were in awe of the Jones team, this group of women from Winnipeg who rose from such humble beginnings to become international stars.

"This is fabulous," Brenda Smith, an attendee to the welcoming event, said. "I couldn't be more proud, especially with being from Winnipeg, and I love the sport of curling. It's a true honour."

The moment had to end sometime, and eventually the crowd started to disperse and the Jones team had a chance to go home. Jones spoke of a new goal as the gold medallists prepared to leave.

"Try to get some sleep and see my baby girl, who I miss," she said. "We haven't slept a lot, so I think sleep will be our priority."

Try as they might, relaxation was not in their immediate future. Starting the day after they arrived home and continuing for a good month, the Jones team was in serious demand. They made TV and radio appearances, attended dinners and received awards and accolades everywhere they went. They posed for pictures and signed autographs on a daily basis, eager to let Canadians enjoy a bit of the magic they had experienced in Sochi. Almost immediately following their homecoming, the curlers got an idea of just how big they had become and how much they had transcended sport into popular culture. They were named as presenters for the Juno Awards, celebrating Canada's musicians, on March 30.

"When they came back and I heard that they were about to be invited to present an award at the Junos, I had a big smile," TSN's Cathy Gauthier said. "When your sport crosses over from a sport to the cultural side or something else, it says to me that you are more than just a curler. You're more than just an athlete, you've become an icon in this country. When they were introduced at the Junos, there were not many people in the audience who would look at each other and say 'Who are they?'

"As Canadians we're all so proud of them and I think the days of those guys being able to go anywhere without being recognized are long gone. And that's awesome."

The City of Winnipeg recognized the efforts of the Jones team immediately, renaming a street in its honour. Regal Avenue, now named Team Jones Way, is home to the St. Vital Curling Club, the team's home rink and the place where Jones had her modest beginnings in the sport.

On March 4, the Jones team was invited to the MTS Centre to drop the puck before a Winnipeg Jets game against the New York Islanders. As the four women stepped on the ice, one of the loudest crowds in hockey roared its approval, standing and cheering for several minutes. It was yet another surreal moment for a team that was pretty well known before going to Sochi but was now part of a city's very fabric. On March 8, they experienced a similar honour, this time at the Air Canada Centre in

Toronto, where the Maple Leafs were celebrating all of Canada's medallists. The curlers shared the spotlight that day with the likes of freestyle skier Alexandre Bilodeau, figure skaters Tessa Virtue and Scott Moir and bobsled champion Heather Moyse.

There were appearances at schools and curling clubs around Manitoba, endorsement offers and invitations to appear in commercials that ran throughout curling coverage on TSN the rest of the season. For the first week, they couldn't even open their email inboxes without crashing their computers or smartphones. Twitter wouldn't load on their devices either because there were so many tweets directed at them in the aftermath of the Olympics.

"The social media was crazy," Jones said. "We couldn't even keep up.

"We do this because we love to do it, and to feel the support of everybody over there was unbelievable. Then to come back and have little kids say that you're their hero and have people all over telling you what they were doing when they watched the gold medal game, you realize that you had this impact that you didn't set out to have but you're so honoured that you did.

"That is probably the greatest achievement that we've had."

To give a sense of the team's popularity, one night in early March, Officer attended the long-running Sons of Italy Gala along with 1,100 other Winnipeggers. As it was described by Mayor Sam Katz, "I swear she got her picture taken with every last one of them." Katz and the Mayor's office had their own honour in store for the team a few days later. Jones, Lawes, Officer and McEwen were presented with Outstanding Achievement medallions in a City Hall ceremony, and at the same time, the Royal Canadian Mint presented them with a framed 2014 Lucky Loonie to commemorate their Olympic victory.

"They were outstanding at the Olympics in Sochi," Katz gushed when asked to sum up the city's feelings for the Jones team. "They impressed the entire nation and made Olympic history by remaining undefeated throughout the Games. We're all proud of them for bringing home the gold and how well they represented us as athletes and ambassadors for our city."

In Winnipeg curling is one of the most popular sports in terms of participation and fan interest; it is only outshone by the Winnipeg Jets of the NHL and Blue

Bombers of the CFL. Many of the masses who help TSN, CBC and Sportsnet achieve big ratings during curling season reside in Manitoba. A Winnipeg band with an international pedigree even saluted the sport musically — the song "Tournament of Hearts" by the Weakerthans pays homage to the roots of curling, its rustic arenas, blue-collar history and love affair with brown beer bottles. For months, you couldn't turn on a TV or radio in Winnipeg without seeing or hearing Jones pitching for a local lottery or auto dealer. You won't find many Winnipeggers who don't know who Jennifer Jones and her teammates are, and there is no shortage of people lining up to shake their hands.

The province of Manitoba was next up, inducting Jones and her teammates into the Order of the Buffalo Hunt in a ceremony at the legislature. The Order of the Buffalo Hunt was established in 1957 as an honour for the province to bestow upon individuals or teams who do Manitoba proud through their service, efforts or achievements. Among those previously inducted were former United States president Jimmy Carter, music stars Randy Bachman and Burton Cummings and NHL stars Teemu Selanne and Jonathan Toews. "It's a great group of people all around the world," Manitoba Premier Greg Selinger said.

On March 30, the Jones team traded in curling outfits and Team Canada jackets — the ones they never wanted to take off — for evening dresses and walked the red carpet at the Juno Awards in Winnipeg. Rubbing shoulders with Canadian music icons like Serena Ryder, Jim Cuddy of Blue Rodeo and Tegan and Sara, the Jones team members were rock stars in their own right. As part of the Junos experience, they had some fun shooting a video with Saskatchewan rock band The Sheepdogs. The curling-themed video was shown during the Junos, which were watched by 1.4 million people on TV. When they were introduced to come on stage and present the Fan Choice Award, they received a one-minute standing ovation from a crowd of music fans. When they announced the award was going to Canadian music bad boy Justin Bieber, the crowd booed lustily. It spoke volumes about the popularity of the Jones team.

There were more honours on the way. Lawes represented the team at the Toronto Blue Jays home opener in early April, along with a handful of other Olympic medallists. Officer had a park in her home neighborhood of North Kildonan named after her as a commemoration for all her national and international success. "I'm very honoured," Officer said. "I played in that park a lot and walked through it every day to go to figure skating lessons." They tried to live normal lives, the way they would have before they became gold medallists, but it was impossible. A simple trip to the mall with her mother and daughter became a major challenge for Jones because so many people wanted to take a picture with her. On one business trip, Jones got her picture taken with every single person in the first-class section of the plane. While grateful for the genuine excitement people felt for her and her team-mates, Jones longed for a bit of anonymity in public places . . . but those days were long gone.

On May 21, Jones was named as a recipient of the Order of Manitoba and received the honour at a ceremony that included Prince Charles in Winnipeg. Among the other notable people receiving the honour that day were NFL player Israel Idonije, curling legend Don Duguid, who won consecutive world titles in the early seventies, and longtime voice of the Winnipeg Blue Bombers, Bob Irving.

More than anything, they made an impact. Almost immediately after the Olympics, Manitoba curling clubs were inundated with calls from people looking to sign up. The provincial governing body of the sport immediately recognized that there was a chance to get some mileage out of the historic Olympic run by four local women. They initiated open houses and spring curling programs — normally reserved for the beginning of the fall season — in order to give new fans of the game a chance to see where it all began for people like Jones, Lawes, Officer and McEwen.

"We think this is just going to bring a new level of interest to our sport," said Craig Baker, executive director of CurlManitoba. "They made history. To win an Olympic event with a perfect record is pretty remarkable. When you go and achieve your dream, they are definitely proud of it and they are sharing it with everybody, which is just going to help us grow and show young curlers what they can achieve. It *is* possible."

Over at the St. Vital Curling Club, where Jones cut her teeth and is still a member, they were planning to have a mural painted of the Olympic heroes. Those who run the club were obviously swelling with pride and were feeling the love themselves.

"This will be an inspiration to the kids that we have curling in our program and to juniors all across the province," said Guy Beaudry, who runs the junior program at St. Vital. "This pushes them farther. It's such a huge moment — the first team to go through the ladies side perfect. There's been so much publicity and I've been getting calls every day from parents wanting their kids to curl."

It's not just the Olympic gold medals that make Jones and her teammates inspiring figures. Their dedication to the sport goes far deeper than that and it's clear they get what it means to be looked up to.

"They're very approachable, very open and giving of their time, before the Olympics and after the Olympics," Baker said. "They know what it means to represent their city, their province, their country and the sport of curling. They are doing so much to continue to promote the sport and to develop the good sportsmanship that curling is known for. They're always willing to attend various events and show off the gold medal and talk to the people and share their experiences.

"I think there will be a spike in all of our programs and we're just going to continue to see that success."

There were so many people who'd played roles in the formation and growth of the team, in bringing it to this point — people like former leads Cathy Gauthier, Dana Allerton and Georgina Wheatcroft, fifth players Tricia Eck, Jennifer Clarke-Rouire and Kirsten Wall, coaches Elaine Dagg-Jackson, Janet Arnott and Earle Morris. One person who'd played a massive role in the development of the team was Cathy Overton-Clapham, but she went away on a holiday instead of watching her old teammates win gold in Sochi. Overton-Clapham and the Jones team had stopped communicating after the split in 2010, but the former third was doing her best to put the bitterness behind her, even if some still lingered. "It's over and done with . . . it's long gone," she said a couple of months after the Sochi Olympics. "How it went about is something that is still hurtful. Things happen and changes are made, you see it happening all the time now with the Olympics, it's just . . . yeah

. . . how it was done." That being said, Overton-Clapham could not deny that the Jones team was deserving of its success.

"Any time Canada is out there trying to win a medal, you are wanting them to win the gold," Overton-Clapham said. "There's no question they are a team that has worked harder than anyone else to get to that point. As far as Jen, Dawn and Jill go, I know how much time and commitment we put in. I can't say there was another team at those Olympics that was more deserving to win than they were. I certainly can vouch for how much time was spent away from home and family and everything else and it's nice to see it pay off for them.

"There's no question that watching the Olympics is hard when you're not there and you've been trying to be there. But I certainly know that there wasn't a team more deserving to win than they were."

While it took them until 2014 to finally put it all together, the Olympic gold medal was a decade in the making, from The Shot in St. John's to the Parody in Paisley to the world championship in Vernon to Olympic Trials disappointments in 2005 and 2009. "We learned a lot playing together," Overton-Clapham said. "I think that team is above and beyond everyone else because of all the building and learning we did as a team. I think Dawn McEwen is a big, big, big key to that team. She was good when she joined us, but now she's amazing."

Jones and her teammates were basking in the glow of their gold medals, enjoying the spoils of their fame and reliving every moment of the Olympic dream on a daily basis. Life had changed immeasurably for four regular people from Winnipeg. Jones in particular now had this iconic status and a reputation for fierce competitiveness, ruthlessness and iron will. The very thought of that made her laugh.

"I'm probably one of the most sensitive people that you'll ever meet," Jones said in an interview with CBC. "I'm still super shy and a lot of people don't realize that about me, but on the ice my role is to lead and try to inspire confidence out of the girls. Sometimes you have to fake it to make it and I've learned to do that. I've got a pretty thin shell around me but I've got a great support team and people that will pick me up when I'm down.

"I don't think of myself as a fierce competitor. If you ask my team I don't think they would say that either because I'm a big puddle. But I honestly never want to let my team down. At the end of the day it comes down to that. I don't want to let anybody in Canada down."

One person who never let Jones down was her longtime coach Janet Arnott, who joined the team in 2007 as a fifth player and wound up playing a season at lead before becoming an off-ice mentor. Arnott coached the team from 2008–10, when it won three Canadian championships and a world title. She was replaced by renowned curling coach Earle Morris in 2011 but hung around as a fifth player and returned as coach in 2012, staying on through the Olympics in Sochi. Coaches don't get medals at the Olympics but the 57-year-old Arnott deserved one in Jones's eyes.

"I don't want Janet to go forgotten," Jones said. "She's a huge member of our team. She's kind of my person on the ice. I make eye contact with her and it just gives me that feeling of confidence. We couldn't have done it without her."

Cathy Gauthier, who played with Arnott on a Canadian championship team in the 1990s, said the coach deserved much more credit than she received from the curling public.

"I'll see Janet out there holding the broom for the girls as they throw, and she provides that sort of coaching role, but I think besides doing those things, she's there to remind them that this is a choice and to have that passion for the game because it obviously makes you play a lot better," Gauthier said. "They went into the Olympics with that attitude. 'This is a great opportunity, let's enjoy it.' Not, 'this might be the only chance we ever get, so if we don't win, oh boy, we're in trouble.'

"It struck such a chord with me because playing with Janet in the past, she was very calm. Canadians, worlds, it didn't matter. Janet would just enjoy, and she would laugh and have some fun out there. She was very matter-of-fact about it and she never really lost her mind. I remember thinking 'I wish I could be more like that.' Obviously, because she's been there and done all the stuff they've done, other than the Olympics, she's able to impart that. They believe in her and what she's sharing."

Now that they were gold medallists, having gone 17-1 through the Trials and the Olympics, many people wondered just what the difference was between this team and the one that simply couldn't get things going in previous Olympic years. There were several answers, not the least of which was the attitude they carried into the Olympics, but perhaps the most obvious was this: Kaitlyn Lawes. The 25-year-old had proven to be the perfect addition to the Jones team. She wasn't necessarily better than Cathy Overton-Clapham, but she fit in better and proved to be just the kind of vice-skip Jones needed to find success.

Because she was so much less experienced than Overton-Clapham, Lawes was open to doing whatever Jones wanted. She tried her best to let Jones know that she appreciated the opportunity to be a part of the team and developed a familiar unquestionable loyalty to the skip. For Jones, who had encountered some difficulties with teammates in the past, having a third who didn't question her, supported her unwaveringly and believed in her and her abilities was immensely helpful. The range of Lawes's shot-making, from finesse draws to big-weight takeouts, certainly didn't hurt.

"There wasn't fighting on the team when Cathy O was there but the team chemistry was not what it once was," Gauthier said. "When teams are together for a long time, inevitably that happens. You bring in a breath of fresh air who brings a ton of ability, a ton of youth and energy and excitement about everything, it just brought positive energy back to the team. There were no issues amongst the players. Everyone wanted Kaitlyn to have a great experience and Kaitlyn was also giving them something they had not had before, which was the fun without any stress because it was all new. No one can ever question what Kaitlyn has brought to this team."

Jones, who had been on a leave of absence since giving birth to Isabella, planned to go back to work at National Bank Financial in May 2014. In the meantime, she had become a partner in a venture called Golden Girl Finance, an organization providing information and support for women to take charge of their finances.

In the immediate aftermath of the Olympics, Jones was once again bombarded with questions about her future. She'd always said a decision about where she and Brent Laing would settle down to raise Isabella would have to come soon. She had not had any serious discussions about it with her teammates as they chose to focus entirely on the their Olympic quest, but that day was coming. No matter what, she planned to let Laing pursue his Olympic dream, since she had already realized hers.

"I told him after we won the Olympic Trials, he gets to decide first because I would like him to be able to experience this."

"Right now I love playing with the girls," she said before leaving Sochi. "I feel like I'm in some of the best shape of my life and I still feel like I can compete at the top level. I know I could go another four years, if I set my mind to it. It's just a question of whether I want to take time with my family right now or wait another four years. There's just so many logistical things with my life that need to be sorted out. It's more than curling for me."

Obviously the other three curlers wanted to keep playing — who wouldn't want to have the best skip in women's curling history on their team? But they had to wait a couple of months for Jones and Laing to make a decision. As promised, Laing chose first, announcing he would be joining 2014 Brier champion Kevin Koe's team from Alberta. That immediately fuelled speculation that Jones would be moving west. Though Jones hinted that her team would return intact for at least the next season and likely for the entire Olympic quadrennial, there were many people who were certain she would move to Ontario or Alberta or somewhere other than Manitoba. However, just before the Grand Slam of Curling's Players Championship in Summerside, Prince Edward Island, in mid-April, Jones put all that speculation to rest.

The team announced on its website that it would stay together for another four years, taking advantage of funding provided to Olympic medallists by the Canadian Olympic Committee and, more importantly, planning on taking another run at the Winter Games in Korea in 2018. Jones planned to keep her Manitoba residence and continue to represent the province in major curling events.

"It does feel great," Jones said. "I can't say enough great things about the girls, just how easy and enjoyable curling is. It's hard to walk away from.

"There weren't very many hurdles. We all really wanted to play together. But we had decided heading into the Olympics to make sure we gave ourselves some time after the Olympics to let it all sink in and see what we wanted to do, and if we wanted to commit for another four years. And to be honest it was a pretty easy decision for all of us."

As for the family situation, Jones and Laing figured they'd been doing the long distance thing for a couple of years already, what was a few more while they were both still young enough to be competitive athletes. "We're pros, now," Jones said. "Wily veterans at it. There's a lot of women who curl with kids. I'm really lucky that my mom and mother-in-law are willing to help out for another four years. So that makes a big difference. Brent and I will just figure out the logistics of it. Just lots of travelling and lots of making sure you enjoy every moment when you're together."

In early May, while in Costa Rica for a speaking gig, Jones and Brent Laing decided to make it official and got engaged. The big moment for Isabella's parents came at a private tiki-torch dinner on a Costa Rican beach. The best year of Jennifer Jones's life got even better.

For good measure, Jones and Company capped their storybook 2014 season with yet another victory, topping Rachel Homan 5-2 in the final of the Players Championship in Prince Edward Island. They won $23,500 and earned an additional $12,500 in bonus money for leading the Grand Slam of Curling in points over the course of the season. "It really has been an unbelievable season for us," Jones said. "We've won all the events we've set out to win and to end with another win is a perfect way to head into summer."

It seemed pretty obvious that the Jones team was ready to ride the wave of momentum for years after the Olympics, taking an amazing experience, a dream come true and then some, and building on it. "It was everything we hoped it would be and so, so much more. But to be honest, it's curling with the girls that's addictive. We have so much fun. It's easy to go on the ice and laugh and enjoy every second of living your dream. It doesn't get any better than that with the team. It's so easy on and off the ice. It makes practicing enjoyable, playing enjoyable and just the whole life experience enjoyable. So that's hard to walk away from."

Of course, alongside Jones every step of the way will be her trusty sidekick, Jill Officer. They have played together for so long that neither of them could even imagine doing so with anyone else. They shared every iota of their success together and just wanted to keep it going and perhaps even get better if that was possible.

"We've had a lot of fun over the last four years," Officer said. "And we still can make some improvements. We're kind of in a really good place with our team, and we weren't ready to walk away from it. The thought was always if we were going to continue to curl, it would be these four people. We decided to go for it. We've had an amazing time together. The Olympics was the pinnacle of it. We're hoping we can do it again.

"It's been almost 20 years that Jen and I have curled together, so being able to go to the Olympics together and win a gold medal is incredibly special. We all have put a lot of time and effort in but obviously Jen and I have been together a lot longer. She's done a lot for me as a curler, she's been a great leader and she's motivated me to be a better athlete. I often think about it because how far we've come in that time is just crazy. How much we've accomplished in that time is crazy to think about, and I can't imagine being at this level with anybody else. I wouldn't be here without her and I would imagine it would be the same for her."

Announcing her return for another four years was almost surreal for Jones, who'd been ready to walk away from the game in 2010, when curling just wasn't fun for her anymore. She'd had to convince herself to come back for even one more Olympic run, which she fully expected to be her last. "If you asked me four years ago if this would be the last four years, I would have said 'Absolutely.' Now all of a sudden we're having the time of our lives, so it's pretty hard to walk away from that."

If the Jones team is lucky enough to get back to the Olympic Trials in 2017, the skip will be 43 years old — hardly over the hill for a curler. Colleen Jones had most of her best years in her forties and Cheryl Bernard skipped a team to an Olympic silver medal at age 43. Colleen Jones also pointed to men's curling greats like Stoughton, Kevin Martin, Glenn Howard and Russ Howard for the success they all had in their mid-to-late forties. "She's got a good 10 years to build on the legacy that she's got already," Colleen Jones said.

As they embarked on yet another Olympic run, the future remained bright. Jones would not likely have any interest in continuing if they weren't all physically capable and mentally committed. "I know the moment that a decline starts to happen, when I feel like I can't get better anymore, then I'll retire. That was always what I wanted to do. Right now I feel as good as ever. I came off one of the best years of my curling career. I still have the potential to get better. That's really what excites me about sports."

Those who were paying attention were not surprised in the least that Jones and Co. decided to stay together and keep playing for at least four more years. Former silver medallist Mike Harris said they'd be crazy not to. "For the last number of years, Jennifer and this team have been at or near the top of women's curling, so there's no reason to think they would stop. They've got a great opportunity moving forward to stay at the top. I'm really happy to see them stick together. They played as well as I've ever seen them play in Sochi, and talk about peaking at the right time. Good for them.

"Bad news for all the other women's teams."

But great news for four friends who shared a special bond that could never be broken. There was something truly special about the relationship of the four women, forged in times of glory and anguish, cultivated on turbulent airplanes, in cramped hotel rooms and on pebbled ice surfaces around the world and solidified in gold.

"We've been together for so long, through the ups and downs, and we've made difficult decisions together, and we've made easy decisions together, and we've gone through greatness, and we've gone through sadness together," Jones said, emotion creeping into her voice once again.

"When we're done, we're going to be friends forever and sisters forever, really. We're going to be there for each other, no matter what. That's truly special in life, and I'm fortunate to be part of that."

CHAPTER TWELVE

PRIDE OF
THE SOO

The calendar belied the truth. Brad Jacobs could stare at it as long as he liked but it would never change the fact that his team had defied time and logic in becoming Olympic champions. On February 21, 2013, one year to the day before they won the Olympic gold medal, Jacobs and his teammates were simply Canadian curlers who had never been able to escape the fringes of the sport and join the inner circle. They had come close at a few Briers, but few people really believed they were contenders, not when the likes of Jeff Stoughton, Kevin Martin, Kevin Koe and Glenn Howard were still competing. Just 12 months later, there was no question which was the best team in the world. It was almost hard to comprehend for a 28-year-old bank accounts manager from blue-collar Northern Ontario.

"I really never saw in my wildest dreams that this would happen so quickly," an astounded Jacobs said. "You always hope you can win a Brier or an Olympic Trials or a gold medal but you never know if anything is going to happen. You just hope. It's crazy how far this team has come, how much we've grown together as a team and as individuals. I'm very proud of what we've accomplished to this point."

So much of the success over that past year could be traced back to that 2013 Brier, specifically to the round-robin game where Jacobs was perilously close to being knocked out of the playoffs but came up with a huge, momentum-turning win over Stoughton to stay alive and then went on an epic run that is still going today.

"Our team can take some credit for springboarding them to their success," Stoughton reflected. "If you look at that 2013 Brier final, if our team wins that game, the Jacobs team might not be Olympic champions. Once they got through winning the Brier, they definitely became a better team, and since then there's been no stopping them, that's for sure."

They encountered some gut-churning adversity early on at the Olympics, but once they got going there was no team in the world that could run with them. Power, finesse, peak fitness, experience and youthful exuberance were all on display, and it made the playing surface uneven.

"Their power game is unmatched," Canadian national team coach Rick Lang said. "The game has been transcending that way for 10 years and they've taken it another notch with their power, the way they can move rocks around and control the house and maintain leads. The guys just had that same confidence that they had in the Canadian Trials and they're hard to derail. No one in Canada can beat them and now no one in the world."

While Mike Harris said the Jacobs team came out of nowhere to reach these incredible heights, many other curlers were not as surprised. Not surprised to see them win the Brier, nor the Trials, nor the Olympics. You can recognize great curlers when you see them, and sometimes all it takes is for one missing piece to be put into place to make incredible things happen.

"They weren't one of the favourites on paper but I'd say no, I wasn't surprised," 2006 Olympic gold medallist Brad Gushue said. "Because I've been through it before and the Olympic Trials are a different beast and sometimes it's just a matter of who handles it the right way, not even who is playing the best or who is the best team. When they won the Brier last year, I knew they were good, but it took me by surprise a little bit. I thought they were maybe a year or two away from really being competitive at the Brier, but they got hot at the right time, they really continued it for a year."

Of all the things the Jacobs team had accomplished in just a year, perhaps the most incredible was what it did for the game itself. "What they've really done is changed the way the public looks at curlers," Mike Harris said. "I think that's their legacy. People look at them and say, 'You know what? They're athletes.' I think that's going to be their greatest legacy. They've definitely changed the perception of curlers with the general public. It's a huge thing to accomplish, and all the rest of the curlers will benefit from that."

Ryan Fry was one of the Buff Boys from his arrival. He fit in on and off the ice, in the gym, at the bar after the game, at the family dinner table. He influenced the game in many ways, showing younger curlers that you can achieve your goals if you are willing to work at it, devote your entire life to it, pick up stakes and move across the country to make it happen. His perseverance was inspiring, especially considering he started out as a player with a reputation as bad as his temper and a penchant for partying as hard as he curled.

"All this just comes with maturity and growing up, 100 percent," Fry said. "I think I always knew, even at a young age, what it was going to take to get to this level and what sort of team we needed to have. I searched for it for a long time, and there's only so many openings along the way. You can't just handpick your team because some of the teams I might have handpicked might not have wanted me. So I was very fortunate to find a spot with this team."

Fry saw it immediately, before the team even hit the ice. Jacobs and the Harnden brothers were his type of people. Curlers yes, but also athletes and determined to be damn good ones. Fry believed in what a person could achieve in the weight room and the gym and so did his new teammates. Fry was also unique in that he considered curling a full-time job. He managed the team, tried to find sponsorships, arranged travel to cash bonspiels. "I'm curling for a living," he said. "With the help of the other guys, we get through it, and we work our butts off to be able to make a go of curling. For me, it's a full-time job and for the other guys it's a three-quarter-of-the-time job. They're very lucky that their employers give them the time they need to be able to pursue this dream."

Good luck is a big part of any team's success and so is good timing. Jacobs had plenty of both when Fry became available at just the right time and proved to be a perfect match for the team. Few people believe this team would be where it is today if Fry had not joined up.

"We didn't know it would be the right fit," Jacobs said. "But with everyone's desire to prepare, everyone's passion for winning, wanting to be the best team, everyone is very like-minded . . . We'll get together on the weekend and hang out, outside of curling. We're truly buddies, on and off the ice, and that's the chemistry that we have. We didn't know that we were going to run into that, so when we brought him on and started playing, we had to figure things out, and now our chemistry and our dynamic are better than ever."

Curling analysts across the country agreed that Fry was the difference-maker. Although he had to be a great third, his biggest role was acting as a mediator between three players who had all the tools but perhaps not the level heads to find success. "What he did for that team was he was the buffer between Brad and the Harndens," Mike Harris said. "Those guys are brothers and cousins and when you curl with your family, you're not as nice to them. When things start going south, it's easy to blame each other and act emotionally rather than being a little more level-headed.

"He was the perfect fit for them. He's like-minded, you know, they work out together off the ice and he's a good shooter with lots of experience from playing with Stoughton and Gushue at the Brier. He brought a lot to the table with those guys. His biggest strength was dealing with the relationship between the Harndens and Brad Jacobs, and I thought he was a calming influence on Brad. You could almost compare him to what Russ Howard brought to Brad Gushue in 2006. I thought that was a huge, huge thing and I don't think they would have done what they did without him."

TSN's Cathy Gauthier saw it the same way. She had known Fry since he was a little kid and had seen him grow through good times and bad. She sometimes found it hard to believe this was the same person as the one who'd had so much trouble controlling his temper and been so wild off the ice earlier in his career.

"His ability to absolutely know when to push Brad, when to back off and when to take on that front end, which is a pretty fearsome duo, and say 'Back off' and not be offensive and to do it at the right times, that's the full, full package. Most really great teams don't have a third with all that skill set."

By no means did Fry's influence take away from what everyone else on the team brought to the table. The Harnden brothers were and are one of the best front ends curling has ever seen and they would never settle for anything less. Jacobs himself had become Cool Hand Brad, a skip with all the shots and the ability to focus on getting the job done. "When everything is all said and done, I want our team to be known as one of the most dominant curling teams to ever play the game," E.J. said.

There were so many people to share the credit for the team's success. Jacobs pointed to his mentors, people like Soo Curlers Association ice technician Ian Fisher and his uncle Al Harnden. The Harnden brothers obviously thought of their father, Eric, who had always been their hero and had been their inspiration to get into the sport. They all felt love for their longtime coach, Tom Coulterman, who had been imparting them with knowledge since they were little kids. "He's been so good with us over the years," Jacobs said. "It's not easy being a coach, especially when they don't get Olympic medals. But Tom knows how much he means to us, and we're thrilled for him to get some recognition here in Sochi."

Another person all of the curlers felt they owed a debt of gratitude to was sports psychologist Arthur Perlini, with whom they started working with in 2010 after they won a bronze medal at the Brier. Perlini, who was a psychology professor and dean at Algoma University, volunteered his time to help the team learn how to manage emotions, deal with stress, show resiliency and control their tempers. "Their ascension has been nothing short of spectacular," Perlini said four years after he first started working with the group. "They truly have distinguished themselves amongst the elite in the sport. Their resilience and mental toughness are what make them stand out."

The Jacobs team received their gold medals on the evening of February 22 at the plaza in Olympic Park and repeated their patented jump up onto the podium.

The pride of a nation, the four "brothers" enjoyed every minute of the festivities, knowing the odds were against something like that ever again happening again. They partied — "Like true Canadian boys, we definitely had some beers together" — with their families, their friends and the victorious women's curling team. It seemed nothing could top that moment in time. Well, almost nothing. On February 23, they attended the men's gold medal hockey game at the Bolshoy Ice Dome and cheered on Canada as it squashed Sweden 3-0. It was Canada's second consecutive gold in men's hockey and it was a thrill for the curlers to cheer on the same players who'd attended their games earlier in the Olympics and who shared their accommodations in the Athletes' Village. As millions of fans watched that game in the early morning back home, the Jacobs boys had seats in the house and even made an appearance on the scoreboard for an interview during a break in the action.

More than immediately after the hockey game ended, the Buff Boys were off to the Fisht Olympic Stadium for the lavish Closing Ceremony. Jacobs had said the Opening Ceremony was his "Welcome to the Olympics" moment. This certainly was even more uplifting, with a gold medal in tow, marching side by side with other conquering heroes. Jacobs had the evidence to prove it, posting a photo of himself with hockey icon Sidney Crosby — both of them in their HBC gear and sporting their medals — on Twitter. "They were having the time of their lives . . . they just couldn't believe the people that were there," coach Tom Coulterman said. "It was fantastic."

More than 2,000 people back home in Sault Ste. Marie had crammed into the Essar Centre to watch Jacobs win the gold medal, so there was little doubt a major celebration was planned for them when they returned home from Russia. They headed for home on February 24, the day after the Olympics ended, and after flying for many hours, found themselves surrounded by adoring fans at the airport in Sault Ste. Marie at 12:30 in the morning. There were hundreds of red-and-white-clad supporters chanting the name "Jacobs, Jacobs" over and over again, belting out "O Canada" and generally making Brad, Ryan, E.J., Ryan, Tom and Caleb feel like heroes. With the heavy gold medals around their necks and the kind of pride in their hearts only people who have just admirably represented their country can feel, the teammates waded into the throng and joined the celebration.

"This gold medal is for everyone in this community to share," Jacobs said above the din in the crowded airport arrivals area. "This is not just for us. Everyone in this community can take a picture with the gold medal because I'm sure everyone has a story of where they were and what they were doing when we won it. We look forward to hearing those stories.

"We could feel it in Sochi. There were a lot of people sending us messages, emails, tweets. Especially when we were 1-2, no one gave up on us, they just supported us more. I never would have thought I'd be standing here at this airport, 28 years old, being an Olympic gold medallist."

It seemed all of Sault Ste. Marie was basking in the glow of the Olympic gold medal. People had taken their children out of school to watch the gold medal game and had shed tears when the Canadians leaped onto the podium. Now they were getting a chance to let their heroes know firsthand just how they felt. "It's a pretty proud moment for our city," curling fan Tim Jackson told the *Sault Star*. "It's a good moment for everyone in our city."

"The energy level in this city, I've never seen it like this," added city councillor Terry Sheehan.

The celebration lasted for weeks as the city planned out the best possible way to do the accomplishment justice. It was not just Sault Ste. Marie that wanted a piece of Brad Jacobs and his teammates, however. Just a few days after they arrived home they spent a media day at CBC in Toronto, which included an appearance on the popular talk show *George Stroumboulopoulos Tonight*. Jacobs walked onto the set of the show wearing one of the signature Rock Head hats that had become popular in Sochi. Bearing the Team Jacobs name, the foam hats were shaped like curling rocks and were very popular with fans of the team, including some of the Canadian hockey players who attended games at the Ice Cube Curling Center. Clearly the Jacobs boys were basking in the glow of their gold medals, and the feeling was only accelerated by how nervous they'd been heading into the Olympics.

"That was the toughest event that we've ever played in," Jacobs told Strombo. "Each event that you go to, each big event, it's tough in its own way, and the Olympics is its own beast, and I'm just happy to have made it through that. There's a lot of pressure on you being Team Canada going there. You're expected to win gold — especially in curling."

They shared some of the lighter moments of the Olympics, disclosing that they'd downed a few Red Bulls before every game and suggesting that curling could never be a part of the Olympics if alcohol were a banned substance. They also talked about the perception of curlers among the other athletes at the Olympics, a perception they believed they might have changed. "Ryan [Harnden] was asked at the Olympic Games if he was one of the bobsledders or a hockey player," E.J. said. "No one would have ever guessed us as being curlers."

"I got asked if I was a figure skater," Fry joked. They were loose and comfortable on national TV. Clearly, the limelight didn't look bad on these four curlers. Jacobs admitted to being nervous about the appearance: "It's a pretty huge show. But once we got out there and started chatting with George, it was a lot of fun . . . He really gets curling. He's a really bright guy . . . The crowd was good. It was just a really great experience.

"Life has been busy. There's obviously a lot of attention on us now because we won at the Olympics. This is something that we've been working toward our whole lives, being at the pinnacle, the top of the game. We're there right now, and we're just soaking it in. It's all new to us."

The following day they were whisked off to Kamloops, British Columbia, where the Brier was going on without the defending champs. Because of the Olympics, Jacobs couldn't participate in the Brier, and that meant Northern Ontario had a different representative for the first time in seven years. The Buff Boys still made a splash though, arriving with gold medals in tow and giving the Canadian crowd one more chance to celebrate their achievement. "We kind of wish we were out there playing, but being a gold medallist and having to come here and make an appearance isn't a bad thing at all," Jacobs told the *Sault Star*.

There were appearances at schools, endorsement deals and even an opportunity to drop the puck at an Oilers game in Edmonton. They were invited to the Toronto Blue Jays home opener and publicity events with other Olympians. It seemed everyone wanted a piece of their time, and they were certainly enjoying their 15 minutes of fame. "There's a lot of demands," Jacobs told Sean Fitz-Gerald of the *National Post*. "And I want to be able to meet those demands as much as possible." That may be the most difficult challenge for a triumphant Olympian. Just ask Brad Gushue, who went through the same experience in 2006.

"First and foremost you get presented with so many opportunities that it's overwhelming," Gushue said. "For me there were times when I just craved to not be known and just be able to go about your life as it was before you went to the Olympics. But you realize that what you did is pretty special, and the opportunities far outweigh the negatives that come with it. You have to learn to say no a little bit and really just enjoy it. Take the opportunities that you want, go and have fun with them, because really, in a year or so, people move on to something else. You've got to enjoy it while you have the opportunity, but you can't run yourself down and do everything."

There was no question they were feeling the effects of everything they'd been through — the travel, the magnitude of their quest and the demands on their time at home. Perhaps the best thing for them was to get back out on the ice. Their first opportunity to do that came just a few weeks after they returned to Canada, at the Grand Slam of Curling's The National in Fort McMurray, Alberta. The rust was evident immediately, and, after they bowed out of the tournament with a 2-3 record, Jacobs admitted he and his teammates were mentally drained. "We didn't play close to our best," he said. "We didn't have any time to recharge mentally after the Olympics and that absolutely makes curling at this level difficult."

They'd been home for a few weeks already, but the party was far from dying down. Sault Ste. Marie had not yet shown its full appreciation for the efforts of the Buff Boys, but they did it in style on April 4. On that night, about 3,000 people, many wearing Team Canada hockey jerseys or simply red and white clothing, came out to the Essar Centre to celebrate the achievements of the city's Olympians. The Jacobs team and coach Tom Coulterman were feted, along with Paralympic skier Mac Marcoux and hockey coach Ted Nolan, who'd coached the Latvian hockey team at the Olympics. Mayor Debbie Amaroso summarized the city's sentiments about the curling champions. "Team Jacobs has transformed this hockey town into the curling capital it is now."

Their win meant so much to a community that, curling-wise, had not seen much success in its history and to Northern Ontario, with its 7,000 registered curlers and a collective desire to be nationally relevant. "This puts curling and Sault Ste. Marie on the map on the national stage," Soo Curlers Association manager Ian Fisher said. "Now the word's out there across the nation that these guys are the best and they're from Sault Ste. Marie, and it makes everybody excited here. When those guys come in the building, the kids get excited as soon as they walk in.

"Our Learn to Curl Program probably doubled in size last year because of them, and I can see us maintaining that size, which is at our limit. I can see a lot of growth over the next year in the junior area because there are so many youngsters looking at them and wanting to be the next Jacobs."

Spurred on by the proclamation from the Mayor, Jacobs assured the crowd that his team planned to be around for a while. "We're not content . . . we want more," he said. It was not the first time Jacobs or his teammates talked about going after an Olympic gold medal again in 2018 and even in 2022 for that matter. At 35, Fry was the oldest of the four team members and would be only 43 come 2022. In curling, that's nowhere near the end of the line. While many Canadian teams, even the one skipped by 2014 Brier champion Kevin Koe, were breaking up and reforming with an eye on the 2018 Winter Olympic Games in Korea, Jacobs and his teammates had all the faith in the world that they had the right formula to keep on winning. And after their performance over the past 12 months, no one could possibly argue that this team did not have what it takes to win another gold medal. "I think we can," Jacobs said before even leaving Sochi. "We plan on staying together for at least another Olympic run, until 2018 at least. We just want to keep on building, keep growing and stick together, and hopefully we'll see you all here in four years."

Time will tell if this team can become a dynasty, but it's certainly not out of the realm of possibility. Up until this point they've done well for themselves, and by no means are they likely to rest on their laurels. "We're gonna keep working hard, and we're gonna try to elevate our game, and we'll be ready to go for next year," Fry said. "Our goal is to give it our best shot at becoming one of the best teams that has played the game. I think we're on our way now, but we've got a lot of work to go."

That's part of the beauty of this team — there is still so much to look forward to in the future. With youth, skill, confidence, know-how and athleticism all on their side, there is simply no telling how far the Buff Boys can go. "We don't want to ever put a limit on the success that our team is going to have," E.J. Harnden said. "We're going to enjoy this as much as possible, let it sink in and then enjoy it with our family, our friends, Sault Ste. Marie, all of Canada, but we're not ever, ever going to stop. We're not going to hold back and just rest on the success that we've already had. We're just going to push forward, and I think that's how you excel as a team."

Perhaps it was the fact that they had reached the Olympic pinnacle so quickly that made Jacobs and his teammates feel like they had the makings of a dynasty. Guys like Jeff Stoughton and Glenn Howard had been to five Olympic Trials without a single Olympic appearance. Kevin Martin didn't make it to the Olympics until he was 35. The Jacobs team should have just been starting out in their careers and were already at the top. They deserved to be satisfied with their success but wouldn't allow themselves to be.

"Curling's not only a sport to me," Ryan Harnden said. "It's my passion. I want to set up every end perfectly and be known as the best sweeper in the world."

All this talk of dynasties and repeat gold medals and staying together for more Olympic quadrennials was fine and dandy but much easier said than done. One person who could say so from first-hand experience was Gushue, who won a gold medal at age 26 and has had nothing but heartbreak since in his attempts to regain that glory. Gushue pointed out that things change, and sometimes other priorities get in the way of curling.

"It's not going to be as easy as the first time," Gushue said. "If you look at that team, none of them have kids yet. E.J. and Brad are the only ones that are married and the responsibilities are not quite at the level of what some of the other teams out there have. Sometimes life gets in the way. For me, over the last eight years, it's been a challenge. I've got two kids, have some businesses on the go and I'm still really focused on curling and I still work really hard at it but it's no longer the number one priority for me, the way it was back in 2006. It's probably number three behind my family and my business. Your priorities change, your perspectives change. Once the kids start coming and things like that, it will be a little harder."

Perhaps the biggest obstacle will be that all the other Canadian curlers are now gunning for the Jacobs team. "They're not sneaking under the radar anymore," Mike Harris said. Sure, the Jacobs team was likely to be back at the Brier sooner rather than later — after all, it had owned Northern Ontario for the better part of a decade — but it would no longer be able to hide in the shadow of Stoughton, Martin, Koe and Howard.

"Those days are gone for them," Harris said. "Time will tell where their spot in the game is long term, but it's going to be interesting to see how they do. They're not a dominant team like Martin or Howard. They're very streaky. When they're at their best, they're as good as those guys, but they're not at the same level of consistency. That's going to be their challenge."

For all the happiness in his life — an Olympic gold medal, a new bride, the adoration of Canadian curling fans — Brad Jacobs still had a major concern on his mind a couple of months after the Olympics. His mother, Cindy, who had pleaded guilty to defrauding Algoma University out of $390,000 to fuel a gambling habit, was due to be sentenced in late April. Brad attended all of her court hearings, including the one on April 29 when she was handed a conditional sentence of two years less a day, followed by three years of probation. If she could stay out of trouble, she could stay out of jail. While Justice Melanie Dunn called the offence a large-scale fraud, she didn't see it as an elaborate or sophisticated scheme, the *Sault Star* reported. "Ms. Jacobs was not motivated by greed, nor living a lavish lifestyle," Dunn stated in her written decision. "She suffered an addiction and stole to feed that addiction. Her family relations and personal finances have been affected. She has brought ruin and humiliation on herself."

It's a credit to Brad Jacobs that he was able to keep his focus through the Olympic Trials and through Sochi 2014 despite the family crisis going on at home. The same goes for E.J. and Ryan Harnden, nephews to Cindy Jacobs. Now there was great relief that Brad's mother would not be going to jail, though she had to live up to stringent conditions to remain a free woman.

The question was, would the curlers be free to come and go as they pleased, living in a fish bowl like Sault Ste. Marie where they were heroes of rock star status? Would life ever be the same?

"They're not anonymous anymore," said Mike Harris, who had a similar experience after returning home from the 1998 Olympics with a silver medal. "For me, living in Toronto, it was easy because nobody cares about curling. I can walk down the street a week after the Olympics and not get recognized. They're from a small city, and they won't be able to go out at all without getting recognized. They're born and raised in the Soo, there's demand on their time, there's expectations to appear at certain things, and they are going to be busy. It's good though . . . it's what they always wanted. It opens a lot of doors. They're going to be doing it for the rest of their lives.

"The Olympics really change your life in all the best possible ways."

When the 2014 season ended, there was a major shakeup of teams on the Canadian men's scene. Martin planned to retire, Howard's team broke up, Stoughton's team broke up, Kevin Koe left his 2014 Canadian championship team to form a new team, and John Morris replaced Koe on Team Canada. As much as the Jacobs team wanted to stay together for decades, there was plenty of history that suggested it would be unlikely. "There's always an expiry date with teams," Stoughton said.

Not everyone agreed with that assessment. National team coach Rick Lang worked with the Jacobs team at both the world championship and the Olympics, and what he saw was a group of curlers who were continually maturing, growing and developing. He believed they would become the model for young curlers in a game that was continually evolving and was ready to enter a new era. "They're unusual in curling because they play better when they're amped up and stoked than when they're not," Lang said on a Canadian Olympic Committee blog. "I know some people criticize them for that, but it's not fair. That's what works for them — high energy, staying pumped and maybe even a little bickering. It just keeps them on edge, in the game and fired up." They had one more chance to get "totally stoked" that year, at the Players Championship in Summerside, Prince Edward Island, in mid-April. It was the perfect way to cap off their brilliant season, playing for cash against a field of great curlers, one more time. This time, the fatigue was passing, the Olympic hangover dissipating, the rust slowly returning to a brilliant shine. Jacobs and Co. made it all the way to the final at the Players Championship, and, most fittingly, went up against the Old Bear, Kevin Martin, who planned to retire after playing that one last game. How perfect to have Jacobs, the 28-year-old reigning Olympic champion, against Martin, the 47-year-old former Olympic champ who had seen enough of the Olympic qualifying grind. In the end, Martin won 4-3 and went off into the curling sunset with one last victory against the future of curling.

Yes, the Jacobs team ended its remarkable season with a loss, but there could be no disappointment. They had so much glory still to bask in and even a little cash for finishing second in the prestigious bonspiel. Most importantly, the final game was symbolic of the state of curling as a whole, a matchup between the old guard and the new.

The torch had officially been passed.

ACKNOWLEDGEMENTS

This book could not have been completed without access to the extensive story archives of the Sun Media Corporation, and in particular, the *Winnipeg Sun* and *Sault Star*. Few newspapers in the world cover curling as extensively as those two publications and none have done more stories on the Jennifer Jones and Brad Jacobs teams. I would like to thank all of the *Sault Star* sports writers over the years, as well as some of the people who work for me in the sports department at the *Winnipeg Sun*, including Kirk Penton and Ken Wiebe and particularly Jim Bender and Paul Friesen. Jim, after decades on the curling beat, was a wealth of knowledge about Jennifer Jones and her teammates, and Paul has always had a unique ability to get the best quotes out of his interview subjects. I'd also like to thank my bosses, Mark Hamm and Kevin Engstrom, for putting up with me while I worked on this project, and the same, of course, goes for my family — Tammy, Chris and Emily. Thanks to Bill Pierce and Glenn Garnett for giving me a chance to cover the Olympics in

Sochi, and getting this ball rolling, and to Laura Pastore and Jack David at ECW Press for picking me to write the book. I'd like to give special thanks to, in no particular order, Cathy Gauthier, Colleen Jones, Mike Harris, Jeff Stoughton, Kim Fedick, Brad Gushue, Terry Jones, Jeff Wyman, Steve Simmons and Cathy Overton-Clapham. Special thanks to four-time world champion Glenn Howard for writing an eloquent and informative foreword. And thanks, of course, to all the curlers who are featured in this book for giving me such a great story to write about. It's been a pleasure.